PRAISE FOR OWN THE WOR

GW00383236

"As someone deep into economic advice, people always ask me for invest-
ment advice. Two different things. My personal views aside, the underlying
theory in this book accords with my own, including my personal investment
strategy. Craig supports an "Own the World" strategy - basically sensible and
well thought-through diversification over the long term. He also encourages
the reader to get a grip, early, on their own long-term investments in order to
harness the power of compound growth and avoid the sapping of compound
professional fees. If you want just one book on investment from the cacophony,
you couldn't do much better."

– Michael Mainelli, co-author of "The Price of Fish", November 2012

"Andrew Craig clearly has an amazing financial knowledge and talent for
writing. This book presents some remarkable facts on global financial issues
that you cannot ignore. The way Andrew simply explains financial concepts
from the ground up is the reason you will close the book feeling confident
handling your own financial future and gain the benefits of doing so. Andrew
needs to do no convincing - the facts he presents speak for themselves. Not
only will this book provide you with a great understanding of investment but
also the motivation and ability to secure a better financial future for yourself.
Overall an amazing resource and a great companion to Rich Dad Poor Dad
to show you how to make your money work for you."

– Amazon review, November 2012

"Finance was a black hole in my knowledge, and for some reason I never
sat down and thought, "Hmm, this is an area that's going to have a huge
impact on my future; maybe I should learn something about it". Then I read
Andrew's book and what could have been dry or intimidating was presented
so clearly and logically that I've been recommending it to everyone I talk to
ever since. It was invigorating to learn how easily I can take control of my fi-
nancial future, and how many common assumptions about finance, investing
and property are wrong. The book maps out a very clear overview of finance
and gives step by step instructions to sensible investing. A life changing book."

– Amazon review, October 2012

SO WHO DOES ANDREW CRAIG THINK HE IS?

Andrew Craig graduated in Economics and International Politics in 1997. His first job took him to Washington DC where he worked for a US Congressman on Capitol Hill. Since then he has spent over a decade working in financial markets for various finance firms in London and latterly New York. These included UBS, Credit Agricole (France's biggest bank) and two smaller boutique firms. Andrew doesn't claim to be a "financial guru" but he is confident he can help you. As he says: "You didn't need to be taught by Einstein or Newton to get an "A" in physics or by Shakespeare to get an "A" in English." Andrew passionately wants you to get an "A" in personal finance. Reading "Own The World" will go a long way towards helping you achieve just that...

A Plain English Finance Guide

OWN THE WORLD

By Andrew Craig

Own The World – A Plain English Finance Guide.

Written by Andrew Craig.

First published in Great Britain in 2012 by Plain English Finance Limited.

http://www.plainenglishfinance.com

DEDICATION

To Neville, Gillian, Michael and Joanna.
I couldn't have asked for a more wonderful nuclear family...

To my cousin Mary Trease with enormous thanks for your invaluable input
and feedback over the last two years.

To Timothy James Peacock, Non-Exec Extraordinaire.
Plain English Finance and Own The World simply could not have happened
without your tireless enthusiasm and world-beating work ethic...

...and to everyone else who has contributed their tuppence worth: Friends,
former colleagues and even those more recent acquaintances whose passionate
belief in Plain English Finance and "Own The World" has helped make them
a reality. There are too many of you to thank individually but I very much
hope that you know who you are...

CONTENTS

WHAT IS GOING ON?

#1

WHY YOU CAN AND SHOULD INVEST YOUR OWN MONEY

"There is an essential life skill that has never been and still isn't taught to the masses: How to manage, control and invest money to protect and provide for your financial future…"[1]

— Mark Shipman, one of the UK's first hedge fund managers, "retired" at 35[2].

---

1 From "Big Money, Little Effort", by Mark Shipman, p.1 of the Preface.

2 I have put "retired" in quotations on this page to denote the fact that I take it to mean you no longer have to worry about working for money. At this point you are free to do whatever you want to do with your life. For many people this will entail more than playing golf and taking cruises, especially if you are able to "retire" in your thirties or forties.

The above quote goes some way to capturing the fundamental gist of this book: That you can and should look after your own financial affairs. As you read what follows, I will present evidence for the following "Eight Fundamental Truths" of finance.

OWN THE WORLD'S "EIGHT FUNDAMENTAL TRUTHS"

1. No one is better placed than you to make the most of your money.
2. You have major inherent advantages over finance professionals.
3. Making money from your money (investing) is far easier than you've always thought. If you managed to learn how to drive, you can look after your own money. It is no harder.
4. You can make far more from your money than you ever thought possible.
5. It is realistic for you to target making more from your money than from your job. This is the money secret understood by virtually every rich person in history.
6. Achieving the above is possible almost no matter how much you currently earn.
7. The Good News: Doing this today is easier than ever before: The tools available to you are the most powerful and the cheapest they have ever been.
8. The Bad News: It has never been more important to take charge of your financial affairs. If you are under the age of about fifty today, there is no chance that you will receive a government funded pension you can actually live on at retirement.

Perhaps the best definition of a truly wealthy person is that they are able to live on the money they make from their money rather than the money they make from working. If you are contributing to a pension, you are already planning to do this, you're just aiming to get to this point in your fifties or sixties rather than any sooner.

There are two problems with this traditional approach to money: First, as we shall see, the vast majority of people in the UK are not making nearly enough of their pension arrangements to end up with a decent income in retirement. Unless you are in a small minority, it is very likely that you will have a very low income in retirement – not the most enticing of prospects and something we will address.

Perhaps more important, wouldn't it be preferable to get to the point of making a meaningful amount of money from your money a decade or two before traditional retirement age? Can you imagine the quality of life you could enjoy if you were able to create true financial freedom and live a great life on the money you make from your money sooner than by the time you are in your fifties or sixties?

The best news is that this is actually possible. It is an incredible shame that so few people realise this to be true. You just need to decide right now that you are willing to put a little time in, understand a bit more about investment and take the steps required to optimise your financial affairs. If you do, you have a far better chance than you ever realised of enjoying genuine financial freedom and doing so sooner than you think.

I think it worth noting that this is true even if you are at or near retirement age already. It is never too late to implement the ideas that follow.

The "Eight Fundamental Truths" on the page above might seem rather far-fetched to many people. Nevertheless, I am confident that you will find sufficient evidence in the pages that follow to back them up. As you read on, your common sense alone will be enough for you to see the inherent truth in the book's message.

The information in this book and the accompanying website will:

- Give you confidence in your ability to look after your own financial affairs.
- Help you learn how to make serious money from your money no matter what your financial background or what happens in the future.
- Ensure that you take the steps required to make the changes you need to make.
- Do this in the shortest time possible using the easiest language possible: Plain English.

WHY YOU MUST UNDERSTAND WHAT IS HAPPENING IN THE WORLD TODAY

We will deal with each of the "Fundamental Truths" in what follows. In the fine tradition of dealing with bad news first, however, let's get the depressing stuff out of the way as quickly as possible and look at the last of them immediately: It has never been more important for you to take charge of your financial affairs.

I am deadly serious when I say that if you do not have a solid grasp of what is happening in the world at the moment, you are very likely to be in the process of becoming poorer and this process is set to accelerate. The good news is that understanding what is happening and what to do about it is not nearly as difficult as you might think.

At this very moment, we are living through a complete change in how the world economy is structured. This has far-reaching consequences for your ability to survive and thrive in the years ahead.

What is currently being described as a "financial crisis" is actually a huge structural, that is to say inherent change in how the world economy works. What we are living through today is not some temporary, cyclical blip. It is not just part of a normal business cycle. Things are not going to return to "normal" and the economy is not going to "recover", at least not to the way it was between about 1945 and 2007.

What is actually happening is that we are living through nothing less than a complete paradigm shift in finance and economics and in how money works. The seeds for this change were sown in the early 1970s since when, a combination of the actions of politicians and central bankers and the impact of rapid technological change have driven us to where we are today. We will look at these ideas in more detail later in the book.

For now, it is enough to understand that this game change in finance and economics is already having a huge impact on politics and society and the pace of change is only going to increase. If you aim to survive and thrive in the years ahead, you will need to get to grips with what is going on and you will need to take action.

I acknowledge that forecasting the future is never easy. However, I would argue that if you have a basic grasp of economic history and a real understanding of what is happening in the present, you can get reasonable conviction that certain things have a higher probability of happening than others. You can then run your money accordingly.

As an example: If it is a statement of fact that government, corporate and private debt levels today are the highest they have ever been, this information can be used to make assumptions that give us a better chance of investment success. Economics is not rocket science, despite what some economists would like you to think and history provides us with plenty of examples of change similar to what we are experiencing today. We can then use that knowledge to help us run our money more successfully.

Conventional wisdom holds that "no one" predicted the financial crisis of the last few years. This is simply not true. A brief look at the bibliography section at the end of this book reveals plenty of people who have seen what has been happening, made a great deal of noise about it and, in many cases, made a great deal of money as a result. We might call these folk "the smart money". The goal of this book is to give you the best chance possible of being on the side of the smart money in the years ahead.

As you read what follows I hope you will find that it intuitively makes sense. It is also crucial to understand that "the genie is out of the bottle" and absolutely, positively cannot be put back in. The change you see around you cannot be reversed. Things have gone too far and the implications are with us for good. The only sensible action you or anyone else can take is to make the limited effort required to get to grips with what is going on and make the very best of it. You can only play the hand you are dealt.

DON'T PANIC. CRISIS EQUALS OPPORTUNITY.

Thankfully and perhaps somewhat ironically, many of the very same forces that have caused the global financial meltdown you are living through can be harnessed to help you most effectively navigate it.

Happily, there has never been a better time for those who do understand what is happening to turn this to their significant financial advantage. The great news is that the road to gaining this understanding is not as long or as scary as you might think. You just need to settle down for a few minutes a day and go through what follows. The information should make sense to you as you go along. At the end of the book I imagine you will be genuinely excited about making the positive changes you can make to help you ride out the storm and end up in a stronger position than ever.[3]

You may know that the Chinese symbol for "crisis" is the same as for "opportunity". Throughout history it has always been the case that those who make an effort to understand what is going on around them have come out of the other side better off than before and, obviously, far better off than those who don't.

Reading this book and taking action will place you in a minority of people who stand to weather the incredible economic, financial and social storm already breaking around us. Anyone who does not get to grips with our current predicament is likely to see a truly horrendous erosion of their wealth and standard of living over the next few decades. This is not some pie in the sky academic argument. This is a statement of cold, hard, fact as you will see. Millions of people in the world are already feeling the painful consequences of what is happening. You can see this every time you watch the news. You may even be one of them.

So let's get started. Make yourself a cup of something. Get comfortable and commit to making a meaningful change to your understanding of what is going on in the world and what you can do about it. I have every confidence that you will find it easier than you previously thought and find the results inspiring.

---

3 If anything does not make sense to you then please don't hesitate to contact me through: www.plainenglishfinance.com

TWO SPECIFIC REASONS YOU MUST UNDERSTAND YOUR FINANCES TODAY

There are two specific reasons why it has never been more important to understand your finances than it is today.

ONE: THE REAL INFLATION STORY

> *"By a continuing process of inflation, governments can confiscate, secretly and unobserved, an important part of the wealth of their citizens. There is no subtler, no surer means of overturning the existing basis of society than to debauch the currency. The process engages all the hidden forces of economic law on the side of destruction, and does it in a manner which not one man in a million is able to diagnose."*
>
> – John Maynard Keynes.[4]

Real inflation today is far higher than you think it is and this is destroying your ability to get wealthy. I will explain this in more detail later but for now you absolutely must understand that the "inflation" numbers produced by many governments are very misleading. This is very bad news for your wealth.

Many people think they understand what inflation is but few truly grasp how rapidly it can make you poor or how misleading the published numbers are. Iron, steel, coal, cotton, wheat, sugar, coffee, uranium, gold, silver, rice, the list goes on and on. The prices of all of these things have increased by at least 100% in the last few years and many are up by multiples of that. Below is a chart showing how much many of these things went up just in the year 2010. Crucially, check out the right-most column, which is an official government inflation number.[5] How can it be 1.1% when everything else has increased by so much more?

---

4 One of the most influential economists of the twentieth century.

5 CPI = Consumer Price Inflation, one of the key measures of inflation.

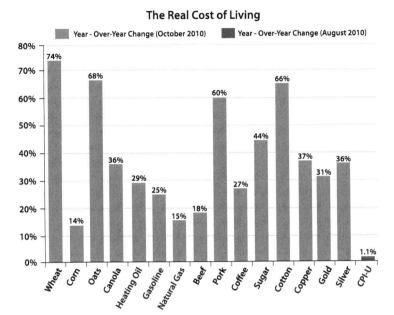

It is worth noting that the price of many of these commodities is extremely volatile and does not go up in a straight line. Nevertheless, the general trend of the last several years is very discernibly up. Despite such large increases in the price of the large majority of things you or I might want to consume, government inflation numbers on both sides of the Atlantic continue to come in as low single digits. Even these sorts of numbers are bad enough to destroy your wealth but the real picture is far worse. I will explain below why this is the case and why many financial analysts, journalists and politicians simply don't understand what the real numbers are.

As a statement of fact, with very few exceptions (consumer electronics for example), the price of nearly all of the things you actually need in your life: Food, fuel, shelter, medical care, insurance, education and so on are going up in price in leaps and bounds and by substantially more than would be suggested by what we might call the "science fiction" inflation numbers ("CPI" or "RPI") published by authorities on both sides of the Atlantic.

"Things" have been getting more and more expensive in terms of most of the paper currencies on the planet, which means that unless your salary is going up at least as much or you're making money from investment, you are getting poorer every day in real terms. This is only going to get worse. Any money you have is being gradually destroyed. If you have any savings in the bank you are losing real wealth every day and losing more than you think. This is one of the many reasons people are feeling poorer without really understanding why.

If you take the richest top 1% of people in the US and Britain out of the numbers, the other 99% have been getting poorer in real terms for nearly 40 years. In the US, the average salary peaked in 1973. The UK is no different. Today the richest 1% of Americans are worth more than the bottom 90%. This is one of the reasons why over forty five million Americans are currently living on food stamps, a situation actually worse than the great depression.[6]

You need to understand this and you need to do something about it. We will look at real inflation in more detail later in the book.

TWO: PENSION SYSTEMS ALL OVER THE WORLD ARE BANKRUPT
This is a controversial statement but completely factual nevertheless. With very few exceptions (Norway for example) and unless you are only a few years from retirement, wherever you live in the world today you absolutely cannot count on being able to live on hand outs from your government for the rest of your life when you stop working. It just can't happen, yet most people are relying on just such handouts.

Nearly every western government is effectively bankrupt. As we shall see, this actually includes America, Britain and Japan as well as the more obvious countries you have been reading about such as Greece, Ireland, Spain, Italy and Portugal.[7] All of these countries are totally incapable of funding the promised pension and medical needs of the hundreds of millions of people set to retire in the next few decades. This is a mathematical inevitability, not some grey area to be debated. National debts in all of these countries are now so high that many western governments can't afford their interest payments without printing money, let alone pay back the entire loan.

Once in this position, the only way they can pay back their loans is by creating money out of thin air. When governments invent money, it causes inflation, which is precisely what has been happening as described in the section above.

At the same time that western governments have mismanaged things to such an extent that they can't provide for your retirement, people themselves have made a completely inadequate private provision for their old age. In the UK, over 50% of people have no effective private pension at all. They are relying on a state that categorically cannot afford to pay for them.

---

6 Source: "The Price of Civilization" by Professor Jeffrey Sachs, Chapter 2.

7 Debt per capita in America is $44,215 at the time of writing compared to $39,937 in Greece. How often do we see the American or British press examine this reality?

Sadly, the vast majority of the other 50% have made completely inadequate pension provision such that they will find their standard of living in retirement to be far lower than during their working lives, particularly given where real inflation is as already discussed.

Most people are looking at a retirement lived, quite literally, in complete poverty. At the time of writing the average British adult has about £30,000[8] saved by retirement. This is enough to buy them a pension income of about £930 a year at current annuity rates. That is £77.50 a month. I would imagine that you would like to have a great deal more than £77.50 a month plus a tiny or, more likely, completely nonexistent state pension to live on for the last thirty or forty years of your life.

This disastrous situation is true for nearly every single country in the world. As you might imagine, the ramifications of this reality could be pretty frightening. History has taught us time and again that an impoverished population is an unstable one. We have seen this reality in several Arab countries in the last year and more recently in Greece, Spain, Russia and even Canada.[9] At worst, the pension situation all over the world could very well be a "blood in the streets" problem before too long.

I fervently hope this does not end up being the case but the only way we can deal with this problem effectively is if as many people as possible take personal responsibility for their own financial situation right now. What follows will empower you to do just that.

To put things in perspective: If you want to have a pension income equivalent to the average British salary of roughly £26,000 per year you will need to have saved up a pension pot of around £900,000 when you retire rather than £30,000 which is the current UK average.[10]

Although this might seem rather frightening, the good news is that sorting it out is actually far easier than you think, no matter what you earn. You can do it. You just need to know how and you need to get started. The sooner the better…

---

8 Frighteningly this is an average of women having less than £10,000 and men just over £50,000.

9 There are compelling arguments to say that one of the key causes of the Arab Spring was the inflation (in food prices, primarily) we have already been speaking about.

10 Annuity rates are currently just over 3%. £26,000/0.03 = £866,666.

WHAT THIS BOOK IS *NOT* ABOUT

Crucially, what follows is absolutely not about trusting some "guru" to show you "an incredible system" to make money. This is not a get rich quick scheme but you will get rich. It is about showing you that making a good return on your money and becoming truly wealthy as a result is easier than you ever thought. The knowledge in this book is not particularly complicated but it is incredibly poorly distributed throughout the general population.

In my opinion, true financial literacy should be taught as a compulsory subject in every secondary school in the country.[11] The reality is that it is only really taught at major investment banks and the best investment and hedge funds. As with most things, the knowledge is available in books for those willing to seek it out (see the bibliography section below for more detail) but there is obviously an enormous amount of ground to cover. I have done my best to cover that ground for you, save you a great deal of time and present you with only the most relevant and actionable information.

If most people understood what follows, financial crises of the kind we are currently experiencing would be far less likely to happen. We can focus on greedy bankers and corrupt or incompetent politicians but neither would have been able to get us to our current predicament were it not for another key ingredient: Financial illiteracy on the part of the great majority of people. The result of this has been literally millions of individuals all over the world making bad personal decisions about their finances year after year.

"Bankers" have only been able to make big bonuses because much of the industry has been selling bad products with high costs for decades and we have let them get away with it. If the car industry consistently sold us terrible cars that broke down all the time but still cost an arm and a leg we wouldn't buy them. We have allowed most of our financial service providers to do just that ever since financial products were invented.

Why has this been the case and how have we let them get away with it? I believe the answer is quite simply because the vast majority of people have never taken the time to understand finance or financial products in anything more than an incredibly simple way. To go back to my car analogy: Many people are interested in cars. They buy magazines about them and do a reasonable amount of homework before they buy one. If people did the same before buying financial products, including property, we couldn't be where we are today. Sadly most do not undertake such homework as a result of a dangerous combination of fear and

---

11 There are signs this might actually happen in the future thankfully.

boredom and because they were never taught the basics at school.

This is what I want to change. Like anything we know nothing about, once you spend a little time on it, finance is much easier and much more interesting than you thought. It is also worth highlighting that if you can be bothered to apply the same effort to buying financial products as you do to buying cars it won't be long before you are buying far nicer cars than you were previously and doing so without using debt.

The reason so few people optimise their finances and become wealthy is because they never spend any time learning about it and never properly try their hand at investment. If you read on, however, you will see very quickly that with a relatively small amount of effort you can do a superb job with your money and a better job than nearly all professionals you might have turned to in the past.

WHAT THIS BOOK *IS* ABOUT

This book will have succeeded when you have a number of "eureka" moments and find that you "get it". You won't need to trust me or think I'm particularly clever. You will feel confident in your own ability to arrange your financial affairs in a way that will make a huge and lasting difference to the rest of your life. Using the information that follows, your minimum goal should be to target building a pot of at least £1 million by the time you retire.

Actually, a far better target would be to achieve this sort of number a long time before you reach retirement age and significantly more by the time you retire so that you can start enjoying your wealth much sooner. As you will see, this is entirely possible.

All you have to do for this to happen is read on and:

1. Realise that finance is easier than you ever thought and why most people never work this out. The reason is extremely obvious: Most people never spend any time at all learning about it. This is one of those strange aspects of human nature. Learning how to run your own financial affairs is a life skill which must rank up there as one of the very best for having a positive impact on all other areas of your life yet most of us invest our time learning about a vast range of other far less useful life skills and totally neglect finance.
2. Learn "Two Amazing Facts About Finance".
3. Understand "Two Crucial Investment Themes for Today".
4. Take simple steps with arranging your financial affairs and start making money.

After you have finished this book, optimising your financial affairs will very possibly take less time than you spent last time you watched a bad film. It will certainly take less time than it took you to learn how to drive a car. Sorry if I'm labouring the automotive analogy a little but the point stands.

As "repetition is the mother of all learning" let us end this introduction by repeating the quote from the beginning of this chapter:

"There is an essential life skill that has never been and still isn't taught to the masses: How to manage, control and invest money to protect and provide for your financial future…" [12]

I firmly believe that if we can change this reality, not only can you personally make a huge difference to the rest of your life but a huge difference to the fortunes of the entire country. Good luck. I know that reading what follows and acting on it will do nothing less than change your life…

---

12 From "Big Money, Little Effort", by Mark Shipman, p.1 of the Preface.

#2

WHY YOU WILL DO BETTER THAN THE "PROFESSIONALS"

"No one cares more about your money than you do. With a basic under-standing of the investment process and a bit of discipline, you're perfectly ca-pable of managing your own money... By managing your own money, you'll be able to earn higher returns and save many thousands ... in investment costs over your lifetime..." [1]

– Alex Green, top US investor, "retired" at 43.

1 From "The Gone Fishin' Portfolio", by Alex Green, p. 4. See bibliography at the end of the book.

Most people do not have confidence in their ability to invest their own money.

Be honest: Did you spend more time researching the purchase of your last car (or pizza delivery or pair of jeans for that matter) than you have ever spent learning the best way to look after your money or reading a solid "how to invest" book? Do your eyes glaze over when you hear words like "bond", "equity" or "commodity"?

If you answered "yes" to the above questions, don't worry, you are in good company. In my experience the above is true of the vast majority of people. Crazy as it might sound this includes many financial advisers and people who work in the City for reasons we will examine shortly.

This is a huge shame given that the number one secret of most rich people throughout history is that they do understand money and how they can make more from it.

Over time, it is actually far easier, quicker and less hassle to have your money (capital) make you money than to make money from your work (labour). Whether we like it or not we live in a capitalist era. One of the fundamental truths of capitalism is that capital makes a great deal more money than labour: It should be pretty obvious to you that people who own businesses tend to make far more money than people who work for them. This is truer today than at any other time in history, primarily because capital is more mobile today than ever before.[2]

The great news and what so few people realise, is that the stock market and other forms of investment are fundamentally just fantastic innovations that enable anyone to become a business owner almost no matter how little money they have to start with. It has also never been easier to invest thanks to inexpensive and extremely powerful online tools that have only been around for the last decade or so.

The fact that making money from money is ultimately easier than making money from work is entirely logical when you consider that you only have a limited number of hours to work. Your money, on the other hand, "never sleeps" as the old saying is quite right in telling us. Money also breeds like rabbits if you know what you're doing. Even multi-millionaire actors, businesspeople and rock stars have very frequently made vastly more money from their money than from their acting fees, salaries or record sales.

It is not an exaggeration to say that virtually every very wealthy person in history

---

2 At the time of writing recent figures show that capital's share of overall wealth in the world relative to labour is the highest it has ever been. This is one of the reasons why the rich who own businesses are richer than ever before relative to people who only work for them.

has accrued far more money from their investments than from being paid for their work. It is also worth noting that they have invariably spent far less time making money from their money than on pursuing their career or passion. Once your money starts making you money you find yourself with the freedom to do anything you want whether you get paid for your time or not. To become rich, you need to get into this mindset.

It is a tragedy that most people do not understand this and the main reason so many people struggle financially. Because they have never studied it, most people have extremely unfortunate, incorrect and limiting beliefs about how money works: "The stock market is a casino," "investment is risky," "cash is safe." All three of these statements are inherently untrue in one way or another, something that is often well understood by the rich.

You might find it hard to believe but: "You can't go wrong with bricks and mortar…" is also a dangerous statement much of the time. Many people throughout history, including in the last few years, have gone horribly wrong with bricks and mortar and many more will do so in the future. We will look at this in more detail in chapter six. It is also fair to say that cash is nowhere near as safe as you might think it is given what is happening to real inflation these days.

The reason why many people have come to believe "the stock market is a casino" is very simply because most people know nothing or incredibly little about it. Amazingly this includes many of the people investing in it.

I have lost count of the number of people I have met over the years who buy and sell shares without understanding almost any of the things that you should before investing in the stock market. This is why "average" investment performance numbers are of no use to you and you should ignore them. A top sprinter who can run the hundred metres in under ten seconds doesn't care that the "average" adult human can run it in tens or dozens of seconds. The fact that there are large numbers of slow people bringing down the mathematical average has no impact at all on the professional athlete's ability to run at his speed. We forget this logic when we think that investment is really difficult because the "average" return is only x%. This number includes a vast number of people who have no clue what they are doing. I hope this makes sense to you.

A BRIEF NOTE ON THE "EFFICIENT MARKET HYPOTHESIS"

A minority of readers who might have studied finance or economics at university or might work in financial services may have read the last few paragraphs and disagreed with my argument. Such a person might refer to something called the "Efficient Market Hypothesis" to suggest that what I have said above is incorrect. Given this possibility I must digress briefly to deal with just such an objection.

The Efficient Market Hypothesis (EMH) is a theory about financial markets that has been around for many years and has been extremely fashionable (arguably with disastrous results). The basic idea is that no one can outperform the stock market by choosing the right investments. That is to say that in financial markets averages *are* important and no matter how much training you get you will never be able to beat them. This is precisely the reverse conclusion to the one I have drawn above using a professional sprinter as my example.

The idea is that the price of any asset will always be exactly where it "should" be because there are lots of intelligent, professional people involved in any given market who are reacting to a wealth of good quality information about where that asset should trade. The theory then concludes that an investor will never be able to get an edge or advantage such that they might buy a share and make a greater return than the market as a whole.

There are still many folk who believe in the EMH. Everyone is entitled to their opinion but I feel strongly that the theory has been widely discredited (as do many of the very best investors in the world). There is a vast amount of evidence and academic work which demonstrates that the theory simply doesn't hold up. As with many of the topics we will cover in this book, there have been hundreds of books written about the EMH and we don't want to waste time going into any great level of detail.

I would simply hope to strengthen my contention that it is entirely possible for you to be a "professional sprinter" amongst investors by giving you a couple of brief examples. Hopefully these will make sense to you whether you have a financial background or not.

ASYMMETRIC INFORMATION

The main reason that the EMH doesn't work in reality and why you can hope to make great returns on your money has to do with human nature and the existence of what is called "asymmetric information". The key point here is that people involved in markets demonstrably do not have perfect information about the things they are investing in as the EMH would have you believe. Some people have far more information than others – that is to say that information is "asymmetric".

As I have already said, many people who are investing have almost no idea what they are doing. I would argue that it is this reality more than anything else that lead to the dot.com boom and bust, to the subprime housing crash and, arguably, to all other boom and bust events in human history.[3]

EXAMPLE ONE: THE DOT.COM BOOM

Later in the book we will learn the basics of how to value a share. If you have a grasp of notions such as p/e ratios, dividend yield or book value[4] you can get a good idea of when a share is "cheap" and therefore more likely to be worth buying or when it is "expensive" and, therefore, more likely to be worth selling. You will never have 100% conviction that you are correct in your analysis but if you do not understand these things, you are at the very least at a huge information disadvantage to those who do.

The "smart money" understands these "valuation techniques". A large number of people investing in the very same market do not. This meant, for example, that in the dot.com boom when dot.com shares were trading at a price light-years more expensive than any shares had ever traded in the history of stock markets the smart money really did understand this to be the case and knew that those prices were entirely unsustainable. The amateur investor who was buying technology shares because a friend told them a share was "hot" did not. Many, probably most, lost a great deal of money as a result. As ever, their loss was the smart money's gain.

The recent stock market flotation of Facebook gives us another example of this sort of mania.[5] The stock market valuation of the company equates to a very high multiple of the profits and sales it is forecast to make in the years ahead (the main method of valuing a company).[6] In the long run these sorts of multiples are almost never sustainable. The share is just too expensive. The main reason Facebook is able to achieve such a valuation is because a very large number of people investing in it simply do not understand valuation multiples.[7] This suits the finance industry because their fees are a percentage of the value of the company but is very bad for the small investor who is pinning their retirement hopes on something which is highly likely to become cheaper in the years ahead (i.e. lose them money).

---

3 If you want some fun and have a spare fifteen minutes, google "tulip bubble".

4 Don't worry if these sound complicated. We will demystify these ideas later in the book.

5 At the time of editing Facebook has fallen about 30% since it was launched.

6 Again, please don't worry if this sounds complicated. You won't think it is once you've finished the book.

7 There are also plenty of "professional" investors putting money into the share because they are second guessing the impact that the herd will have. This is a dangerous game and, arguably, gambling rather than investing although it is fair to say that some people do play this game successfully, at least for a while.

It is worth noting that if enough people who do not understand valuation fundamentals keep buying the company, the price might go up for a while. All those people will then think they've done the right thing and made a solid investment. As a result of human nature, other people (who don't understand share valuation either) see the price going up and decide they need to jump in or they will miss out. This pushes the share price from very expensive to crazily expensive which is exactly what happened in the dot.com boom. This reality strongly illustrates what a weak theory EMH is in the real world. The long term end result of a share being crazily expensive is inevitable: The stock market has its own gravitational pull. What goes up (beyond sensible levels) must, inevitably come down.

If you look at many decades of stock market data, it is abundantly clear that no company should ever be worth twenty five times the value of its sales or a few hundred times the value of its profits. Any that do trade at these levels are doing so because there are a sufficient number of investors who do not understand this truth. The share will eventually come back to earth, losing most of them a lot of money. Buying these sorts of companies simply isn't investment. It is gambling. People who are informed investors, therefore, tend to leave these companies alone given there are thousands of other ones for which a sensible analysis can be made and an informed decision reached. We will look at how to do this later in the book.

EXAMPLE TWO: THE SUB-PRIME CRISIS
The sub-prime crisis gives us another example of asymmetric information leading to one group of people making a killing and another group losing their shirts. Probably the best selling book about the sub-prime crisis is called "The Big Short" by Michael Lewis.[8] It is well worth a read and basically tells the story of a group of smart investors whose detailed research gave them better information about certain financial products (mortgage backed securities) in the sub-prime market. Their research told them that these products were completely the wrong price.

As a result they were able to make thousands of percent on their money in less than a year and, in some cases, literally billions of dollars betting against these financial assets. This is another glaring example of market inefficiency, asymmetric information and the EMH simply not holding true. It is also perhaps worth noting that wealth is arguably never destroyed, merely transferred to the "smart money" from the less smart money.

I could fill a book with examples of why the EMH, whilst an elegant theory, simply doesn't hold up in the real world of investment but hopefully the above

8 See bibliography.

will suffice for now.[9] The most important point here is that investing in financial markets without knowing what you are doing is like driving on a motorway before you have learned how to drive. You might be lucky and arrive safely at your destination but it is quite likely that you will have a nasty crash and then tell everyone how dangerous driving is. It is only because so many people involved in financial markets do not know what they are doing that so many lose money and come to believe it is "risky" or "a casino".

SIX SPECIFIC REASONS WHY YOU WILL DO BETTER THAN "PROFESSIONALS" WITH YOUR MONEY:

Crucially, there are a number of very good inherent reasons why you should be able to do a better job with your money than finance professionals. There are obviously a large number of areas of your personal finances where, traditionally you might have sought professional advice. These would include: Arranging a mortgage, buying a type of insurance product such as life or contents insurance, critical illness, accident or sickness cover. You might also have gone to a financial adviser to discuss inheritance tax or making a will.

In what follows, however, we are interested in discussing how useful financial advice is when it concerns investment and pensions, that is to say growing your money as effectively as possible. As you have already seen, the whole thrust of "Own The World" is that you can and should look after your own money. Once you feel confident doing this, you may still wish to outsource other more peripheral areas of your personal finances such as those listed above, if only to save you time, but these are much less important than getting investment right.

For what it is worth, my personal feeling is that it is increasingly easy to take care of nearly all of these more peripheral financial products yourself. In recent years we have witnessed a proliferation of online resources such as financial comparison websites which have empowered people to arrange their own will or buy good value insurance products very easily for example.

Whether you choose to go down that route or to use a financial adviser for these sorts of decisions is obviously entirely up to you. My hope is that after you have read what follows, you will at the very least feel empowered to make your own investment decisions. Ultimately, doing the best job with investment is the most fundamental building block of your personal finances.

---

9 If you would like more evidence then please have a look at the Wikipedia entry about the Efficient Market Hypothesis or just google it and do some of your own research.

So, let us now look in more detail at why you are truly inherently best placed to look after your own investment decisions. Entire books have been written on this subject[10] but the main reasons are:

REASON 1: A SIGNIFICANT CONFLICT OF INTEREST AND LACK OF KNOWLEDGE...

One of the key reasons why you should find it easy to do a better job with your money than if you use a professional is concerned with the traditional structure of the whole UK finance industry.

Because most people do not feel confident making their own investments, they will tend to seek the services of a financial adviser of one kind or another. To see why this might be problematic we need only consider the training traditionally received by most UK financial advisers and the way in which they have been paid.

Later in the book we will look at the various different types of investment available to you and their relative merits. One of the best things about investment today is that there is a vast range of things you can invest in: Bonds, equities (shares), commodities, currency (foreign exchange), real estate (property) and funds, to name some of the main categories.

Each of these has very different qualities and, as we shall see, the successful investor must ensure they are using the right mix of all or at least most of them. Arguably the biggest reason why most people fail in investment is they fail to own a sufficiently wide range of investment products. As we shall see, owning a wide range of shares from all over the world, property, bonds and commodities gives you a far better chance of consistent success. Very few people do this, even those who work in financial services.

One of the reasons for this is that few financial advisers are likely to recommend this sort of mix. Nearly all traditional advisers will want you to invest in funds or insurance products of some kind and very little else. This is entirely logical (for them) since:

- Most financial advisers have traditionally been paid a cut of the products they sell and the only two main product groups where this has been practicable are funds and insurance products.
- The majority of financial advisers have little or no understanding of any of the other products. Hardly surprising since they struggle to make any money from them.

---

10 Two of the best of which are Peter Lynch's "One Up on Wall Street" and Alex Green's "The Gone Fishin' Portfolio." See the bibliography for full details.

To elaborate:[11] For the last several decades, most financial advisers have been paid on a commission basis. That is to say that they have been paid a percentage of whichever product they suggest you buy.

As you can imagine, this led to a worrying conflict of interest. You may be aware that the Financial Services Authority (FSA) is the body tasked with looking after consumer's rights in the UK finance industry. The body which the FSA uses to examine people who work in finance is called the Chartered Institute for Securities & Investment (CISI) and the CISI themselves acknowledge that: "…there are incentives for the intermediary (adviser) to recommend a product that offers the highest commission rates…"[12]

In June 2006, aware of this problem and in the wake of a number of mis-selling scandals you may have read about (endowment mortgages, payment protection insurance, etc.), the FSA published a review of how financial products are sold to UK consumers. This review concluded that because: "…many consumers rely heavily on advisers… and there can be a misalignment of advisers' interests with those of consumers…" there is a "…risk that substantial consumer detriment will occur…"[13]

In Plain English, that is to say that even the government body in charge of regulating the financial services industry freely admits you are at risk of getting bad financial advice from financial advisers. This is certainly borne out by my experience and the experience of most people I have ever spoken to about financial advice after over a decade of asking the question. Whilst I acknowledge that this is anecdotal, the subject matter here will no doubt resonate with many of you.

This state of affairs is pretty incredible when you think about it and one of the reasons so many people have had a bad experience with investment over the last few decades. The good news, however, is that once we understand this reality we are equipped to do something about it.

So, the traditional model for financial advice in the UK has meant there has been a risk that financial advisers might recommend products that pay them the highest commissions rather than those best suited to your needs.

---

11 To be fair, there are truly independent financial advisers. They will ask you to pay them an hourly rate or a lump sum for evaluating your financial affairs, rather than take a cut of your investment funds (although the very worst of them will do both if you're not careful). Even though these sorts of IFAs exist, so many consumers are unwilling to pay for them that they have traditionally made up a fairly small part of the market. Ironic given these are often the best types of advisers to use.

12 From the Chartered Institute for Securities and Investment's "FSA Regulation and Professional Integrity" work book, p. 7

13 Again: From the Chartered Institute for Securities and Investment's "FSA Regulation and Professional Integrity" work book, p. 76.

Whilst this might seem bad enough, I would argue that there are even more serious structural flaws in the industry. For example, many financial advisers have traditionally been described as "tied". That is to say that they are only in a position to sell you the products of one company or a small group of companies (to whom they are "tied").

This is generally the case if you look for financial advice from a high street bank, for example. If, as many people naturally do, you go into a high street bank looking for investment advice, their staff will often only be able to suggest products offered by that bank.

This means that you will only be able to choose an investment from a laughably minuscule sub-set of what is on offer in the world of investment as a whole. In addition, you will usually end up paying higher fees than you need to, as these products tend to be inherently expensive. It is entirely possible for a tied adviser to do the very best they can within the constraints of the product range they have at their disposal and for you to end up with a very poor result for your financial affairs compared to what is possible.

All of the above might seem bad enough but regretfully I would go even further and say that another problem with financial advice in the UK in general is that many of the people involved in the industry have a woefully inadequate understanding of finance as a whole. In the past it has been entirely possible to become qualified as a "financial adviser" without needing to have any detailed understanding of the wide variety of financial markets we described above and will look at in more detail below.

As we have seen, many financial advisers have only ever been trained on the products their employer sells and have quite literally no knowledge about the thousands of other products that might be better for your purposes. At my first ever meeting with a financial adviser in a high street bank, the person I spoke to wasn't even aware that products existed other than the ones their firm sold.

As an example of how problematic this can be, as we shall see in more detail shortly, gold has been one of the best performing financial assets in the world for the last decade. If you had purchased gold ten years ago you would have made around six times your money by now whilst stock markets have hardly budged.

For all the reasons outlined in this section, it is unlikely that any financial adviser in the UK would have suggested you invest in gold. Many would have no idea how to do it to start with and even those who would have known which vehicle would give you exposure to gold would have had little incentive to suggest that product since they would be unable to earn any commission.

As we shall soon see, one of the key things that differentiates the very smartest and most successful investors in the world from everyone else is their understanding and use of all the main asset classes. If you walk into a high street bank today and ask to see one of their advisers, it is not an exaggeration to say that you have virtually no chance whatsoever of speaking to someone with this level of knowledge. The same is true of many independent financial advisers (IFAs).

Remember, this isn't just my opinion. The Financial Services Authority themselves have identified these very issues in recent years, one might suggest not a moment too soon. To quote the CISI's own examination materials again: "Those providing advice can do so with relatively little training and testing when compared to other professions..."[14]

This point is especially well made when you consider that an accountant must endure three years of study and professional exams in order to gain their qualification, a financial analyst at an investment bank or investment fund will often have had to complete the Chartered Financial Analyst (CFA) qualification (which also takes at least three years and is famously difficult) and a lawyer will have, at the very least, had to complete a degree in law or a conversion course and further years of professional training before they are able to practice.

For what it is worth, those in charge of regulating UK financial services are in the process of addressing these issues. From the 1st January 2013, financial advisers will have had to demonstrate far more knowledge about investment and financial markets than previously and passed much more rigorous exams. As a result, some firms in the industry expect that as many as 40% of financial advisers will leave the industry this year.

Having already passed these exams myself, however, I would argue that there is still a significant gap between the subject material examined and the knowledge required to understand the investment methods used by the world's very best investors which we will look at in this book. It took me six months to complete the new exams and I could have completed them a good deal more quickly had I not been writing this book. Compare this with the several years of study other professions have had to complete described above.

In conclusion, it should be clear having read the above that you will very possibly be better off making the limited effort required to understand financial products yourself than you are using most financial advisers.[15]

---

14 CISI "FSA Regulation and Professional Integrity" work book, p. 77.

15 If you intend to seek financial advice any time soon, please have a look at the www.plainenglishfinance.com blog article "Questions for anyone who wants to give you financial advice."

Before I go on to our next section, I would like to make an important additional point: Which is to say that as with any profession, there is obviously a wide range of ability amongst financial advisers. I stand by the arguments I have made so far in this chapter and I am strongly of the opinion that the market for financial advice in the UK has many inherent flaws which increase the risk of you receiving sub-optimal financial advice. Nevertheless, there are of course financial advisers who are extremely competent and will do a good job for you.

At the very least then, reading this book will equip you to identify the best financial advisers, fully understand their charging structure and get the best value out of them as a result. That said, I would argue that once you have acquired the level of knowledge required to identify a top quality financial adviser it isn't that much more of a leap to have acquired the knowledge required to run your own financial affairs. The point still remains that doing so will save you a great deal of money over the years and no doubt make you feel far more empowered and in control of your life.

To go back to my driving analogy: Most of us learn how to drive, rather than employ a driver. I would repeat that if you were able to learn how to drive, you are able to learn how to invest. It is no harder and will not take any longer. Whether you decide to employ a financial adviser or not is obviously entirely up to you and you will be very well placed to make that decision by the time you have finished this book.

The eagle-eyed amongst you may have spotted a paradox in the above section: How can I complain that financial advisers haven't spent enough time studying and then say that you don't need to spend that much time learning about finance to do well? The answer is that those of you who don't want to spend much time learning about money can still do very well with a formulaic approach we will look at later in the book. It won't take you long to get this level of knowledge. To be fully up to speed on finance, such that you can give advice to people, however, should be a much longer road to travel. Hopefully this makes sense. It certainly should do by the time you've finished the book.

By learning a little about how to look after your own money you can ensure that you give consideration to the full range of financial products available in the world today, benefit from the very best investment methods available and maximize your chances of saving thousands of pounds or more in commission and fees. This leads us neatly on to the next reason why you will do a far better job than many professionals you might use:

REASON 2: CHARGES / FEES / COSTS

As MoneyWeek[16] magazine puts it:

"If the evidence is any guide at all, then there is one thing that all investors should watch out for before they put their money to work: Costs."

When you use a financial adviser you will pay for that advice. Often their charging structure is hard to understand. They will generally take a cut of your money to put you into a given product (usually a fund or insurance product as explained above) and this product will, in turn, have its own set of additional charges attached.

What this means is that if you give your money to a professional investor they might charge as much as 5% or even more of your capital up-front for the privilege of putting your money to work and a chunk of your money every year for the life of the product.[17] This can mean that if you sign on the dotted line for a fund, endowment or similar insurance product that looks as if it has no fees, the reality is that over the next few decades the adviser and provider of that product will skim literally thousands of pounds from your money. This will have an extremely detrimental impact on your returns.

For example, if you buy a fund in an ISA you are likely to pay between 1.5-5% of the money you invest to your adviser and the manager of the fund. This amounts to about £170 - £560 of your money if you are managing to save your annual ISA allowance of around £11,000.[18]

As we have seen, those professional investors will then charge a percentage of your money every year. This is very bad news for how quickly you can have your money making money since small changes in the percentage return you make each year have a huge impact on how quickly you become wealthy over time. We will see just how powerful this impact can be in chapter four when we look at compound interest. Over a lifetime of investing, the difference can quite literally amount to a seven-figure sum (that is not a typo). Hardly surprising that so many people are disappointed by their investment results when these largely hidden fees are eating into your returns that aggressively.

16 Please see the resources section of the website for more about MoneyWeek magazine.

17 As part of the research for this book I approached a number of IFA firms. As examples of the sorts of fees they are asking: I was told by one IFA firm that I would need to pay 4% of my funds to them as a fee up front and 0.8% per annum going forwards. Another asked for an £800 flat fee for a review. This book will show you how to avoid these sorts of costs entirely. These fees are on top of fees built into the products they would have told me to buy.

18 We will look in more detail at what an ISA is below. I acknowledge that few people are able to save the full £11,000 or so pounds (for now) but have used this number for illustrative purposes.

As we shall see later in the book, if you have even a basic understanding of where to go, today there are ways of investing which cost as little as £1.50, saving you hundreds of pounds to begin with and many thousands over several years (and possibly as much as a million or more over a lifetime, without exaggeration).

As you can imagine, these better value ways of investing are not promoted very well by the financial services community for the reasons outlined above. You are unlikely to hear about them from your high street bank or local IFA. This is another reason so many people have a dim view of investment: They automatically go to their high street bank for financial advice, which is almost always a bad idea as we have seen.

REASON 3: "CAREER RISK"
The third reason that many professional money people suffer from a structural (inherent) tendency to perform poorly with your money is known as "career risk". Assuming you have gone to a financial adviser and purchased a fund on their recommendation, there is a good reason why even the best of those funds may not do as well with your money as you will.

Simply put, a fund manager who does what everyone else does tends to have a lower risk of getting fired. If that person owns big blue chip stocks in a terrible year like 2008, for example, they will lose the same amount of money as everyone else who owns big blue chip stocks. There is safety in the herd. With everyone having had a terrible year, "the market" gets the blame and everyone keeps his or her job. This is good for the cautious fund manager but clearly no good to you if you have lost a large chunk of your money as so many people did in 2008.

Nearly all professional investors are limited to certain investment categories. They might be in charge of a "UK equity fund" or a "Global bond fund" for example. We will learn more about what these are later. For now, we need only understand that in a bad year for the UK, no matter how good a professional investor is in their own niche, you will very likely lose money if you are in a UK fund. This problem can be dealt with by ensuring your money is well spread around the world and across different asset classes. Again, we shall see more about how important this is and learn how to do it later.

A good example of the "career risk" problem is the case of a fund manager called Tony Dye. Mr. Dye was a top fund manager in the 1990s. During the dot.com boom of the late 1990s he was quite rightly highly critical of what he saw as the crazy increase in the share prices of technology and dot.com companies. As a result he refused to buy any of these sorts of companies. Sadly for Mr. Dye, this meant that he made significantly lower returns than his peers who had jumped on the dot.com bandwagon at the time. Even though he was correct in his analysis (that dot.com and technology shares were crazily over priced) he lost his job in 2000 a month before the market peaked. This is a good illustration of how "safety in the herd" for the fund manager often means a serious lack of safety for you and your money. People who were invested in the funds which outperformed Mr. Dye in the late 1990s lost a great deal of money when the market crashed.

REASON 4: LIQUIDITY OR THE "SUPER-TANKER-TURNING-CIRCLE" PROBLEM:

The fourth big reason why you have a very good chance at becoming a better investor than the well paid professional concerns the amount of money you will be looking after compared to them. If you have only a few thousand pounds or even only a few million (!) to invest, you are mostly able to buy and sell things without causing the price of those things to move much if at all.

If a big famous investor who is looking after billions of pounds decides they want to sell one of their investments, it may take them several weeks, or even longer for some investments, and push the price down. You or I might be able to buy a "cheeky" little biotechnology or mining stock and benefit from a huge short term move in the price. The big money professional can seldom buy and sell enough of that sort of stock to make much of a difference to the return on their fund as a whole which means neither can you if you are invested in that fund.[19]

REASON 5: EXCESSIVE SPECIALISATION AMONGST FINANCE PROFESSIONALS

"The most powerful tool an investor has working for him or her is diversification. True diversification allows you to build portfolios with higher returns for the same risk. Most investors… are far less diversified than they should be. They're way over-committed to stocks…" [20]

– Jack Meyer, manager of Harvard University's multi billion dollar investment funds, produced 15.9% per year for fifteen years (a 910% compounded return).

Another important reason why you will be able to do a much better job than many City professionals with your money:

People who work in financial services, even those in top investment banks making the large bonuses we are constantly reading about, are almost always incredibly specialised from very early in their career. This means that there are relatively few who are able or even inclined to see the "big picture" and it is truly the big picture that you need for consistent investment success.

19 Again, please don't worry if this terminology is alien to you. Soon you will be familiar with it all.
20 Jack Meyer quoted in "The Ivy Portfolio", p. 50.

Many investment professionals are just like those doctors who tell you how bad drinking and smoking are for you and then nip to the pub for several drinks and a few good strong cigarettes at the end of their day. Over the years I have lost count of the number of incredibly smart City folk I know who have all their money in the one asset class they know about with the result that even they are heavily punished in a bad year for that asset class.

At the risk of being a little on the repetitive side, one of the most successful investing strategies over many years is being properly diversified. This means that you should ensure that you own a wide variety of assets rather than just shares or just property for example. To repeat our example from above but make a subtly different point, you will recall that over the last decade gold has performed exceptionally well. It is amazing, however, just how few investment professionals have owned gold.

Any detailed study of the best thing to do with your money will suggest that you should have at least some of your money in precious metals but relatively few investment professionals who work exclusively with other asset classes such as equities (shares) or bonds would even have thought about gold. I know this from first hand experience. As a result they have missed out on part of their portfolio rising 600% over the last decade.

REASON 6: THE WAR BETWEEN FUNDAMENTAL AND TECHNICAL ANALYSIS

Another important disadvantage of finance professionals becoming highly specialised is that almost all of them end up subscribing to one or other of the two main categories of financial analysis (fundamental and technical) and are rabidly and, to my mind, irrationally critical of the other. It is very often the case that finance professionals who see themselves as using what is called fundamental analysis feel the same way about finance professionals who use technical analysis as cats feel about dogs. This is a great shame for both of them.

I have quite literally heard the former describe technical analysis as "black magic" and heard technical enthusiasts say that fundamental analysis is "totally pointless". Both of these are literal quotes from serious and highly paid City professionals and these sorts of views are the norm not the exception. It seems to be another manifestation of human nature that people tend to choose a "church" at some stage of their career and are then at risk of "doing an ostrich" going forwards.

We will explain more about what these two approaches are later in the book but for now it is enough to make the point that many of the very best investors in the world use both of these types of analysis. A very good example is Anthony Bolton, one of Britain's best ever fund managers. Mr. Bolton has a very fundamental approach to picking shares but is on record as describing his use of technical analysis as his "secret weapon".[21]

Using a combination of the two techniques he returned 19.5% per annum over 28 years, a 14,460% compounded return. This turned £10,000 into £1.46 million. Interestingly, for those of you who know that his subsequent track record running a China fund has been pretty awful, this is further evidence of the importance of geographical and asset diversification.

I think it is a great shame that most investment professionals tend to choose one or other of fundamental or technical analysis to the total exclusion of the other when the use of the two together is so self-evidently more effective.

IN SUMMARY

1. Most investors are at risk of losing money and making bad investments because they really don't know what they are doing.
2. Even professional investors can have the cards stacked against them for the reasons described above.
3. This means that if you can be a well-informed "amateur" you have a huge advantage over both of these other groups. You are truly in the investing sweet spot.

This is extremely exciting news and what is even more exciting is that learning how to get into that sweet-spot is far easier than you think. To continue with my driving on the motorway analogy:

I would argue that learning how to make a huge difference to your finances is no harder than learning how to drive safely. It is because virtually no one does it that so few people find this out.

People who do spend a little time learning about money often find that life gets a great deal easier and a great deal more fun. The day you make several thousand pounds from a phone call or mouse click is a truly wonderful one and opens your eyes to a world of possibility...

21 http://www.fool.co.uk/news/investing/2012/01/16/anthony-boltons-secret-weapon.aspx

#3

WHO AM I AND WHY DO I THINK I CAN HELP YOU?

"Andy's drive is not just to inform, but to genuinely benefit those who engage with his material. Having dabbled in the stock market for a long time, but with limited success, the clearly outlined strategies in "Own The World" have made a huge difference to the way I personally think about investing".

– Tim R. Commercial Insurance Professional

"Andy Craig's mission is to remove the blanket of confusion and secrecy that covers our understanding of money, finance and the economy. He is giving us the tools to do a crucial job - take control of our own finances, and our futures. He is passionate that this mission succeeds. And if he succeeds, we all will."

– Tom S. Broadcast Journalist

So far I have highlighted how vital it is to get to grips with your finances, suggested this is much easier to do than you might previously have thought and promised that I can help. I have also explained the various reasons why much of the financial advice you will find in the UK is inherently unlikely to help you achieve the very best result for your finances.

It is entirely natural for you to want to know why I feel qualified to do this and why I am any different to the rest of the finance industry. There are a very large number of people working in finance who promise the earth and then fail to deliver, why should I be any different?

My first answer is that the most fundamental difference between me and any financial adviser you might go to is that my goal is for you to learn how to look after your own money, not for me to look after it for you.

Hopefully this much was clear from the first page of this book.

In terms of why I feel qualified to help you achieve this goal, obviously the traditional approach is to tell you about my educational and career background in order to establish my credentials and I will get to that in a moment. Before I do, however, I want to repeat the point made earlier in the book: It is my fervent wish that as you read what follows you will find the material sufficiently compelling in its own right that it won't really matter to you what my background is. The information in this book should appeal to your common sense such that you don't really care who the author was.

That said, for the sake of tradition I will now say a bit about why I feel qualified to write this book. Feel free to skip ahead to the next chapter if you are bored by "about the author" pieces.

I started taking an interest in economics, economic history, politics and finance from what might be considered a freakishly young age. My father might not thank me for saying this but it is not an exaggeration to say that he used to take me through magazines like the Economist and the Sunday papers with him from about the age of nine or ten.

Inevitably, I chose to study Economics and International Politics at University, graduating in 1997. My first job then took me to Washington DC the day after my last exam at University to work as an intern for a US Congressman (the American equivalent of an MP).

Rightly or wrongly, the Chief of Staff in my Congressional office was convinced that a half British, half Irish person like me was inherently better at writing than any of the Americans on her payroll despite my tender years. This was fantastic news and meant that I managed to gain rapid promotion from "…'executive' intern in charge of opening mail and getting coffee…" to actually writing serious policy speeches for the Congressman almost from day one. As you can imagine, this was an incredible experience. The key benefit of my time in DC was that it gave me an early idea of how important politics and politicians can be when thinking about finance and investment.

Happily my stint in the US Congress meant that I was lucky enough to be asked to interview by the vast majority of the companies I applied to back in London: Investment banks, management consultants and accountancy firms as well as the UK Civil Service (Foreign Office et al.). I eventually accepted a job with what was then SBC Warburg (now UBS Investment Bank). Since then I have spent more than ten years working for various finance firms in London and latterly New York. These included the aforementioned UBS, CA Cheuvreux, the European equity arm of Credit Agricole (France's biggest bank) and two smaller boutique firms.

I started my career in the bond market at UBS before moving into equities (shares).[1] You will recall from the last chapter my point that many finance professionals become specialised very early in their careers, often from day one. Although I am by no means unique having worked in bonds and equities, it is nevertheless reasonably rare and means I don't have quite the cat vs. dog approach to people who work in another branch of finance that many finance professionals do.[2]

Perhaps even more importantly, however, when I moved into equities my area of specialism was called "pan European small and mid caps". Although something of a mouthful, this simply meant that I dealt with companies from all over Europe and the UK that were less than about £2-3 billion in size.[3] This meant that I was able to personally meet and travel (around Europe and the US) with the very top management teams (CEO, CFO, Chairman etc.) of several hundred companies from every sector imaginable and was involved with the stock market flotation (IPO) of dozens of high profile companies including the likes of Burberry, Campari, easyJet, HMV, lastminute.com, Carluccio's and the Carbon Trust.

The key point here is that working in "smaller" companies meant two things: First, that I got high level access to the very top management of hundreds of companies, an incredible learning experience as you might imagine. Secondly, the

1 We will look at bonds, equities et al. below.

2 I'm being rather tongue in cheek here but it is true that many City employees tend to perpetuate generally hilarious stereotypes about other City employees working in different asset classes.

3 Measured by market capitalisation. Under about £3 billion is called "small and mid cap" where "cap" stands for "capitalisation".

price of smaller companies tends to be more volatile than the bigger household names in the FTSE 100 such as Tesco, M&S, BP, Shell or Vodafone. This means that I witnessed some companies appreciate in value by dozens, even hundreds of percent and, equally, saw others lose a huge percentage of their value, sometimes overnight.

This experience was key in my developing a belief in the amazing possibilities of investment. I saw first hand how much money the very best investors were able to make, something very few people in the general population ever do. I was also in a front row seat when certain investors lost a great deal of money very quickly which developed in me a keen desire to work out how to avoid this if at all possible.

My reaction was to read widely about investment outside of my day job and to start investing my own money. Thanks in great part to the returns afforded by those investments I have been able to spend around five of the last fifteen years outside of conventional employment (i.e. not having to earn any money). This has given me the time I needed to read a few hundred books on finance, trading, economics, history and economic history.

In fact, if you were to ask me the number one reason why I feel qualified to present you with what follows, it is the bibliography at the end of this book and the fact that I have also read dozens of emails about finance and economics nearly every day for the last decade. More than my degree or over ten years of working in banking, it is the time I have had to read the very best books and other information sources about investment and economic history that has enabled me to put this book together.[4]

I came up with the idea for Plain English Finance and "Own the World" in November 2007. Whilst on holiday I found myself in yet another discussion with someone who was extremely bright and had a great job but went to great lengths to tell me they had no clue about finance and investment and were too scared and distrustful of the industry to ever invest. For the umpteenth time I thought what a tragedy it was that so few people realise how relatively easy it is to learn how to look after their own money and decided there must be something I could do about this.

I spent another three years working but realised in early 2010 that I had enough saved up to give me the financial security I needed to leave stockbroking and work on launching Plain English Finance and on this book.

---

4 You will find recommendations for what I consider the very best books for your purposes in the resources section of www.plainenglishfinance.com.

You can be the judge of whether the result is that I am able to bring you information that you will find useful, even life-changing. I very much hope you will. So without further ado, let us look at the first of our amazing facts about finance with a view to your having some "eureka" moments about money as soon as possible…

#4

TWO AMAZING FACTS ABOUT FINANCE

"Those who understand compound interest are destined to collect it. Those who don't are doomed to pay it…"

– Tom and David Gardner, founders of top financial website The Motley Fool (www.fool.co.uk).

"It is only in the relatively recent past that the financial services industry has developed to the point that people from any background can invest in almost any country or asset class (shares, bonds, commodities etc.) easily, quickly and cheaply…"

– Andrew Craig, this chapter.

I believe there are two "amazing facts about finance" to focus on immediately. Once you understand these, you should very quickly start to see the incredible possibility that effective investment offers you.

FACT ONE: COMPOUND INTEREST: "THE EIGHTH WONDER OF THE WORLD"

One of the main objections I hear when I share my excitement about the wonderful world of investing with people is: "But that won't work for me, I make too little to have enough to have left over to invest."

Wrong!

Many people believe they need a big lump sum or the ability to save a large amount of money every month to make investment worthwhile. This is absolutely not true. As with so many things in life, it is the tortoise that generally wins the money race, not the hare. People who understand money and end up with lots of it tend to be those who understand that little and often wins the race.

You are much more likely to save a small amount of money right now than you are to save a large amount of money some time in the future. I'm sure you are familiar with this psychology: It is exactly the same with going to the gym, revising for exams, doing housework and so on.

As you are about to see, time is one of your biggest allies in becoming wealthy so you must take action now or as soon as possible. Start small but start now. If you do start small, no matter how small, you will immediately enable yourself to benefit from the magic of compound interest:

SO, WHAT IS COMPOUND INTEREST AND WHY IS IT SO IMPORTANT?
None other than Albert Einstein described this amazing fact about finance, compound interest, as "…the Eighth Wonder of the World".

If you take nothing more away from this book than an understanding of the incredible power of compound interest you will have joined a lucky and generally wealthy few. As Tom and David Gardner, founders of top financial website The Motley Fool put it:

> *"Those who understand compound interest are destined to collect it. Those who don't are doomed to pay it…"*

Compound interest is, quite literally, a form of free money… and it is free money that grows like a weed over time. How can this be?

Imagine that you invested £1,000 today. Imagine too that whatever you invested it in went up by 10% this year. In this scenario you would have £1,100 one year later: Your original sum, plus £100 of interest or return on a share or other investment. Simple so far.

Now comes the free money part: Assume you invested that £1,100 for another year and achieved 10% again. The following year you would have £1,210. This time you have made £110 of interest (1.1 x £1,100 = £1,210) but £10 of that interest is essentially free money. It is the interest you have been paid on your interest or, put another way, the return on your return.

At first glance this may not seem particularly exciting but over time the effect is incredibly powerful. Let's look more closely at some examples to see just how:

THE POWER OF COMPOUNDING

Let us say you decided to have a go at this investment thing. For the sake of argument, you started with £5,000 and managed to invest £250 per month going forwards. These might seem like numbers too small to make you a millionaire but are they?

Let us assume that you were to put your £5,000 lump sum into a current account that, as is effectively the case today, is paying no interest whatsoever. You then added £250 a month into the same current account each month going forwards. Let us look at what happens over the next few years if you are a straight "saver" in that current account compared to what you might achieve as an investor with compound interest on your side.

After one year the saver would have £8,000 squirrelled away: The £5,000 he or she started with, plus twelve payments of £250 totalling £3,000 more (12 x £250 = £3,000).

That is certainly "better than a punch in the face" as a City trader might say but now let us see how this compares with someone who had decided to invest their money: Let's look at the difference assuming a few different rates of return for the purposes of illustration.

At 0% the saver would have £8,000 as we have established.
At 8% the investor would have £8,584.33 at the end of the year.

At 10% they would have £8,737.17.[1]
At 12% they would have £8,892.80.
...and at 20% the investor would be sitting on £9,544.29.

We can immediately see a meaningful difference between what the saver has managed to achieve after a year versus the investor. Of far more interest, however is what happens over a number of years. The table facing illustrates the incredible power of compound interest.

If you start saving £250 a month at the age of 30, for the sake of argument, keep at it and pay it into top-performing assets you would end up with nearly *eight million pounds* by the age of 60. That is not a typo...

---

1 Some of you might think that a 10% return on £8,000 will give you £8,800 but remember that we are starting the year with only £5,000 and adding £250 as the year goes along, hence the difference.

£5,000 lump sum to begin and £250 saved each month...

	Saver	Investor			
Year	After X Years	0% return	8% return	10% return	12% return	20% return
2012	1	£8,000	£8,584	£8,737	£8,893	£9,544
2016	5	£20,000	£25,991	£27,816	£29,796	£39,568
2021	10	£35,000	£57,214	£65,286	£74,752	£132,538
2026	15	£50,000	£103,731	£126,936	£156,423	£383,182
2031	20	£65,000	£173,035	£228,370	£304,794	£1,058,910
2041	30	£95,000	£430,117	£669,845	£1,064,024	£7,792,017

COSTS ARE KEY

Crucially, please note the huge differences that a small change in the percentage return can make over time. For example, over twenty years the difference between making 12% and 10% is nearly £76,500 and this is when using reasonably small numbers. Just a 2% change in your return makes a huge difference. Ten years later the difference is closer to £300,000. This is why, as noted above, it is very important to watch the costs of any financial product you are buying. It is fair to say that very few people even understand what the costs of their financial products are, or how to find them out, let alone the impact they will have on their ability to make money. This is a key reason why so many people suffer poor performance when they invest.

Many of you will be looking at these numbers thinking that these kinds of returns are impossible. There is no question that statistically it is hard to achieve a reliable 8, 10, 12 or even 20% return on your money. That said it is entirely possible to achieve them if you are prepared to look at the world in a certain way and learn a little. Simply investing in gold in the last ten years would have achieved these sorts of returns as we shall see. Timing your entry and exit with a technique that I will show you later would have achieved substantially higher than even 20%.[2]

There are also many investment professionals who have made these sorts of long-term returns. The table on the next page gives just a few examples. There are plenty more.

For simplicity I have given you an illustration of the money you would have made simply investing a £10,000 lump sum with these folk at the start of their run. If you had been making regular contributions, you would most likely have made significantly more than the number in the right hand column. Hundreds of pounds would have turned into millions of pounds.

It is also worth noting that these investors have achieved these incredible returns over many decades and in spite of the inherent disadvantages confronted by professional investors that I outlined in chapter two. You have none of these disadvantages.

So you can see that the difference between someone keeping their money in a savings account, or "under the mattress" and someone who invests their money is completely life changing, even if you are starting with relatively small amounts of money.

For what it is worth, let us look at what could have been achieved if you were able

---

2 Please see the section on using the RSI in chapter twelve.

Top Fund Managers

Investor	Company	Average % Return	Time Period	% return Start/Finish	So £10,000 became
Warren Buffet	Berkshire Hathaway	20.20%	1965 to 2010	394000%	£39,400,100
Anthony Bolton	Fidelity London	19.50%	1979 to 2007	14660%	£1,466,100
Joel Greenblatt	Gotham Capital	50%	1985 to 1995	5766%	£576,700
Jim Rogers	Soros Quantum Fund	38%	1969 to 1980	3456%	£345,700
David Swensen	Yale Endowment Fund	16.20%	1985 to 2008	3160%	£316,100
Peter Lynch	Fidelity Boston	29.20%	1977 to 1990	2795%	£279,600
Seth Klarman	Baupost Group	20.20%	1982 to present day	2076%	£207,700
David Einhorn	Greenlight Capital	21.60%	1996 to present day	1879%	£188,000
Benjamin Graham	Columbia University	14.70%	1936 to 1956	1553%	£155,400
Jack Meyer	Harvard Endowment Fund	15.90%	1990 to 2005	915%	£91,600

to save your entire UK ISA allowance of £890 per month. This is the amount you can invest each month at the time of writing in the UK without having to pay tax on any gains you might make. The final table on the next page illustrates this for you.

Please take a moment to look at these three tables. It is very important that you get a really good sense of just how powerful an effect investment can have on your wealth. Very few people realize the enormous numbers you can generate over time.

Cynics will say that the above examples are misleading because I have highlighted the best investors of all time and most investors fall far short of these sorts of returns. All I am asking for you to do is acknowledge the possibility of making great returns on your money. There is plenty of research that says that, on average, you can't beat the market over the long run. To me that is like saying: "Research shows that the average adult takes 35 seconds to run the one hundred metres."

I am not interested in averages. I am interested in doing my best to work out who the "fastest runners" of the investment world are and, having done so, to invest with them or invest like them. There are ways of consistently achieving the sort of returns highlighted above, you just need to find them.

FOR EXAMPLE: A STRATEGY THAT HAS MADE 13.9% FOR 11 YEARS RUNNING
An example of a very simple but effective way of making these sorts of returns is called "Dogs of the DOW" or "Dogs of the FTSE". Every year you simply buy the ten stocks in the FTSE with the highest dividend yields[3] hold them for a year and then sell them at the end of the year. You then repeat the same process each year. Simply doing this with no more thought at all has produced an average return over the last 11 years of 13.9%.[4] Not bad, better than most professional investors and powerful enough to make you millions by the time you retire, especially if you are keeping your costs low by investing yourself.

You will have bad years. There is no guarantee that you will always invest in the correct assets at the right time. What I hope is clear, however, is that if you are invested you have a much higher chance of making serious returns on your money than if you are messing about holding your money in cash or just cash and property which is the case for so many people. I will elaborate more on this below.

---

3 We will look in a little more detail at what dividends and dividend yields later on for those who are unfamiliar with what they are.

4 You should be able to find details about the "Dogs" strategy quite easily online if you are interested. These specific numbers appeared in the 12th January 2012 edition of MoneyWeek Magazine (p.12).

£5,000 lump sum to begin and £890 saved each month…

Year	After X Years	Saver	Investor			
		0% return	8% return	10% return	12% return	20% return
2012	1	£15,680	£16,605	£16,846	£17,091	£18,109
2016	5	£58,400	£73,329	£77,788	£82,587	£105,779
2021	10	£111,800	£175,080	£197,479	£223,449	£377,251
2026	15	£165,200	£326,672	£394,408	£479,351	£1,109,130
2031	20	£218,600	£552,521	£718,416	£944,249	£3,082,257
2041	30	£325,400	£1,390,306	£2,128,613	£3,323,169	£22,742,930

COMPOUNDING WORKS BOTH WAYS. DO NOT BORROW MONEY IF AT ALL POSSIBLE

Very importantly, it is worth noting that if you borrow money, the power of compounding hits you in reverse: Over time you end up paying more and more to whomever you are borrowing from. Luke Johnson, the entrepreneur behind Pizza Express and ex Chairman of Channel 4 refers to this as "...the gruesome mathematics of leverage in reverse."[5]

This is why you must eliminate debt, get invested as soon as you can and make lifestyle changes to achieve this if needs be. We will see how to do this shortly. Nearly all debt is very expensive. It is challenging to make a 15-20% return on your investments but almost certain you will pay at least this on your debt. Another reason why so many people fail at the money game is that they use far too much debt in their life. Please note that I am talking about credit cards and loans here, rather than mortgage products. Mortgages are a special case which we will also think about in more detail below.

IN SUMMARY

So we can see from the power of compound interest that if you can achieve a half decent return on your money, even a relatively small amount can become a very large amount in time...

This is arguably the most important thing you will ever learn about money.

Got it? Then let's move on to the second amazing fact about finance and see how you can very easily start making this free money from your hard-earned cash...

FACT TWO: TODAY'S BEST FINANCIAL PRODUCTS AND INFORMATION SOURCES ARE BETTER THAN EVER BEFORE

One of the paradoxes of the last few years is that people have been so focused on the "global financial crisis" they have generally missed some very interesting developments in the finance industry as a whole:

It is only in the relatively recent past that the financial services industry has developed to the point that people from any background can invest in almost any country or asset class (shares, bonds, commodities etc.) easily, quickly and cheaply.

Let's say you thought that the price of oil was going to go up. Don't worry for now

---

5 From "Start It Up: Why Running Your Own Business is Easier Than You Think." By Luke Johnson. P 178.

about how you might come to form this opinion, we will come on to that. Today, you can own some oil with the click of a mouse and with far lower fees than in the past. Perhaps you believe that Brazilian farmland is going to increase in value as the world's population grows from seven to nine billion and Brazilian crops are in more demand? You can own your very own piece of a Brazilian farm from the comfort of your home.

Not that long ago, these sorts of investments were very difficult, even impossible to make. If you wanted to benefit from growth somewhere like India, China or Singapore or make money from gold, oil or Brazilian farms, you needed a large amount of money, a relationship with a private banker somewhere like Switzerland and a willingness to pay high fees and deal with lawyers. In the last few years, thanks to the internet and intense innovation from financial services companies around the world, these hurdles have pretty much disappeared.

This is an extremely exciting development that very few people understand.

Today, if you have a basic grasp of what you are doing, you can easily and cheaply become an owner of almost anything you might think of. You have never been in a better position to make money out of a good idea than you are today. Sadly, very few people have any idea how to do this.

The reason for this is that the vast majority of people fall into one of three categories:

1. Those who do not invest any money at all.
2. Those who do invest but use their high street bank for financial advice.
3. Those who do invest and use an Independent Financial Adviser (IFA) for advice.

Today, there are almost as many financial products available in the world as there are wine producers. Sadly,

...the main high street banks and many IFAs are like a wine merchant who sells a very limited range of mediocre wines expensively...

There is a wonderful world of investment opportunity available out there if you know where to go. The key is choosing the right things to own, knowing how and where to buy them and paying the right price to own them. This is certainly no walk in the park but it isn't the Herculean task that many people who work in finance would have you believe. You are also better placed to solve the puzzle than many financial advisers for the reasons presented earlier in the book.

With a little bit of knowledge you can soon arrange your financial affairs to benefit from the incredibly exciting diversity of investment opportunities available today. You can keep your costs low, minimize the tax you pay and even make money when your investments fall in price as well as when they rise.

MOVING SWIFTLY ON...

So now you are up to speed on the power of compound interest and the fact that it is easier and better than ever before to invest. Knowing these two facts alone gives you a huge advantage over most people.

Now we shall turn our attention to two incredibly important big picture investment themes.

#5

TWO CRUCIAL INVESTMENT THEMES FOR TODAY

"...barring the cataclysmic unforeseen, the outlook for business is good and will become even better as time goes on..."

– John Paul Getty, "How To Be Rich"

These were his views at the time of the Great Depression when many people felt as pessimistic about the world economy as they do today. How right he was.

"The nominal inflation number is cooked like a thanksgiving turkey..."

– Byron King, publisher of top performing investment newsletter "Outstanding Investments"

This is where things get exciting. If you got your head around the two amazing facts above and can now get to grips with the two themes below, your knowledge of finance will quite literally be in the top tiny percentage of people in the world and you will be very well placed to make a superior return on your money as a result.

Our two crucial themes are:

1. THE WORLD ECONOMY KEEPS ON GROWING:

Forget the "financial crisis" or the "recession". The fact is that the world as a whole continues to grow. If you are invested in this fact you stand to benefit enormously. One fundamental truth about investment is that "…there is always a bull market somewhere…"

2. THERE IS SIGNIFICANT REAL INFLATION IN THE WORLD:

We already met this point in the introduction. We will look at it in more detail in this chapter. In recent years governments all over the world have been inventing vast quantities of what I call "fictional" money. I use the word "inventing" rather than "printing" because very little of this new money is even actually printed as notes or minted as coins, it is simply "invented" in computers.[1] This creates inflation. It is vital to know that this is happening and understand what to do about it.

The inflation caused by all this new money is very bad news for anyone who doesn't understand it. It can, however, be reasonably good news for the tiny minority of people who do because they can choose investments that benefit from it. They can "own" inflation.

To see an excellent example of this reality take a look at this chart of the gold price over the last ten years. This incredible performance is a direct result of what I am talking about. People who understand this theme have owned gold for several years and made around 600%.

---

1 This is what Quantitative Easing is (QE). We will look at this in more detail.

$GOLD (Gold - Spot Price (EOD)) CME

The above shows the progression in US dollars but the same phenomenon has happened in every major paper currency in the world as we can see from the table below. This is a direct result of inflation all over the world.

Gold's 11-year run against the U.S. Dollar and other currencies...								
Gold % Annual Change								
USD	**AUD**	**CAD**	**CNY**	**EUR**	**INR**	**JPY**	**CHF**	**GBP**
2001	2.5%	11.3%	8.8%	2.5%	8.1%	5.8%	17.4%	5.0%	5.4%
2002	24.7%	13.5%	23.7%	24.8%	5.9%	24.0%	13.0%	3.9%	12.7%
2003	19.6%	-10.5%	-2.2%	19.5%	-0.5%	13.5%	7.9%	7.0%	7.9%
2004	5.2%	1.4%	-2.0%	5.2%	-2.1%	0.0%	0.9%	-3.0%	-2.0%
2005	18.2%	25.6%	14.5%	15.2%	35.1%	22.8%	35.7%	36.2%	31.8%
2006	22.8%	14.4%	22.8%	18.8%	10.2%	20.5%	24.0%	13.9%	7.8%
2007	31.4%	18.1%	11.5%	22.9%	18.8%	17.4%	23.4%	22.1%	29.7%
2008	5.8%	33.0%	31.1%	-1.0%	11.0%	30.5%	-14.0%	-0.3%	43.7%
2009	23.9%	-3.6%	5.9%	24.0%	20.4%	18.4%	27.1%	20.3%	12.1%
2010	29.8%	15.1%	24.2%	25.5%	40.2%	25.3%	13.9%	17.4%	36.3%
2011	10.2%	8.8%	11.9%	5.1%	12.7%	30.4%	3.9%	10.2%	9.2%
Av.	17.7%	11.6%	13.7%	14.8%	14.5%	19.0%	13.9%	12.1%	17.7%

Let's look at each of these themes in more detail:

THEME ONE: THE WORLD ECONOMY KEEPS ON GROWING

THE WORLD IS GETTING RICHER...

The world is much richer today than it was ten years ago and much richer than it was twenty, fifty or one hundred years ago.[2] This should be obvious if you think about it. Crucially, the world will continue to get significantly richer due quite simply to population growth and economic and technological development.

...BUT YOU ARE GETTING POORER...

In recent years people in many modern western countries might be forgiven for having lost sight of the inherent truth of the world getting richer. Many in the developed world are poorer today than they were ten years ago having suffered dot. com and property crashes, the "financial crisis" since 2008, rising job insecurity and the significant "stealth" inflation we are looking at.

In fact, westerners are quite right to feel as if things have been getting harder economically: As we discovered in the introduction, if you take out the richest 1% of the population, the other 99% of people in the UK and America have been getting poorer in real terms for several decades. The inflation-adjusted wage of the average American has not increased since 1973 and the UK is no different.

Why?

Because globalisation has meant that billions of people elsewhere in the world have finally been able to compete for the world's inherently limited resources. These include oil, fresh water, agricultural products, timber, metals and so on. For centuries, the markets for all of these things were completely dominated by people from developed countries. This should be obvious since we were the first to industrialise and were able to use our technological and military superiority to build empires and take a great deal more than our "fair share".

However, further technological and societal developments have meant that in the last few decades, roughly since the end of the Second World War (WWII), people in the developing world have increasingly been able to compete for jobs and capital with those of us in the west. This has increased the real cost of things. With China's decision to pursue economic development in the late 1970s and the

---

2 An amazing fact: The last decade has seen humanity produce 25% of all economic output ever in the whole of human history. It seems rather incredible that at the same time this cornucopia of wealth has been created so many people in the west see ourselves as mired in a terrible "economic crisis". Humanity, in aggregate is the richest it has ever been.

fall of the Berlin wall a decade later, this process has accelerated.

This is a key part of the paradigm shift I referred to in the introduction. Like it or not, those of us in "rich" countries are losing our relative and absolute economic power to billions of hungry, aspirational and hard working people elsewhere.

With peace and an increased promotion of free trade after WWII, the global shipping industry and international trade exploded. To begin with, developing countries were able to catch up with the west in the relatively unskilled agricultural and extractive primary sectors such as mining.

Increasingly, however, they made great strides in many more lucrative manufacturing sectors: Think of Japan after WWII, the Asian Tiger economies of Taiwan, Korea and Singapore after that and, more recently, another wave of countries like Brazil, India, Vietnam and Turkey, to name only a few. We are all intuitively aware of how successful they were in this, just think about where so many of the products in your home come from.

Today, further technological developments, primarily in telecommunications and travel, mean that a tidal wave of people in scores of countries are also competing with westerners for highly paid jobs in a wide range of white-collar sectors: IT, engineering and business services such as finance and consultancy.

All of this has driven very strong economic growth in the developing world: Most notably in the BRIC countries: Brazil, Russia, India and China but in many others too: Thailand, Singapore, Indonesia, Vietnam, Turkey and many other parts of Asia, many South and Central American countries, many countries in the Middle East and even, more recently, some of the more stable African nations.

Countries that previously simply didn't have a "middle class" now have one which numbers in the tens, even hundreds of millions. Statistics such as the growth in car ownership in places like China and Brazil have been astonishing as people in these countries have started to catch up with the developed world. Today Brazil is a larger economy than the UK. China buys more cars than America and has eight thousand miles of high-speed train track, more than anywhere else in the world. Twenty years ago they had no high speed rail at all. This has happened incredibly quickly.

LET'S SEE THIS IN NUMBERS
To show this idea in numbers: Global Gross Domestic Product (GDP)[3], the total of all economic activity in the world, increased from about $32 trillion (thirty two

---

3 GDP is just a measure of the total amount of wealth generated by a country each year.

thousand billion dollars) to $74 trillion between 2000 and 2010.

That is to say that the world economy as a whole grew no less than 131.25% (from $32 to $74 trillion) in ten years. If you had been able to simply "own the world" your money would have increased by at least 131.25% (more with compounding, that is to say re-investing the income you would have earned).

In contrast, this compares to having owned the main shares in the UK or even the US: If you had owned a basket of the main shares in the UK or US such as the FTSE 100, Dow Jones or S&P 500, you would have lost a significant chunk of your money in the same time frame (true at the time of writing after accounting for real inflation). This is just the sort of investment you would most likely have owned if you had spoken to a financial adviser at a high street bank and the sort of product you are likely to have in your pension fund if you have one. Once you've accounted for inflation and the fees attached to such a product you would have lost a large chunk of your real wealth owning only British or American shares.

Furthermore, whilst you should never trust forecasts blindly, it seems highly likely that the trend for the world economy to grow will continue because of population growth and technological development: The International Monetary Fund (IMF) estimates the number will be $82 trillion by 2015.

As the title suggests, therefore, one of the key things this book will teach you is how you can "own the world". Given the improvement in financial products already highlighted, it has never been easier or cheaper to do so.

AN ENVIRONMENTAL ASIDE...
As a brief aside, for those of us who care about the environment, these global growth numbers might be seen as potentially very bad news. After all, the more the population and economy grows, generally the more raw materials we use and the more pollution and waste we generate. This has been a serious personal concern of mine for a long time. As the Economist magazine has put it:

> *"If China's consumption of raw materials and energy were to rise to rich country levels, the world would not have the resources to supply them..."*

You could argue that this fact is hugely worrying when you add in India, Pakistan, Indonesia, Latin America, Africa and all of the other hugely populous and rapidly industrialising nations in the world. A full discussion of the ecological and environmental impact of global economic growth is beyond the scope of this book but I would like to point out that it is possible for there to be economic growth which actually improves our environment, otherwise known as "sustainable development". An example of this would be the growth in companies which facilitate fractional car usage. Many readers will be familiar with Zipcar, a company which uses clever IT so that you can pick up a car, use it for a few hours and only pay for that time. Today, Zipcar operates in over fifty cities in the US and UK.

Zipcar estimates that each of their vehicles takes at least twenty personally owned vehicles off the road. As their model is replicated across an increasingly urbanised world, their growth and the growth in companies like them will add to GDP numbers but result in a better result for the environment. Advances in IT systems will hopefully facilitate these sorts of business models, sometimes referred to as collaborative consumption, developing across a wide range of human activities.

It is these sorts of developments that give me more confidence than ever that human ingenuity and scientific breakthroughs will enable the whole world to grow economically in the future without destroying our planet.

There are a number of books in the bibliography below and in the resources section of the Plain English Finance website that deal with these issues. Perhaps the best of which are "Sixth Wave. How to succeed in a resource limited world." By James Bradfield Moody and Bianca Nogrady and "What's Mine is Yours: The Rise of Collaborative Consumption" by Rachel Botsman and Roo Rogers.[4]

IN CONCLUSION
Despite what many of us feel in the west, the world is still growing and will very likely continue to do so. People in the developing world will get relatively richer and people in the west will very possibly continue to get relatively poorer.

SO, WHAT CAN I DO?
There is very little the west can do about growing competition from the developing world. Sadly, over the last twenty years, individuals and governments in the west have avoided the inevitable erosion of their living standards from increased global competition by "doing an Ostrich" and borrowing vast sums of money, primarily from the developing world. This is one of the reasons we find ourselves in our current predicament.

Rather than borrowing vast sums of money, a far better option for anyone in the west is to invest in the dynamism, ingenuity and hard work of these developing countries. Doing this is one of the main reasons the top 1% of people in the west are richer today than ever before as previously mentioned. They have been shareholders in the explosive growth of the emerging world. You need to "own

---

4 See www.sixthwave.org and the bibliography below for more details.

the world" to make superior returns on your money and we will look at how to do this below. For now, however, it is time to look at our second crucial theme:

THEME TWO: THERE IS SIGNIFICANT REAL INFLATION IN THE WORLD

I believe it is worth repeating the following quote we saw in the introduction given how important a point it makes:

"By a continuing process of inflation, governments can confiscate, secretly and unobserved, an important part of the wealth of their citizens. There is no subtler, no surer means of overturning the existing basis of society than to debauch the currency. The process engages all the hidden forces of economic law on the side of destruction, and does it in a manner which not one man in a million is able to diagnose."

– John Maynard Keynes.

Since the early 1970s, central banks (governments) all over the world have been "printing" money at a faster and faster rate. More accurately put, they have been "inventing" money rather than printing it. They don't physically print much of it these days but simply add some zeroes to accounts in a central bank computer. Below is a chart showing this phenomenon in the US.

The sheer scale of the acceleration in recent years is extraordinary, just look how steep this graph is from 2008:[5]

---

5 Please don't be confused by the fact that this graph alludes to the "St. Louis Adjusted Monetary Base". This is simply because it is the St. Louis branch of the Federal Reserve that publishes this data.

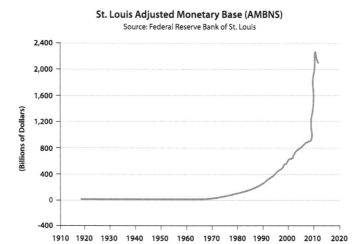

The situation in the UK is no different, as we can see from this graph:

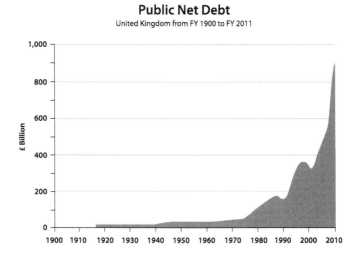

This causes inflation. It is not really necessary to understand exactly why this has happened, but it is very important for your financial future that you understand it is happening, very important indeed. To explain:

"WHEN I WAS A LAD..."

Stop and think for a moment about what all the most important things you need to buy in your life cost and compare this to what they cost ten years ago or when you were a child perhaps. You should really get a feel for what has been happening and the point I am trying to make here. How much did your parents buy their first house for? How much did you if you are a homeowner? How much does that house cost now? Does this mean that "...you can't go wrong with bricks and mortar..." or is there actually something more complicated going on?

Now think about how much your first pair of jeans cost, or your first ever car, or pretty much anything you can remember: Chocolate bars, pints of milk, loaves of bread. Hopefully you get the picture. If you really think about it, nearly everything you need to buy has gone up in price very significantly. Pretty much the only exceptions to this trend have been consumer electronics products such as televisions and computers.

This is inflation at work. Many people think they understand inflation. I would argue that the reality is that most people have only a vague idea of its existence and absolutely don't "get" its sheer magnitude and what this means for their long-term financial situation.

This is extremely bad news for most people but relatively good news for the small minority who do understand. The value (purchasing power) of one pound or one dollar has fallen by around 90% since 1971.[6] Worse, this negative trend in the value of money is accelerating thanks to the actions of politicians and central banks all over the world as they continue to invent large amounts of new money out of thin air. In the UK and the US this is called quantitative easing (QE).

BUT WHAT IS INFLATION?

"But inflation is still really quite low. 4% or something isn't it?" I hear you ask. Yes but what is "inflation" as reported by governments? Here is a little story that may help explain why "inflation" numbers as produced by governments are of very little use to us. This is incredibly important for your financial future.

In the 1980s the British government changed the definition of "unemployment" on numerous occasions. Each time the unemployment number "fell". It is not hard to argue that all that was going on here was that people we would most likely understand to be "unemployed" such as adults who didn't have a job and wanted one were no longer defined that way and so dropped out of the numbers.

Some were re-classified as "disabled" (those earning "disability benefit"), now a

---

6 Source: http://www.measuringworth.com/ppoweruk/

huge number in the UK, others as being on a "youth training scheme" or any number of dubious ways to take them off the headline unemployment numbers discussed on television and in newspapers.

At the time of writing, the UK has about 2.7m "unemployed" people but quite literally another several million who do not have a job but are classified differently, on disability benefit for example. On the other side of the Atlantic, the US authorities play similar games with their unemployment numbers. Perhaps the best example of this is that anyone who has been out of work for longer than a year drops out of the statistics entirely. Because they are no longer eligible for any state support they are no longer "unemployed" according to the definition the US government uses.

This leads to the ridiculous situation where the US government reports a fall in unemployment and the stock market rallies (goes up) when the only reason the number has fallen is that 300,000 people have been out of work for more than a year, are still unemployed but are no longer in the numbers discussed in the press.[7]

This results in the US currently claiming they have about an 8% unemployment rate. If you actually work out the percentage of working age adults who don't have jobs and want them the real number is currently closer to 16% (and north of 20% if you use the methodology that was used until the early 1980s). You can see this in the graph below:[8]

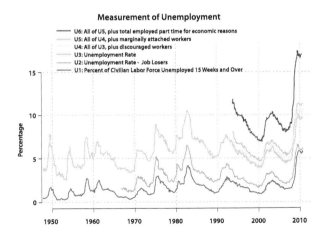

7 Since originally writing this chapter this situation has become even crazier. In February 2012 1.2 million more people "fell out" of the numbers and the market didn't bat an eye. Those people still don't have jobs but the official unemployment number fell.

8 Source: US Bureau of Labour Statistics. More information can be found here:
http://en.wikipedia.org/wiki/Unemployment#United_States_Bureau_of_Labor_Statistics

Amazingly enough the US authorities don't even try to hide this higher number. It is called "U6" unemployment. The 8% number is called "U3". I am consistently amazed by the fact that the media and politicians focus on U3 and ignore U6. By definition U6 seems a far better representation of what unemployment actually is (people who don't have a job). This is just another example of our press and much of the financial analyst community being asleep at the wheel. The only benefit of this reality is that you can use it to your investing advantage.

Below is another way of looking at the same thing. Note the huge difference between today and past US recessions. This difference is not captured if you only look at the "official" U3 number:

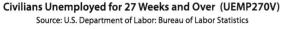
Civilians Unemployed for 27 Weeks and Over (UEMP270V)
Source: U.S. Department of Labor: Bureau of Labor Statistics

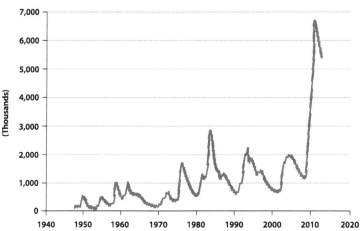

UNEMPLOYMENT? I THOUGHT WE WERE TALKING ABOUT INFLATION?

"Why is this relevant to inflation?" I hear you ask.

The answer is that for many years now governments all over the world have been playing the same trick or worse with their inflation calculations as they have with their unemployment numbers. The US authorities made the biggest change to the calculation in 1996 when President Clinton implemented changes recommended by something called the Boskin Commission. If the pre-1996 method were still being used, US and UK inflation today would be closer to TEN percent as you will see below.

I cannot stress how important it is to understand this. In my experience almost no one understands this reality. At the very least they do not understand the scale of the problem. I have been constantly amazed by the complete ignorance of what follows amongst the general population and investment professionals alike. Very few journalists seem to understand this reality, neither do virtually any of my ex-colleagues in the City, many of whom are analysts and economists at major investment firms.

Understanding why today's inflation numbers are complete science fiction gives you a serious advantage whilst everyone else fails to. It is one of the reasons why gold and silver have gone up so much over the last several years for example.

It is not difficult to find an explanation online as to how nonsensical today's inflation numbers are. Rather than summarise the arguments myself, I have simply reproduced one such explanation below as I could not have made the argument better. Please note that although this article is focussed on the US numbers, the same points are broadly relevant to the UK calculations. It is also worth noting that US inflation numbers are important for the entire global economy given it is the US dollar which is the most important currency in the world (for now).

SUBSTITUTION, WEIGHTING AND HEDONICS[9]

"Trickery and treachery are the practices of fools that have not the wits enough to be honest."

– Benjamin Franklin.

"...It always amuses me when the government releases certain data, such as inflation data. There is a bevy of economists and market mavens, who draw all kinds of conclusions, then make forecasts as if the data was accurate. I think at this point there is enough evidence that proves Washington manipulates the numbers for their own agenda. A good question to ask would be "What would the inflation numbers really look like without government adjustments?"

Inflation is basically upward pressure on prices due to large amounts of money in the system and expectations of future inflation. The government regulates the first component by regulating the money supply, but how do they regulate people's expectations?

By lying... Little by little, over long periods of time, they have manipulated the public into believing that inflation is always lower than it really is. Richard Nixon began the camouflage with the "core inflation" buzz phrase, which is effectively reporting

9 Source: http://viewpointsofacommoditytrader.com/1717/substitution-weighting-and-hedonics/

inflation minus inflation. Imagine reporting inflation but excluding food and fuel. Is that any way to work up the family budget?

In any event, our traditional numbers are reported by The Bureau of Labour Statistics, or BLS, in the form of the Consumer Price Index, or CPI. As Chris Martenson notes on his site:

"If you were to measure inflation, you'd probably track the cost of a basket of goods from one year to the next, subtract one from the other, and measure the difference. Your method would, in fact, be the way inflation was officially measured right on up through the early 1980s. But in 1996, Clinton implemented the Boskin Commission findings, which now have us measuring inflation using three oddities: Substitution, weighting, and hedonics.

To begin with this list, we no longer simply measure the cost of goods and services from one year to the next, because of something called the "substitution effect." Thanks to the Boskin Commission, it is now assumed that when the price of something rises, people will switch to something cheaper. So any time, say, that the price of salmon goes up too much, it is removed from the basket of goods and substituted with something cheaper, like hot dogs. By this methodology, the BLS says that food costs rose 4.1% from 2007 to 2008.

The Farm Bureau, which does not do this and simply tracks the exact same shopping basket of thirty goods from one year to the next, says food prices rose 11.3% over the past year. That's a huge difference. In my household, the Farm Bureau better matches our experience.

Next, anything that rises too quickly in price is now subjected to so-called "geometric weighting," in which goods and services that are rising most rapidly in price get a lower weighting in the CPI basket under the assumption that people will use less of those things. Using the government's own statistics from two different sources, we find that health care is about 17% of our total economy, but it is weighted as only 6% of the CPI basket. Because healthcare costs are rising rapidly, the impact of including a much smaller healthcare weighting is a reduction in reported inflation. By simply reinstating the actual level of healthcare spending, our reported CPI would be several per cent higher."

Although I find substitutions and weightings very amusing manipulations, my favourite is hedonic adjustment. What did you call me? What in the world is a hedonic adjustment? Well, here goes:

"Tim LaFleur is a commodity specialist for televisions at the Bureau of Labour Statistics, where the CPI is calculated. In 2004 he noted that a 27-inch television

selling for $329.99 was the same price as last year, but was now equipped with a better screen. After taking this subjective improvement into account, he adjusted the price of the TV downwards by $135, concluding that the screen improvement was the same as if the price of the TV had fallen by 29%. The price reflected in the CPI was not the actual retail store cost of $329.99, which is what it would cost you to buy, but $195.

At the BLS, TV's cost less and inflation is heading down. At the store, they're still selling for $329.99. Hedonics is a one-way trip. If I get a new phone this year and it has some new buttons, the BLS will say the price has dropped. But if it only lasts eight months instead of thirty years, like my old phone, no adjustment will be made for that loss. In short, hedonics rests on the improbable assumption that new features are always beneficial and are synonymous with falling prices. Over the years, the BLS has expanded the use of hedonic adjustments and now applies these adjustments to everything from DVDs, automobiles, washers, dryers, refrigerators, and even to college textbooks. Hedonics are now used to adjust as much as 46% of the total CPI."

Considering these adjustments and manipulations, are the figures released by the BLS meaningful at all? I don't think so, but you should draw your own conclusions. I would certainly consider the old method when planning for future inflation. Below is a chart from shadowstats.com, where they run the numbers like they used to be run. Honestly..."

Monthly Inflation: 1872 to Present

Official (BLS) Annualized Inflation = **3.57%**   ShadowStats.com = **11.15%**

Here is a more recently updated chart where the picture is even clearer.

The bottom, darker line is the "official" number after the various cheating mechanisms used to keep it artificially low, the top line is the real number.

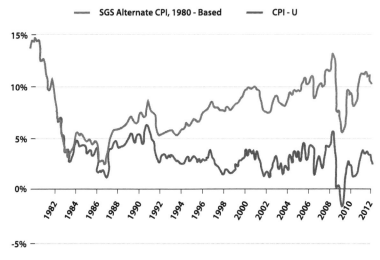

Annual Consumer Inflation - Official vs SGS (1980-Based) Alternate
Year to Year Change. Through Feb. 2012. (BLS, SGS)

Published: Mar. 16, 2012

HIDDEN INFLATION

Another important source of "hidden inflation" which doesn't make it in to the "official" numbers occurs when companies give consumers less of a product without changing the price, something which has been prevalent in the last few years. Some readers may remember a major national pizza chain in the UK being accused in the press of making their pizzas smaller whilst keeping the price the same.

Equally, although this may seem like a strange example, an American friend of mine recently pointed out that a standard packet of a famous US brand of cookies currently contains 39 cookies. This compares to 45 a year ago. This is a 13.3% reduction in the amount of the product you receive with no change in price. This is exactly the same as 13.3% inflation in that product.

If you start paying attention to these sorts of things you realise that these examples can be found across a wide variety of products. Many companies are dealing with severe input-cost inflation and one of the easiest ways for them to keep their historical profit margin is, quite simply, to give you less for the same money in the hope that you won't notice.

As a result of the above, as Bryon King, publisher of top rated investment newsletter[10] "Outstanding Investments" puts it:

"The nominal inflation number is cooked like a thanksgiving turkey…"

It is quite incredible that the figures quoted above are understood by so few people, especially journalists and senior finance professionals. Suffice to say inflation and unemployment numbers regularly discussed in the media are essentially science fiction. This is important because, as we have already seen:

"By a continuing process of inflation, government can confiscate, secretly and unobserved, an important part of the wealth of their citizens…"

This is precisely what is happening today and why governments on both sides of the Atlantic do such a great job of producing nonsensical numbers: So they can get away with it. "But why don't financial analysts, economists and journalists call these numbers into question if this is the case?" You ask, and well you might.

The first thing to say in answer is that many do. I am calling the numbers into question in this book. In addition, a brief internet search will rapidly unearth independent and extremely well qualified analysts trying to put the right numbers into the public domain. Perhaps the best of these is the website www.shadowstats.com as mentioned above but there are plenty of others.

With the above sort of work widely available it does consistently amaze me how nearly all mainstream analysts and journalists seem to be asleep at the wheel. I confess I find it vexxing when I hear a politician talking about 8% unemployment in the US or 4% inflation in the UK and the journalist just accepts these nonsense numbers at face value.

It is also worth noting that GDP numbers are "inflation adjusted". If you accept the premise that there are serious flaws in the inflation numbers, then, by extension, the GDP numbers are also inaccurate. If, for example, you use what I deem to be the "real" inflation numbers published by www.shadowstats.com, then many western economies are actually going backwards in real terms (in recession) whilst their politicians claim they are growing.

Every cloud has a silver lining, however and the good news is that if you understand the real numbers, you have an information advantage over those who don't and can use this to make more money from your investments.

10 Byron King publishes Outstanding Investments. See the resources section of the website.

HOW DO THEY GET AWAY WITH IT?

For what it is worth, explanations that occur to me for why so few people take this blatant massaging of the numbers to task are:

1. Many analysts and journalists have raw intelligence and a "great education" but are too young or blinkered to see the big picture. They have learned about inflation on the job and never stopped to really look under the bonnet and attempt to understand how the numbers are actually calculated or how this has changed over time. This phenomenon should be familiar to us as an age-old facet of human nature: As Henry Ford put it: "Thinking is the hardest work there is, which is the probable reason why so few engage in it…" Or, as Voltaire would have it: "Common sense isn't so common…" It is also most often easiest to work within the existing paradigm or conventional wisdom rather than have to confront complexity and the disapproval of the "mob" or your boss by rocking the boat. I know from first hand experience that there is no upside for a young analyst at a major investment bank pointing out that, when it comes to published inflation and unemployment numbers the Emperor isn't wearing any clothes.

2. Furthermore, those in the know that "get" this inflation reality such as senior staff at major investment banks, hedge fund managers, commodity traders, some politicians and central bankers, are able to turn it to their significant financial advantage. They have very little incentive to blow the whistle. It is similar to the situation at WorldCom or Enron a few years ago: Much of the senior management knew what was happening but it suited them fine to keep quiet as long as they could get away with it.

SUMMARY

In conclusion, the actions of many governments in recent years have lead to a situation where we are in the throes of very significant monetary inflation. When there is significant inflation the value of cash falls as the price of "things" increases.

The smart investor benefits from this by making sure he or she owns the very things which are going up in price. As a basic rule of thumb, this includes precious (monetary) metals and commodities. We don't need to understand in detail why gold, silver, oil, wheat, cotton, coffee, art and wine and so on go up in price when there is inflation. It is enough just to be aware that this is the case just as we have seen for the last several years.

That said, for what it is worth, it should seem logical that if you have a fixed supply of "stuff" and the supply of money doubles, then the price of that "stuff" will double, all other things being equal: If twice as much money is competing for the same amount of things (bread, milk, eggs, cars, gold) then the person selling those things can put the price up. This is precisely what has been happening in recent years.[11]

Armed with this knowledge and our understanding that the global economy continues to grow, we are now ready to do something about it and start making some serious money.

So let us now look at exactly what to do to benefit from our two facts about finance and our two crucial themes...

11 Some people reading this will be familiar with Irving Fisher's equation $MV=PT$ and argue that I have missed out the impact of Velocity of Money in my argument. I feel that a full discussion of this is too much detail for the purposes of this book and for most reader's interest. For those of you who are interested, however, I am very happy to have that discussion on the website. For what it is worth, my belief in a nutshell is that Velocity is always at least one. This being the case, a doubling in the money supply will always cause at least a doubling in prices (with a time lag). The reality is that Velocity is usually a great deal higher than one. This is why hyperinflation is a far higher risk than "deflationistas" tend to believe. If you disagree, please see Zimbabwe, Argentina, Brazil, Hungary, Weimar Germany, Austria, Conquistador Spain, the Holy Roman Empire and dozens of other historical examples for details.

FINDING THE MONEY, GETTING THE RIGHT ACCOUNTS & UNDERSTANDING THE PRODUCTS

In this section of the book we will look at the specific steps you need to take in order to optimise your financial affairs. Before we do, it is perhaps worth summarising briefly what we have learnt so far:

1. It has never been more important to understand what is happening in finance and arrange your affairs appropriately.
2. It isn't as hard to do this as you might think. You are only a few hours away.
3. You need to ensure you benefit from the incredible power of compound interest.
4. Financial products today are better than ever if you know where to go to find the best ones at the right price. You just won't find them at your high street bank.
5. The world economy is still growing and will continue to do so. You need to "own the world".
6. There is significant real inflation in the world. You need to "own inflation".

So now let us turn our attention to how you can arrange your financial affairs to take advantage of all of this. Getting your house in order is not as daunting as you may have previously thought. We will break down the actions you need to take into the following topics, each covered in their own chapter:

1. Creating financial surplus and the key role played by property in doing so.
2. The types of account you will need and the importance of an ISA.
3. The types of investment vehicle you will need to use.

#6

CREATING FINANCIAL SURPLUS AND THE KEY ROLE PLAYED BY PROPERTY

"If you would be wealthy, think of saving as well as getting..."

– Benjamin Franklin

It should be clear from what you have read above that if you want to be wealthy, if you want to have real financial security and the finer things in life, there is a very simple formula well understood by the rich and unchanged for the several thousands years since humans invented money:

Live on less than you earn and invest the rest...

We have seen how powerful compound interest is. Even if you do not have much money to invest do not let this put you off. Start saving something immediately and let compound interest and time work their magic.

If you want to win at the money game it is absolutely imperative that you create financial surplus in your life and invest that surplus in a good variety of assets. If you have failed to do this in the past, a large reason may have been that, even if you had managed to save some of your income, you wouldn't have known where to invest it and so you felt there was no point. Perhaps you didn't trust the financial services industry to give you good advice?

This is entirely fair enough, but read on and this will no longer be true. Very soon you will have a better idea than most of how to invest your money and feel more confident than ever that you can do it. As such, let us turn our attention first to how you are going to find some financial surplus. In reality, you are going to be best off saving and then investing at least 5-10% of your monthly income.

Many people reading the above will be thinking that they can't "create financial surplus". You might have three kids and you can barely make ends meet at the moment. Saving 5-10% of your monthly income is just completely unrealistic.

Without wanting to sound overly harsh, if this is what you are thinking, then you are highly unlikely to become wealthy. You will have to hope you win the lottery or a long lost relative leaves you some money. Like most people it is likely that this is the only way you will ever get rich. Worse, you may end up having a fairly impoverished retirement.

The truth, however, is that pretty much anyone should be able to arrange their personal affairs so they can live on 95% or less of their income, almost no matter what they earn. If you are reading this and think you can't then, with relatively few exceptions, you are quite simply not prepared to take sufficiently radical action. There is one very simple type of radical action, which can create financial surplus for you rapidly: Move house. If you cannot save money given your current living arrangements, change them. This will put you in a position to save money far more quickly than trying to buy fewer things, spend less in the pub or drink fewer cappuccinos every week.[1]

THE CRUCIAL ROLE PLAYED BY PROPERTY IN CREATING SURPLUS

If you are renting, move, go and rent somewhere at least 5-10% cheaper and invest that difference. Although if you are making the change, why not consider somewhere 20% cheaper, invest 15% and have 5% more disposable income?

If you own a house, and your mortgage payments are eating up so much of your monthly income that you can't find 5-10% of your money to invest then sell the house and downsize. I appreciate this may seem like a fairly dramatic course of action but it is the one course of action which can get you results in a reasonably short period of time and will set you up for life.

One of the primary causes of the financial crises in the US and Britain has been our unhealthy obsession with home ownership and a widespread failure by many people to understand how to value property over time as against the other main assets you might put money into such as shares, bonds or commodities.

We have lived through twenty years or more of most people believing that "you can't go wrong with bricks and mortar" or that "rent is throwing money away paying someone else's mortgage."

These are simplistic beliefs that are often entirely incorrect. Like all assets, sometimes property is good value and worthy of investment, at other times it is dangerously expensive. Many rich people understand this.[2] Given the above, it is worth taking a closer look at property and how to value it. The decisions you make about it will have a huge impact on your wealth over a lifetime and the wrong decision can potentially damage your financial situation for life.

Many people in the English speaking world feel familiar with property as an asset class. There is a long tradition of owner occupancy in countries like the UK,

---

1 That said, self-storage has been one of the fastest growing industries in the last decade and the average Briton has more than a tonne of unwanted possessions. A third of self-storage units in the US are rented by people on an income of less than £15,000 per year. If you think about the amount of useless stuff you have purchased you may surprise yourself at how much you could have invested instead. (Source: "Enough: Breaking Free From the World of More" by John Naish). Sex in the City fans may remember an episode where the lead character, Carrie, can't afford the deposit on her flat but realises she owns thousands of dollars worth of shoes. Please don't be that person.

2 One of the best investors of all time, Jim Rogers, has twice sold all of his property on the eve of a crash (in 1987 and 2007). He regularly describes property as a fundamentally bad investment due to its illiquidity (how hard it is to buy and sell) and the large number of ongoing expenses associated with it. This is a guy who made 4200% on his money in just over a decade.

America and Australia which is less the case in many other countries in the world, including wealthy European nations such as Germany and France where a high percentage of the population rent, often for their entire life.

House prices are a national obsession in the UK and US and regularly discussed in the press. Houses tend to be an individual's biggest asset and there is also an inevitable emotional attachment to one's primary property over and above the attachment one might have to a share or any other type of investment for obvious reasons: Clearly you can't live in a share or a bar of gold.

The problem with this is that many people feel they are "experts" when it comes to property and never more so than in the last twenty years. There is nothing like a rampant bull market in an asset class to make everyone feel like a genius.

In reality, it is consistently amazing to me how many folk prognosticate on the housing market without understanding any of the key long-term measures of value or issues such as the impact of inflation and interest rates on the market. This is a very similar point to the one I made earlier in the book about many people investing in shares not understanding how they are valued. Property is likely to be your biggest investment. It would make sense, therefore, to really understand how it is valued.

Nearly all of the estate agents I have ever dealt with in London who confidently hold forth about the state of the property market demonstrably fail to grasp much, if any of what follows. This is entirely analogous to just how many financial advisers have no broad understanding of financial markets.

The first thing to say is that over the long run and I am talking about over three hundred years of data here, property is absolutely not the "sure thing" which most people have come to believe it is in the last twenty years or so. "You can't go wrong with bricks and mortar..." is actually a dangerous and entirely incorrect statement.

ANCHORING

A facet of human behaviour long highlighted by psychologists, especially in the realm of finance is that we tend to have relatively short memories and this leads to a phenomenon known as anchoring. Basically what this means is that, if something has been true in your personal experience (e.g. ever-rising house prices) you will tend to assume this is the normal state of affairs.[3] We tend to assume something that has been true in our lifetime or an even shorter period will continue to be true. Our current obsession with property is a good example and perhaps understandable given we have witnessed a relatively long and very strong bull market.

A more extreme and potentially more illustrative example of anchoring and the trouble it can get us into would be the dot.com boom of the late nineties. Amazingly, it took only about two to three years before a very large proportion of people and even the supposedly professional investment community had become dangerously anchored, thinking: "Technology stocks always go up and are not subject to the traditional rules of stock market valuation. It is different this time." We are all aware how this ended for most of the participants in that market. Lots of people lost a great deal of money.

It is best we are aware of anchoring and other similar behavioural traits each time we consider a market. To get a truer picture of things, smarter investors will do their best to look at a much longer time frame, difficult though this may sometimes be.

If we do this we will see that as with any asset class, over the long run property performs extremely well at certain times and extremely poorly at other times. Given the experience of the last twenty or so years, it may come as a surprise to many readers that...

...UK property basically did not appreciate in value at all from 1900 to 1960. That is for no less than sixty years...

In the 1965 book "The Economics of Housing", the author, Lionel Needleman wrote:

"There are considerable risks attached to investing in housing. The housing market is both unstable and unorganized. House prices can fluctuate violently and yet houses are much less negotiable than most forms of investment." [4]

How different this stance is to the conventional wisdom of today. People living in the 1960s would have thought you were completely crazy if you had suggested you were thinking of borrowing 110% of the value of a house with a view to renting it out or planning to use a few property investments to fund your retirement.

---

3 The Chartered Institute for Securities & Investment defines Anchoring by saying: "People tend to give too much weight to recent experience, extrapolating recent trends that are often at odds with long run averages and probabilities." Source: CISI Investment, Risk & Taxation book, p 193.

4 Source: MoneyWeek Magazine, 18th November 2011, p. 55.

I do not claim to have a magic formula to predict exactly when property will do well or badly but there are certain metrics and methods for giving us a fighting chance of figuring out whether we are closer to a strong period for housing or to a weak one just as there are for every other type of investment we will look at later.

Given how significant an investment property is and how your choices about property will affect your monthly cash flow and your ability to invest in anything else, it would seem like a good idea to get to grips with these measures of value before we make any investment decisions. Strangely, relatively few people do this. It seems that most people are largely unaware of what follows, including many estate agents. This is one of the reasons we have experienced property bubbles on both sides of the Atlantic.

So let us look at key metrics we might use to understand real value in the property market. Like everything else you will find in this book and on the website, these really aren't that complicated. The tools used by smarter professional investors are simple enough and I would argue that we should all have learned about them at school. However, in my experience they tend to be poorly understood by many people.

INFLATION

First off, I want to revisit the relevance of inflation. We have already discussed just how important inflation is when talking about wealth generally. This is especially the case when considering the performance of a property asset. Economists and behavioural psychologists describe a phenomenon known as money illusion. This basically means that the majority of people do not take inflation into account (sufficiently or at all) when thinking about changes in the value of something. This is particularly the case with property.

You will hopefully recall from the section on inflation above that the value of the pound and the dollar have fallen in real terms by more than 90% since the early 1970s. This is why prices from the early 1970s seem so incredibly "cheap". In 1973 for example, you could buy a decent sized house in London for £10,000.[5] That same house would in all probability cost £500,000 or even more today.

Does this mean that the "lucky" person who purchased a house in 1973 has increased their wealth by a factor of fifty? If you do not take account of inflation then you might conclude that they have. The price in 2012 is exactly fifty times what it was in 1973. Surely they have made fifty times their money?

---

5 For what it is worth, I'm using 1973 because it is the year my parents bought their first house in London.

THE DIFFERENCE BETWEEN WEALTH AND MONEY

But here we look at one of the most important concepts in this book: The difference between wealth and money (particularly paper money). In the example above, if the individual concerned sold their house they would take away fifty times the amount of paper money that they started with (pounds in this example). They have grown their money by a factor of fifty.

But what has happened to their wealth? The key thing here is to look at how much the price of everything else has gone up by. The first and most obvious thing to look at is how much the price of other houses has increased. What I am about to say might seem blindingly obvious to the point of being ridiculous but please bear with me as it is crucial to illustrating a key point: Let us say the "lucky" owner of this house wanted to sell it, cash in his "gains" and buy another house in the same area. Has he or she increased his wealth in terms of houses in the area?

The answer should obviously be "no". If you sell and then buy in the same market then, all other things being equal, the prices in that market will have gone up just as much as the price of your property. This is the most extreme example but the point stands that even though this person has fifty times the amount of pounds sterling they had before, they can still only buy one relatively nice house in this part of London. Another similar house in the same area will cost exactly the same as the one they are selling: Their wealth in terms of number of houses in this area of London has not actually increased at all.

Now, it is quite possible that this person has always wanted to move to rural Scotland when they retire and prices there have only gone up by twenty five times since 1973. This being the case, our lucky seller has increased their wealth in terms of houses in rural Scotland by a factor of two. Thanks to the appreciation in value of their London house being double the appreciation of a house in rural Scotland, they can now buy twice as much house in rural Scotland than they could have done originally. Their wealth in terms of Scottish houses has in fact doubled. This is obviously good news and shows that we should always be thinking about relative wealth when working out if we are doing the right thing with our money.

To continue the analogy, let us say the price of a posh meal out for two in London was £10 in 1973 and today it is £100, which is probably about fair. Then we can see that the owner of the house is better off in terms of meals out given these have gone up by a factor of ten times in pound terms vs. their house which has gone up by fifty times.

Similarly, a flight to New York in 1973 cost about £85.[6] To keep the arithmetic simple let us say that the price today is £850 then the homeowner is five times richer in terms of flights to New York than they were in 1973 (their house is up by fifty times, flights by ten times). Again, there has been far greater inflation in house prices than in flights to New York (for lots of structural reasons).

The point here is that if you want to build wealth you must always be thinking about comparative value and purchasing power. A simple number of pounds actually tells you relatively little about whether you are truly getting richer or not. Perhaps the above examples seem a little esoteric. A more recent example over a shorter time frame might help solidify the point:

IS A £1 MILLION POUND HOUSE STILL A £1 MILLION POUND HOUSE WHEN IT'S WORTH £1 MILLION?

I happen to know a number of people who purchased a house in central London for around £1,000,000 in around 2006 and 2007. They consider their house to be as valuable today as it was then. Even despite the "terrible" economic news we have heard almost every day since late 2008, they can at least content themselves that their property has not fallen in value. Is this correct?

Again, what follows may be a little hard to grasp but it is important we do grasp it. Let us say that someone purchased a house in London in 2007 for £1,000,000. Here is a very important consideration that the large majority of people don't make: At that time £1 was worth about $2 so they had purchased a house worth $2,000,000. This much is easy to follow.

Today, a nice estate agent reassures our property owner that due to all the same good solid reasons trotted out for the last twenty years (constrained supply, foreign buyers galore), their house is still worth £1,000,000. Fantastic. The only problem is that the pound is now only worth $1.55 (at the time of writing). Over the last five years, the pound has been the worst performing currency against the US dollar of the sixteen biggest trading currencies in the world. This means that our friend's London property is now worth $1,550,000. It has fallen in value by no less a sum than $450,000.

You may well ask: "Who cares? This person lives in London, shops in London, sends their kids to school in London. Why is this relevant?"

The answer is that this assessment of value is actually extremely relevant to this

---

6 Source: "Notes From a Small Island", Bill Bryson, p. 17.

person's true wealth, the main reason being that the vast majority of things in the world that this person may want to buy are largely priced in dollars (for now at least): Oil, gas, rice, wheat, cotton, copper, timber, paper – the list goes on and on.

Not many people really, truly notice what is going on but when the pound weakens against other currencies, very many of the things we need to spend money on become more expensive, usually with a small time lag. This is perhaps most obvious at the petrol pump but you can see it in your utility bills and, if you're really paying attention, your grocery bills too. As a result, the fact is that the pound sterling price of your property is a poor indicator of what is happening to your real wealth.

If your property is "worth" the same in pounds today as it was five years ago but nearly everything you need to buy in your life (petrol, bread, eggs, milk, cars, electricity, train fares, insurance, healthcare) has gone up in price by 20-30% then in real terms you are actually 20-30% poorer than you were five years ago.

So we have looked at how important inflation is when considering the true value of property. There are two other key valuation metrics that we must be aware of to give us the best chance of working out where we are in a property cycle: Rental yield and the ratio of property prices to salaries.

RENTAL YIELD

One of the most useful ways of trying to work out if a property is cheap or expensive is the return it would generate for you if you were to rent it out. Working out rental yield is a simple calculation but one that surprisingly few people make when considering the purchase of a property, including many of the estate agents I have ever dealt with in London and New York (I dealt with a number of estate agents in New York who had never even heard of rental yield. To me that is like a Doctor never having heard of a heart. Is it any wonder with "professionals" like this that America witnessed a massive bubble in property prices?).

Quite simply, rental yield is the number you get if you divide the assumed annual rental income from a property by the assumed value of that property. It is a number that you can then use to compare the returns on property to any other asset you might be thinking about, including shares, commodities, bonds or other properties.

Let us assume you owned the £500,000 London property discussed earlier. Let us also assume that you are able to rent it out for £1,500 a month. This means that you will make £18,000 per year. This is the "gross" rental income. Expressed as a "yield" we would say that this property is generating 3.6% of gross rental yield for its owner.[7]

Bear in mind, however, that as a landlord you will usually have to spend a certain amount each year on the maintenance of a property and on fixtures and fittings, boilers etc. There is also a chance that your property will lie void (empty) from time to time as you can't immediately find a tenant to replace one who has left. Both of these will obviously have a negative impact on your rental income.

As such, we might prudently assume that a rental property will be void one month a year on average over time and annual expenditure on fixtures and fittings will usually total approximately another 10% of the gross rental income. Continuing with the example above, this brings our assumed "net" rental income from the property down from £18,000 to £14,700 as we subtract 10% for wear and tear (£1,800) and another month's rent for potential void periods where the house or flat may lie empty between tenants (£1,500).

This gives us a net or real rental income of 2.94%.[8] This number is very useful as you can now compare it to the interest you might get on a current account, the return you might make on a share or the return on a different property.

CAPITAL GROWTH

But the rental yield is not the whole story. When we consider how good an investment a given property might be, we should obviously also consider potential capital growth. Let's take the above example again. Imagine that, as has been the case for some years in London, the price of the property increases. Let us assume it does so by 5%, from £500,000 to £525,000.[9]

So, in this example, the return from the property is 2.94% from rental income and 5% from capital gain. We can say that the total return is 7.94%. Not bad. Except that those of you who have been paying close attention should realise there is one more piece of the puzzle to include in our calculation before we can be confident that we have the right number.

---

7 For anyone who is a bit rusty with maths, we calculate this as (£18,000/£500,000) x 100 = 3.6%.

8 As above, the calculation is simply (£14,700/£500,000) x 100 = 2.94%.

9 Again, with apologies to anyone who thinks this is very easy maths, we calculate a 5% increase in something by multiplying it by 1.05. So, £500,000 x 1.05 = £525,000.

INFLATION AGAIN

Have you guessed what it is? Hopefully many of you will have realised that we must account for inflation. If we do not, then we are suffering from "money illusion" as mentioned above.

Continuing this example, the latest UK inflation number at the time of writing is 5.2%. You will recall from the chapter on inflation above that there are very strong arguments to suggest that even this relatively high number is a serious underestimation of what the REAL inflation number is (I would remind you to look at www.shadowstats.com or re-read the section in chapter 5 to understand why real inflation is a great deal higher than 5.2%).

TOTAL REAL RETURN

Nevertheless, just to keep things simple and because using the official number will still enable us to understand the point, if we now use all three components of the return you make on a property let us see what number we get in our example. A simple calculation of the real return you make on your property is net rental yield + capital gain – inflation.

In this example this gives us: 2.94% + 5% - 5.2% = 2.74%.

Actually, without wanting to complicate things too much, bear in mind that inflation will also affect the value of your rental income throughout the year. With inflation at 5%, the £1,500 you receive in rent in January is worth £75 less at the end of the year. Your real return is, therefore, even lower than the 2.74% above.

TAX

Many of you may already have thought of one final additional consideration: Tax. In the UK any increase in value (capital gain) on the property you live in (that is considered your "primary residence") is free of capital gains tax – the tax on your profit on that property when you sell it.

When considering property purely as an investment, however, (i.e. if you are looking at a buy to let opportunity which you will not live in) capital gains tax will be due on the property when it is sold. The tax paid will depend on your financial situation at the time the property is sold. I will not further complicate this section by going into any more detail. The only point I wish to make is that, if you are considering the merits of a buy to let investment compared to any other investment the 2.74% number above is actually even higher than the real return you will make once you account for the tax you will have to pay if you sell the property.

...AND FINALLY, THE COST OF MONEY

Of course, if you are borrowing money from the bank to enable you to own the above property this is another consideration when working out what your asset is doing for you. Even though interest rates are at a three hundred year low at the moment, you will realistically still be paying a few percentage points to borrow the money required to own the property above if you don't own it outright. This rate will then have to be subtracted from the percentage return we have already calculated above. In this example, this would imply that this property asset is actually making a negative real return after you have accounted for inflation, borrowing costs and tax.

I would note at this point that the real return on property in the UK has been a great deal higher than in this example for several years, hence why it has been a great investment for so many people. It is also worth pointing out that property will still perform a great deal better than cash held in a current account even in the above example given that rental yield plus capital gain is significantly more than the real interest rate (after inflation) you will earn on your money in a bank.

So, crucially, we now understand how to work out the real return on your investment if you buy a property asset. This is extremely useful because it enables us to compare apples with apples if we want to work out the big picture of where it might be best to invest our money at any given time. Let us say that we did some calculations at the beginning of 2012. If we think that a property investment is going to generate a real return of 2.5% before the cost of borrowing money (for the sake of argument) we might consider this a pretty poor investment against a share which is paying a 5% dividend and which we think has a strong chance of going up 10% or more this year (giving a total return of 15%) or against gold perhaps which we see has gone up by around 10-20% every year for a decade (or silver which went up over 160% last year).

When I lived in New York, I worked out that I was paying my landlord a 1.6% gross rental yield based on the asking price of my apartment and not including any assumption for fixtures and fittings or void periods. I confess I was amazed by the real estate agent in the sales office in my building who kept telling me what a great investment it would be if I purchased my apartment from my landlord. In the time I lived there, my gold investments went up over 40%. All I had to do to own gold was click my mouse a few times. Compare this to the large amount of administration and complexity I would have had to worry about if I had bought that apartment (not to mention the tiny return I would have made on it).

PROPERTY IS ALSO ILLIQUID AND COMES WITH A HEAVY ADMINISTRATIVE BURDEN

This is another key point to bear in mind with property: It generates a great deal more work than nearly all other investments. It is very illiquid and costly to buy and sell, taking a long time to transact with large numbers of payments due to lawyers, surveyors, real estate agents and the government.

That said, compare the examples above to the situation in the early 1990s. A good friend of mine's father has always run a small property company. In the early 1990s, after a significant property crash, he was able to acquire properties in and around London that enabled him to achieve 12% rental yields. There was low inflation at the time and given there had just been a property crash, he obviously had a higher probability of making significant capital gains in the years ahead. He could realistically target total real returns on the investments he made at that time north of 20%. Contrast this with the examples above, more in line with today's reality, where the real return is around 2.5% (or even less in New York). It should be obvious that investing in property had a much higher probability of making you serious money in the early 1990s then it does today.[10]

Of course none of us has a crystal ball but by thinking about the simple calculations outlined above, you can hopefully see that it is possible to significantly increase your chances of making better big asset allocation decisions in your life than people who do not. We will see later on how it is also possible to make reasonably good assumptions about the total return you might make on other asset classes such as shares, bonds and commodities in a very similar way to what we have just done for property.

Please don't think for a moment that you can ever get the timing 100% right but you can materially increase your chances of getting the timing roughly right and this fact alone will have a huge impact on your ability to become properly wealthy over the course of your lifetime. Now let's turn to our other useful measure of intrinsic long term value in the property market:

---

10 It is worth noting that at the time of writing it is possible to buy properties in Miami which are yielding 20%. This is a fair indicator that prices in certain parts of the US may have fallen far enough already and it is time for the smart money to buy back into these markets.

RATIO OF HOUSE PRICES TO SALARIES

Another key metric to think about when looking at property is the ratio of house prices to salaries. This is a very important measure of affordability and, again, will help us greatly to work out whether property is fundamentally cheap or expensive at any given time. If the average person in Britain is earning £30,000 and the average house costs £180,000 this ratio is obviously 6:1. Clearly if the average salary is £30,000 and the average house costs £60,000 the ratio is 2:1. Before you laugh, this apparently crazily low ratio has existed in the past. Your imagining that a house couldn't possibly ever only cost two times your annual salary is a result of anchoring, discussed above.

Another very important idea in finance generally is that of "mean reversion". You may remember from maths that "mean" is a type of average. All mean reversion means is that, in the long run, anything measured will tend to go back to its average price over the medium to long term. It is worth knowing that the long run average ratio of house prices to salaries over the last several decades is actually about 3:1. This immediately tells us that when the ratio is 6:1 house prices are arguably fundamentally expensive and likely to fall and when it is 2:1 house prices are fundamentally cheap and more likely to rise.

The following charts neatly illustrate this reality:

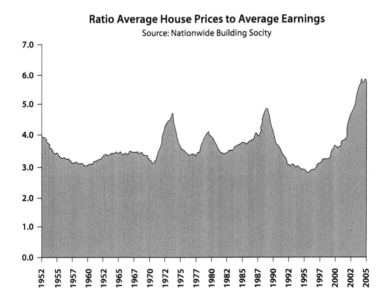

Ratio Average House Prices to Average Earnings
Source: Nationwide Building Socity

We all know that house prices went up a great deal from about 1993 until 2007. Salaries, however, did not keep pace with that increase in price. The result, as you can see in the chart above, is that in that time frame, houses for the average person in the UK became twice as expensive using the ratio we are currently considering.

If you were contemplating buying a house in 2006 and had looked at this chart, it should hopefully have been obvious that, all other things being equal, there was a higher probability that you were buying into the market at a high (expensive) level than at a low (cheap) level no matter what your estate agent was telling you.

Bearing in mind how significant an investment property is, you might have been advised to invest your money elsewhere and carry on renting for a while until the ratio came back down to more like three times. This is what the smart money would have done as we can see from this next chart. So what happened to prices? As the above chart implied, prices were too expensive compared to the long run and the following happened:

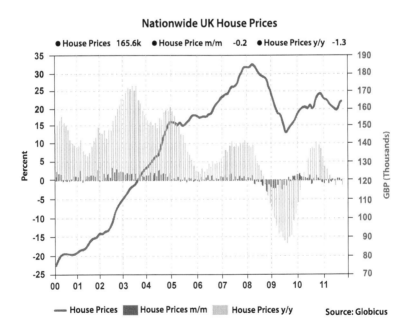

As you can see, 2008 was a difficult year for UK property. Bear in mind the above chart does not account for the substantial weakening of the pound in that time or true inflation so the real story is even worse than it would suggest.

I would repeat that people who look at the pound value of their property today and say that their property is worth the same as what it was worth in 2007 are suffering from money illusion: The fact that their property is "worth" the same number of pounds does not tell the true story of that asset's actual value. It is crucial that you understand this when making vitally important decisions such as when to buy property. Remember that becoming wealthy over your lifetime is a marathon not a sprint.

Again, I do not claim the ability to predict perfectly when it is time to buy and sell property but you should hopefully feel, intuitively, that understanding the above is of significant value when considering the property market.

Of course there are many factors that affect the property market: A big part of what drove the enormous increases between 1993 and 2007 were many commentators claiming that most dangerous of phrases: "It's different this time." Just like they did to justify the dot.com bubble. In truth, there have been many reasons for the historically unprecedented strength of British property in this time period and even more so with regard to London property.

Much has been made in recent years about the lack of supply of property driving the huge price increases we have seen. There is no question that this has been a factor (although there are actually nearly one million empty properties in the UK).[11] Social changes such as higher divorce rates, large scale immigration from new EU countries such as Poland and more people wanting to move out from their parents' and live alone have meant a higher demand for many types of property.

"Prime" central London has also been particularly strong given the explosion in the British financial service industry and its bonus culture and, in addition, vast numbers of global rich who see London as an excellent long-term investment with its favourable tax treatment of foreign nationals, English language, strong legal system and perfect placement for international business above Europe and between America and Asia.

INTEREST RATES

Perhaps even more important than these factors, however, has been the price and supply of money. The price of money, otherwise known as the interest rate, has been held extremely low for a long time by the policies of central banks on both sides of the Atlantic. This fact, combined with financial deregulation and developments in the global debt markets meant that there has been an unprecedented amount of cheap money available to anyone who wanted to buy a house for the last several

11 Source: http://www.moneyweek.com/blog/merryn-somerset-webb-scandal-of-britains-empty-homes-14900

years.

This, more than anything, is why the price of housing went up for so long and by so much. When considering where house prices might go from here it is perhaps most instructive for us to think about whether there will continue to be a vast supply of money at low interest rates. To do so we must understand how interest rates are set and this means we must have a basic understanding of the bond markets.

If we consider interest rates first, we should be aware that governments only have a certain amount of power when it comes to setting interest rates. Governments raise money partially from tax but more and more by selling bonds. If no one wants to buy a country's bonds when they are issued then they are forced to offer them more and more cheaply. Cheaper bonds mean higher interest rates because the lower the price of a bond the higher the implied interest rate. We will explain this in more detail later in the book.

At the time of writing this is exactly what has been happening across Europe. We have seen interest rates in Greece, Italy, Spain and even France get pushed up very significantly by a bond market which refuses to pay as much for these countries' debt as before. The only way for a government to fight against this reality is by inventing money to buy their own bonds. This is essentially what "quantitative easing" is. As we have discussed above, throughout history this policy has always caused significant inflation. As we have seen, higher inflation means lower real returns on property (and most other assets apart from "stuff", ergo, commodities).

It seems, therefore, that at the moment many property markets are caught between the "rock" of rising interest rates or, in those countries which decide to combat this by printing money (particularly the UK and the US), the "hard place" of rising inflation.

We must also consider the supply of money (as well as it's price). With many banks in Europe and the United States technically insolvent, they need to keep hold of as much of their cash as possible. This means that even though the UK and US governments in particular are doing their level best to keep interest rates low by inventing lots of new money, actual bank lending has fallen through the floor as banks make people jump ever-higher hurdles before they qualify for a loan.

The chart below captures this point. Total bank lending in the UK for mortgages has fallen off a cliff:

Gross Advances for House
Purchase in the UK

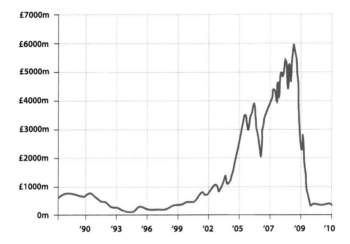

If there is less money available in any market the price of that asset class will fall, all other things being equal. This is a fundamental rule of economics and finance.

At this point in the chapter I would like to stress that it was not my intention in this discussion of property to simply outline a bearish (negative) case for UK property.[12] My aim is simply to ensure that having read this section the reader is better equipped to evaluate the potential outlook for property as an investment over the long run. You must always be thinking about the relative merits of an investment at any given time in your life.

That said, I believe it is not controversial to say that much of the UK property market currently suffers from historically low rental yields and high capital values (as demonstrated by a high multiple of income ratio). Property investors today also confront the twin head winds of the likelihood of increasing interest rates (and inflation) and a financially weak banking sector reluctant to lend money (e.g. to someone who might ultimately buy your property from you).

12 One very important feature of the property market which I acknowledge is that it is the one asset which a private individual can borrow meaningful sums of money to buy. We will say more about this shortly.

THE ENDOWMENT EFFECT

I would argue that another reason UK prices (in sterling terms at least) have held up relatively well so far is due to another facet of human psychology: The endowment effect. This is another phenomenon well documented by behavioural psychologists.

Put simply, the endowment effect is when an individual believes the current price or value of something they own must be the same or more than what they paid for it or, frequently, what the highest perceived value of it was. Human beings are inherently reluctant to acknowledge when they have made a loss. We are hard-wired this way. This is why many people doggedly hold on to shares which are worth much less than they bought them for and watch them fall further and further, compared to professional traders who are often explicitly aware of the endowment effect and ruthlessly cut their losers as a result.

What happens in property markets time and time again throughout history is that when the fundamentals turn bearish (negative), there is quite a long lag-time before prices fall, primarily due to the endowment effect. In more difficult economic conditions the number and wealth of potential buyers falls, for all the reasons mentioned above (less bank lending, less people with high-paying jobs or making bonuses etc.).

People who own properties that were relatively recently valued at, say, £1 million find that no one is actually willing to buy their property at that level but refuse to accept that the property is now worth, say £900,000, the best bid they have actually received. Rather than admit their property has fallen in value, the seller will be inclined to hold out for the number they perceive their property to be worth. Whilst this is happening, it should be obvious that the overall number of transactions falls off a cliff.

This is exactly what we have seen in much of the UK market for the last couple of years: The number of housing transactions has been at record lows in many parts of the UK for some time. There is a "Mexican stand off" whilst sellers refuse to accept their property might be worth less than the high water mark valuation their estate agent gave them in 2007 whilst for their part, potential buyers simply cannot afford to pay that price.

This stalemate is broken in one of two ways: Either economic and lending conditions improve and buyers are now able to pay the asking price or economic conditions deteriorate and more and more sellers are forced to accept the lower prices due to personal circumstances such as losing their job.

You can see that in the second scenario prices may often fall significantly in a short space of time as waves of forced sellers finally cave in to lower prices. This is why we have property crashes as neatly illustrated in the Nationwide chart from a few pages back.

THE SENSIBLE FRENCH

I would like to conclude this section by highlighting an interesting feature of the French mortgage market. The French have a very different approach to mortgage lending than we have had in the Anglo-American world. In France, with very few exceptions...

> *...the basic approach is that the total of an individual's monthly mortgage payments (to include interest, capital and any other borrowing they have) should not exceed one third of the buyer's gross monthly income...*

This approach stands in startling contrast to where the UK and US markets got to in the last two decades and goes some way to explaining why the French property market has not suffered the same level of boom and bust witnessed in the US and the UK. When thinking about the US and UK markets, it is perhaps instructive to realise that until the 1980s their markets were not dissimilar to the French market. I would argue that what then changed has been a key driver of the explosion in property prices on both sides of the Atlantic since then and set the stage for the horrendous crash we have seen in the US and may well see in the UK.

FINANCIAL DEREGULATION MADE BORROWING TOO EASY

In the 1980s both Reagan and Thatcher de-regulated the financial services industry. This was carried on in the 1990s under Clinton and successive UK governments. Prior to these changes, getting a mortgage in both countries had been reasonably hard throughout most of history. An applicant needed a decent deposit, a reasonable track record in their personal finances and often had to demonstrate a grasp of the metrics discussed above to a bank manager they most likely had some previous relationship with before they were able to borrow money. Most mortgages were also interest and capital repayment products.

This all changed from the 1980s. Deregulation meant that it became much simpler for individuals to secure a mortgage. Structural changes in the banking sector meant that mortgage approvals were increasingly a centralized form-filling exercise with borrowers no longer having any sort of personal relationship with their bank manager. In addition, many bank managers and mortgage brokers didn't understand much of the content of this chapter let alone this book.

As more and more people were able to secure funding, property prices inevitably increased. Very quickly a self-fulfilling upward spiral in property markets developed: Prices went up which meant banks relaxed their lending criteria on the assumption that they would always be able to take back an asset which would be worth more in the future than now, thus underwriting the loan. This was only possible given how many bank staff were in their twenties, had only ever seen a rising property market – anchoring at work - and didn't understand most of the contents of this chapter. Neither did most of the people buying properties. The US and UK property markets became a great big game of musical chairs.

Bankers and mortgage brokers got paid more and more as the volume of business, upon which their bonuses were paid, flourished, giving them little incentive to question what was happening. House prices kept increasing which, thanks to a heady cocktail of money illusion and endowment effect made people feel wealthier.[13] This, of course, kept politicians happy as there is no happier electorate than one that feels wealthy.

In the "naughties", particularly after 9/11, the stage was set for an even more frenzied bull market as Alan Greenspan, Chairman of the Federal Reserve, cut real interest rates to less than zero and held them there for years. The real interest rate is the interest rate minus inflation, hence how it can be less than zero as it is at the moment. All over the UK and the US people were effectively being paid to borrow money to buy property. Hardly surprisingly that prices kept going up.

It is not controversial to suggest that on both sides of the Atlantic vast numbers of people who would never previously in history have been able to borrow money to buy a house were able to do so. A significant proportion of these people had no understanding of basic finance, let alone any of the financial metrics discussed in this section. As a result, I would argue that several million bad decisions were taken across the English-speaking world, without which we could never have had such a huge bull market in property.

Many of the best-informed market commentators saw what was happening and started highlighting the likelihood of a crash some years ago. As often happens in such cases, many of these folk ended up looking foolish as they called the top time and again and then saw the market carry on up. As John Maynard Keynes famously said: "The market can remain irrational longer than you can remain

---

13 I fully acknowledge that in the hottest markets in the world, people really were getting wealthier as price increases vastly outstripped inflation. That said, let us not forget that home-owners sitting on huge nominal increases in the value of their property could only benefit from that increase in real terms if they were to sell their property and move somewhere where the increase in prices had been less extreme, as per the example discussed at the beginning of this chapter.

solvent…"

Put another way, this is a classic example of "greater fool theory". As long as there was a "greater fool" and a bank willing to fund them, the market carried on going up even though people were making quite ridiculous decisions about the "value" of the property they were buying based on any of the long term fundamentals we have discussed in this chapter.

The Northern Rock situation in the UK was a direct result of this. In the US the whole edifice came crashing down from 2007, as more and more people were unable to fund their mortgage payments. We have seen how this has played out in the US: The most over-heated markets, such as Miami and Los Angeles have seen price falls as much as 70% and in some instances have still not found a floor. The Case-Shiller index of the twenty biggest cities in the US is down 34% since the peak and house prices are back to where they were nine years ago. One project I am aware of in Seattle was originally trying to sell land for $300,000 a plot. Those plots were eventually sold for $1,500. This is how bad things can get.

I repeat that I do not claim to know whether the UK market will suffer as badly as many markets in the US. There are many arguments to suggest that London in particular will continue to be resilient, the basic reason being that nearly every wealthy foreigner in the world would like to own a place in London (particularly wealthy Greeks, Libyans, Syrians and other people from the Middle-East for obvious reasons). The exceptional growth in the developing world I have discussed above has created thousands of new millionaires and a large number of new billionaires and many of these people see London as a great place for their money, especially with the pound 25% cheaper against a basket of foreign currencies than it was a few years ago.

At the same time, however, a significant crash in global financial markets will rob many of these people of a significant chunk of their wealth, resulting in less money competing for London property assets. In addition, the loss of many thousands of jobs in the London financial services industry and the non-payment of bonuses to many people in that industry, which is happening as I write, implies a huge decrease in the amount of money chasing London property assets. We shall see how this plays out in the near future.

It is perhaps worth flagging that London house prices, priced in gold or a basket of foreign currencies rather than pounds sterling have fallen some way since peaking in 2007. This was also the year that Jon Hunt, the founder of the London estate agent group, Foxtons, sold that business for £390 million. I would argue that this sale will prove to have been very well timed in the years ahead in terms of maximizing his *real* wealth rather than just his number of pounds sterling.

In the rest of the UK, what happens to property prices will as ever depend on supply and demand in each individual market and on where rental yields, total returns and multiples of people's income are compared to the long run average. They will also continue to be influenced by interest rates, inflation and available bank lending.

I hope that this section has been useful in outlining key ways of looking at property and how to value it. Armed with these methods you have a far better chance of making the right decision about when to buy a home and at what price. I fully understand that there is an emotional angle to buying a home that should be taken into account. Property is the only asset where this factor should have an impact on our decision making process. That said, I still maintain that if you want to maximize your chances of building wealth throughout your lifetime you should not be afraid to be patient and rent if the metrics and considerations we have looked at in this section suggest that the asset you are looking at is historically expensive. If you find yourself looking for houses and the only ones you like are priced at six times the combined income of you and your partner or spouse you should almost certainly consider renting for the time being.

BUT RENTING IS JUST "THROWING MONEY AWAY" ISN'T IT?

It is also perhaps worth quickly addressing another fallacious belief that "rent is just throwing money away" or "paying someone else's mortgage". Is it really? Take the example from the beginning of this section: A £500,000 flat being rented for £18,000 a year. Let us imagine that this property loses only 10% of its value in the year ahead: 5% because of the market and 5% due to inflation. Our property is now worth roughly £450,000 in real terms.

This £50,000 decrease equates to 2.78 years worth of rent (£50,000/£18,000). As such, in this scenario, it would have been better to be the renter than the owner over the next three years. I hope this makes sense. This is a fairly conservative example. In the early nineties many British properties fell by 20% or more which would mean the renter could rent for five and a half years in this example and still come out ahead of someone who decided to buy the property rather than rent it. If you buy a property at a historically high price then you would almost certainly have been better off renting.

SO, HOW MUCH SHOULD YOU SPEND ON PUTTING A ROOF OVER YOUR HEAD?

As we have seen above, the French mortgage market will very rarely give anyone a mortgage where the repayments of interest AND capital exceed one third of their monthly income. This might seem crazily conservative to many people in the UK now but it is actually fair to say that it is crazy that this seems crazy (if you get my drift). Any long run assessment of roughly what people should spend to put a roof over their head will come up with the number of "about a third of income".

This is a good rule of thumb. If your mortgage payments are costing you more than one third of your monthly income, then, compared to long run averages, you are likely to be paying more than you should for your home. This is especially true given where interest rates are at the moment.

Remember that interest rates right now are the lowest they have been in quite literally three hundred years. Mean reversion tells us that there is a very high probability that interest rates will be higher in the future than they are today. If you are paying a large percentage of your salary on your mortgage right now with interest rates at an incredible historical low then you are at a high risk of having to pay an even higher percentage of your salary in future.

It is only because Britain has seen such an unprecedented bull market in property that many people have been willing to pay much larger percentages of their salary on their mortgage than historically.

Of course, moving home is a wrench, especially if you have children but the alternative is surely worse. If you have arranged your affairs in the past such that your home is a financial millstone around your neck, please try to inspire yourself by imagining the freedom you will feel if you remove that millstone.

So what if you have to live in a smaller property or a less fashionable neighbourhood? Life is a marathon, not a sprint. The sooner you arrange your affairs so that you create some savings to invest in assets other than property, the sooner your wealth will start growing meaningfully. If your home is only costing you one third of your monthly income then it really shouldn't be that difficult to find 5-10% of your monthly income to invest in other assets.

If you do things properly, longer term you will be able to have a lovely home, spare cash and the peace of mind that you can afford it. This is surely a far less stressful way of living your life than "keeping up with the Joneses" and being stressed all the time. It is also 100% more likely to make you properly wealthy in the medium to long term. If the only investment you have in your life is property you are missing out on substantial opportunities to grow your money and your financial situation is fundamentally imbalanced.

NEGATIVE EQUITY

Importantly, I well appreciate that some people reading this may be suffering from negative equity. That is to say that if you were to sell your house, you would end up with less than you need to pay your mortgage back. I can only imagine just what a horribly stressful situation this must be to have to confront. It is not immediately obvious that you can benefit from taking the radical action I'm talking about. What you decide to do if you are in this situation will be an intensely personal decision based on your own specific circumstances.

Having said that, being completely honest, if I found myself in that position today I would be very worried about two things: (1) The very real risk that interest rates are more likely to increase in the years ahead than decrease. Remember, they are at a three hundred year low and this is not sustainable. (2) Obviously linked to this, the risk that the value of my property will fall further for all the reasons discussed.

There is a small chance that if you hang on, things might get better and the value of your property might bounce, depending on where you are but what if it doesn't? The future is an unknown. There is at least an equal chance that your property will fall further in value at the same time that your mortgage payments rise. I am strongly of the opinion that there is a much higher chance of the latter scenario given the state of the British and global economy. Confronted with this reality, wouldn't it be better to bite the bullet, downsize as much as possible as soon as possible and use the money you free up to pay back the rest of that loan?

TO CONCLUDE ON PROPERTY AND CREATING SURPLUS

Whatever your current living arrangements I would hope that you can see that changing them in order to free up extra money each month is actually quite an exciting proposition and surely preferable to carrying on with a large debt burden and resultant stress.

OTHER DEBTS YOU MAY HAVE

For those of you who have outstanding credit card debts or loans you will want to pay these down before you start investing. This is because the interest rate you are being charged on this debt is highly likely to exceed the return you will be able to make on investing your money.

Free up as much of your income as you can then use it to pay any credit card debt or loans off as quickly as possible. See your new extra 5-10% of cash as a debt-destroying laser beam. Whatever you do, don't despair. Whatever financial situation you are in now, if you take these steps and keep at it, time flies by and one day you will wake up and find yourself in a much better situation than you ever dreamed was possible. Just get cracking and make brave changes as soon as you can. You will feel great as soon as you do.

TAKE SOME ACTION NOW

It is fair to say that a key feature of human nature is inertia. We read things, nod in agreement, realise we should take some sort of action and then switch the television on. We are all guilty of this reality.

Remember that if you want to have an income of about £30,000 a year when you retire you need to build a pension pot of nearly £1 million. You definitely want to take action so that you succeed in doing this...

I would strongly recommend that, whatever your situation, you take some small action now. If you are already able to save and invest 5-10% of your income from this moment then please carry on reading.

If you are not able to save and invest that proportion of your money right now then stop reading, grab a pen and paper and think about how you are going to change this reality. If you need to move house then get online right now and start trying to find somewhere 10% cheaper that you would be happy to live in. Alternatively, you could downsize your car. Where there is a will, there is a way. You should set yourself the target of being able to save 10% of your salary within the next three to six months.

Come back to this part of the book once you have succeeded in this and arranged your affairs to create 5-10% a month of financial surplus… Good luck.

#7

TYPES OF ACCOUNT YOU WILL NEED AND THE IMPORTANCE OF AN ISA

"Start by doing what is necessary..."

– St. Francis of Assisi

So you have managed to free up some money each month. Now you need to optimise your financial services providers. Many people are quite understandably bewildered by the complexity of the financial services industry. Much of the industry likes to keep it that way so they can charge you high fees for bad products.

If you are going to flourish financially you need to have a much better than average grasp of the type of accounts available to you and the best ones amongst them. To optimise your finances, you will need to make the best arrangements with your current account and pension and, most importantly, ensure you have an excellent ISA account.

1. YOUR CURRENT ACCOUNT

You would arguably have to be living in a cave not to know what a current account is. We all have them. It is, however, fair to say that most UK current accounts leave a lot to be desired. First, they offer appalling interest rates: I confess I actually laughed out loud recently when I was waiting in line at a major high street bank and there was an enormous poster proudly advertising an account that paid 1.8% gross interest.

This was for an account that had a monthly charge "from £7.95". Assume, for simplicity, you are a basic rate taxpayer and that you were "lucky" enough to be paying "only" £7.95 a month for this account. Your net interest rate with this bank would be 1.44%. On this basis you would have to keep more than £6,625 in that account just for the interest you earned to pay off the monthly charges.[1] I'm amazed a bank would even advertise such a completely terrible product but there it was on a big poster in their branch. Why do we let them get away with it?

You will probably be aware that the big UK banks have also been caught red-handed time and time again mis-selling bad products. At the time of writing one of the major UK banks has just been fined several million pounds for mis-selling a product to pensioners. There has also been the payment protection scandal and a long standing consumer campaign against unfair overdraft charges.

Importantly, their other financial products tend to be nowhere near as good as those offered by other less well know players in the market. Their ISA accounts for example, tend to offer a tiny fraction of the flexibility and choice of other far better players, often at higher fees. The only reason they can get away with this is because they have such a captive client base. Many people have no idea that

---

1 Twelve months of £7.95 = £95.40. So how much would we need to have in the bank earning 1.44% to earn £95.40? The sum is: 95.4/0.0144 = £6,625. In reality you would need slightly more given the charge is taken monthly so each month your capital sum would be less.

they can (and should) go elsewhere. We will discuss this more in the section on ISAs below.

Despite all the above, I do not advocate changing your current account. In my experience it is virtually impossible to get away from these issues, no matter which bank you use in the UK. What is key, however, is that you optimise how you use your current account. I would hope that, having read this far in the book; you will never accept a return of 1.8% gross on your money. My advice with your main bank is simply to keep as little money with them as possible.

Work out what you need to live on each month, add a margin of error and then ensure that any surplus is automatically paid away every month from your high-street bank to accounts that will enable you to make real money. For most people in the UK, the most important of these will be your ISA account but we should also consider your pension situation, so let us look at that first.

2. YOUR PENSION

I would be surprised if anyone reading this has not heard the word "pension". Nevertheless, I hope you will forgive me if I suggest that the vast majority of people have, at best, only a basic understanding of what a pension is, what they can do with it and what issues they need to be aware of in the years ahead. This fact is another invitation for much of the financial services industry to sell you bad products with high costs.

There are two main types of pension:

1. One provided by the government or state.
2. Private or occupational pensions built up by an individual, sometimes with the help of their employer.

GOVERNMENT / STATE PENSIONS
In the introduction to this book I made the point that state pension systems all over the world are completely bankrupt. To many people this seems like a controversial statement. I think it is worth demonstrating quickly why it is not. The state pension is unquestionably doomed due to a combination of enormous demographic change and a complete failure by a generation of politicians to address the implications of that change.

In the UK, the government started to provide a small pension to people over the age of 70 in the year 1909. If you think about it, this wasn't actually that much of a financial commitment. Life expectancy in 1909 was far shorter than it is today.

Relatively few people survived into their seventies. The ratio of workers to old age pensioners was very high: That is to say that a high percentage of the population were working and paying tax and a very small percentage indeed were retired and drawing a pension.

In the one hundred plus years since then, this reality has completely changed. There is perhaps nowhere more illustrative of this change than Japan. When the Japanese launched their generous welfare state after the Second World War there were around forty five workers for every pensioner. By 2020 this number is forecast to be 2:1. Arguably, it is this fact more than anything which accounts for the fact that Japan's stock market today is still trading miles below it's 1989 peak and its economy has struggled for decades.[2] It is a huge and inescapable black cloud on the Japanese economy's horizon.

Sadly, this same phenomenon is happening all over the developed world. Modern countries are burdened with social security systems that were put in place when the entire structure of those societies was completely different to what they are today.

Faced with this demographic reality, what governments all over the western world needed to do in the last few decades was ensure that, more than ever before, we all saved and invested for a rainy day. Sadly, most of them did the exact reverse.[3] Rather than running budget surpluses and saving and investing to provide sorely-needed capital for our future, governments all over the developing world have consistently spent far more than they have earned in tax receipts and made up the difference by borrowing on global bond markets and "inventing" money.[4]

They have also done a terrible job at ensuring that people make the effort to sort their own financial affairs out, primarily because finance is such an unpopular subject: You don't win elections telling people they need to spend less and save more. Here is a graph showing the sheer scale of what the US have done in terms of borrowing:

2 The Japanese Nikkei index peaked at over 39,000 in 1989. Today it is still below 10,000. Quite incredible.

3 Australia is a wonderful exception. From the mid 1980s, Australians have had an extraordinarily good national pension system which has forced most people to save for their retirement.

4 I stress that I have no political axe to grind here. This gross mismanagement of our financial affairs has taken place under both main parties in the UK and with Democrats and Republicans at the helm in the US.

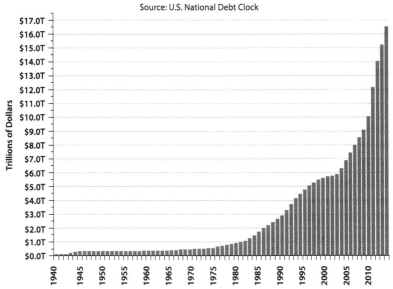

National Debt from 1940 to Present
Source: U.S. National Debt Clock

This graph is pretty extraordinary, especially when you look at the incredible acceleration in borrowing of the last few years, but even it fails to tell the full story. If you add up the unfunded liabilities of the US government, that is to say, the money they are committed to spend on pensions, healthcare etc. in the future, the number is well over $200 trillion.

This is why Niall Ferguson, Professor of Economic History at Harvard University describes government accounts as "essentially fraudulent".

To put this in perspective: The US economy generates about $15 trillion of economic output each year. If we use the $200 trillion number, this implies the US owes 13.3x what it makes.

This is like someone earning £30,000 a year having £400,000 of credit card debt.

The interest alone costs you most if not all of your annual income. Many analysts think the situation is even worse and the $200 trillion figure could be prove conservative in the long run.

Even on the official numbers, below is an excellent illustration of just what a mess American finance is in and, most importantly, how the politicians are totally failing to deal with it:

An illustration of just how little politicians are doing:

- U.S. Tax revenue: $2,170,000,000,000
- Federal budget: $3,820,000,000,000
- New debt: $1,650,000,000,000
- Official national debt: $14,271,000,000,000
- Recent budget cuts: $ 38,500,000,000

Thirty eight and a half billion dollars of budget cuts might seem like a good effort from Washington until you take away eight zeros and pretend this was a normal household budget.

This makes things much clearer. The numbers above are basically the same as:

- Annual family income: $21,700
- Money the family spent: $38,200
- New debt on credit card: $16,500
- Outstanding balance on credit card: $142,710
- Total budget cuts: $385

The point I'm making is that year after year these problems get worse and there is no political will whatsoever to take steps to solve them. The situation in the UK is no different. I find the debate about "austerity" quite maddening given that the current coalition government is actually spending significantly more than the government were ten years ago as a percentage of GDP. On both sides of the Atlantic, the only way out of this situation, for politicians at least, is by printing (inventing) vast sums of money.

The problem with this, as we have seen, is that inventing money devalues it through inflation. We have actually seen this happen time and time again throughout history.

YOU WILL NOT GET A PENSION YOU CAN LIVE ON FROM THE GOVERNMENT
As a result, western governments have basically two choices when it comes to pensions:

1. Own up to the fact that they can't afford to pay people a pension any more, or...
2. ...print vast amounts of "science fiction" money with which to pay people a "pension" thus creating rampant inflation.

The result for you will be the same: Either you don't get a pension, or you get a pension paid in money that can't buy much of anything any more.

So far, governments on both sides of the Atlantic have taken the money-printing option and it is extremely likely this will continue for the simple reason that because so few people understand what is going on they can get away with it.

For obvious reasons a politician who stands up and says: "Sorry, you can't have a pension,[5] we just can't afford it any more" has a much shorter life span than one who says: "We are taking positive steps to solve the financial crisis with a £100 billion package of quantitative easing".

Both statements have essentially the same result but only a small minority of people understands this. Today, no matter what your political inclinations, no matter how you view the role of government, the simple fact is that we can't afford to pay for society's pension and healthcare requirements in the way we have in the last few decades. There are just too many retired and retiring people compared to productive workers. If you are younger than about fifty and want to have enough wealth to live on in the future you will have to make your own provision for that future. Let us, therefore, turn our attention to private pensions:

PRIVATE / COMPANY PENSIONS
Even in the days before the state pension was at risk of disappearing it had the problem that it wasn't very much money anyway. Many people aspired to retire on a much higher income than what they would get from the state.

Understandably, it was realised that it would be a good idea for the state to encourage anyone who wanted to save and invest to provide for his or her own future. As a result, for several decades now governments have permitted individuals to have their own private pension arrangements, often organised through their employer.

The main differences between saving your money in a pension fund compared to elsewhere is the tax treatment and access to your money. Money saved in a pension account is not taxed when it goes in. This is obviously good news. The quid pro quo, however, is that you are not able to touch that money for many years. This is less good news as we shall see.

Many of you will have a company pension scheme where a percentage of your salary and, if you are lucky and have a generous employer, possibly some additional "matched" money from your employer is automatically paid into "something" every month, usually a "fund"[6] of some description. Some of you, particularly if

5 Or a health service for that matter.
6 We will explain more about what funds are shortly.

you are self-employed, may have a private pension scheme. For those of you who do have a pension, do you know what it is invested in? British shares? American bonds? Cocoa futures?

If you are anything like most people, you will either have no idea at all where this money is being invested or only a relatively vague idea. You will also almost certainly have no idea what fees you are paying for these funds. These are often significantly higher than they need to be. Please remember how quickly your money is eroded by high fees. Don't worry, literally only one person out of several hundred I have asked in the last few years has ever had detailed knowledge of their pension arrangements. Amusingly this has included nearly everyone I know who has a high powered job in finance and me for the first several years of my career.

Your pension is the first thing you need to sort out and won't take long. You simply need to ensure that you are doing the best you can with your pension money. If you don't know what your pension is invested in or what costs you are paying, it is unlikely that any pension you are building up is working anywhere near as hard for you as it could be doing. Over time, this could have a seven figure impact on your life.

There are broadly two categories of pension I want to focus on here: Occupational pensions, provided by your employer and Self-Invested Personal Pensions or SIPPs. SIPPs have existed since 2006 and "do what they say on the tin". A SIPP is simply a pension account that gives you the tax benefits of a pension and allows you to invest in a very wide variety of assets and make your own decisions about what to invest in.

Although it is by no means always true, very few occupational schemes are as a good a vehicle for pension investment as a SIPP. This is simply because SIPPs are so flexible and likely to be far more so than the pension scheme your company has. Companies tend to outsource their pension schemes to one pension provider. The result is that employees in a company scheme will tend to have quite a narrow range of options to invest their pension in. They also often have rather high fees compared to what you will be able to pay within your SIPP account and we have seen already what a large negative affect high fees will have on your money over time. This is a very similar point to the one we made earlier in the book about the limited range and excessive fees of most investment products you might be offered by your high street bank.

Those of you who have an occupational pension with your employer are unlikely to have much freedom to invest your money how you like. Your company will most likely offer a limited product with fairly tight parameters on the type of funds you can choose. If this is the case, don't worry too much. There will still be a way to optimise what you do have in that scheme. We will get to this below when we look more specifically at how to invest and what to invest in. Your approach will be broadly the same for your pension and ISA money.

CONTROVERSIAL ADVICE

If you do not already have an occupational pension, I am going to make a controversial suggestion: Which is to say that, if you have less than £940[7] a month to save:

I do not think you should organize a pension at all...

If you are self-employed or working for a company that does not have a pension scheme then I am very strongly of the opinion that your first priority, with any money you can save, is to put as much as you can into an ISA account each month.

The reason for this is quite simple: Although you get a tax break on any money that you put into a pension, you are essentially not able to access it until your retirement, which could be many years from now.[8] Given the uncertainty we are currently dealing with, I would much rather have immediate access to my money.

If you are in your twenties, thirties or even forties, I think it is a substantial gamble to assume that the UK pension system will exist in anything like its present form by the time you retire. Remember that the government is essentially bankrupt. To me, there is too much uncertainty about what may or may not happen to any money you commit to a pension account.

There are many examples throughout history of governments passing laws that permit them to take control of pension assets. If you think this is something that hasn't happened for decades, think again. The most recent example was in Argentina in late 2008 when the government passed a law to nationalize $30 billion of private pension money. Thousands of middle class Argentinians who were saving diligently lost control of their own money.

Closer to home, few people remember that Gordon Brown changed the tax treatment of dividends in pension accounts in 1997. This resulted in £5 billion a year less money for holders of pension accounts. To me this is an excellent example

---

7 This number is calculated by dividing your annual ISA allowance by twelve. In the 2012/2013 tax year the ISA allowance is £11,280, hence £940 per month. As you can imagine the vast majority of people have less than £940 a month to save and invest.

8 This isn't strictly true. It is possible to get your hands on pension money before retirement but only by permitting one of a number of cowboy outfits to take on your pension and pay you out approximately 50% of what you have saved. This option also takes several months and should only ever be considered as a last resort if you are in real financial trouble.

of how careful we must be to assume that highly regulated savings vehicles such as pensions will remain the way they are.

Using Argentina as an example of what might happen in the UK might seem like a crazy comparison but it really isn't. By some measures, Argentina in 2008 was actually in a better position financially than the UK is in today.

It is hard for us to predict the future, which is why, unless you already have an occupational pension arrangement I would far rather you keep your savings as accessible and mobile as possible despite the tax advantages a pension has.

TO CONCLUDE ON PENSIONS

To summarise then, you will fall into one of the following categories with your pension:

CATEGORY ONE:

You have a pension with your employer and can only invest in products offered by your employer's pension scheme.

Action to take: Ensure you own the best funds available to you under your employer's existing scheme. You will understand how to do this once you have read the sections on investment below. If you are paying a reasonable chunk of your salary into the pension scheme and have the option to take that money as cash, you may want to consider changing this and paying that money into an ISA account for the reasons mentioned above. Whether you decide to do this or not will depend on what you think of the pension arrangements your company has after you have read what follows, what your past performance has been and what the costs of the pension product are as compared to your ISA account. You will understand how to evaluate these issues once you have read the sections which follow.

CATEGORY TWO:

You are now self-employed or working for a company which does not provide you with a pension but you have a pension pot built up from previous employment.

Action to take: Do not make any further contributions to a pension unless you can afford to save more than your ISA allowance of £940 a month. With your existing pension pot, ensure you own the best funds available to you within your scheme. Again, after reading the rest of this book, you will have a better idea of how to do this.

You may also consider opening a SIPP account and transferring across what you have saved so far. This will give you enormous freedom with what you can invest those funds in and very likely cut down the fees you are paying, thus improving your performance.[9]

CATEGORY THREE:
You do not currently have any pension arrangements.

Action to take: If you don't have a pension at the moment and have less than £940 a month to save and invest, which describes the vast majority of people, do not open a pension account. Focus instead on your ISA arrangements.

As such, let us now turn our attention to what, for most people in the UK, is the most important vehicle for you to become wealthy: Your ISA account.

3. YOUR ISA(S)

Even if you set aside my thoughts about pensions, if you really want to make giant strides with your financial situation you need to start saving some money from your income each month anyway. No matter what your view of the UK pension system, you basically can't touch pension money until you are fifty five at the earliest.

If you plan on building fun-money sooner than by the time you have grey hair then you will need to save and invest cash separately from any pension arrangements you have. When you see how much you can make doing this you will want to do it. Start as soon as possible.

As you will have read above, if at all possible you should aim for at least 5%, preferably 10% of your salary after tax being automatically paid into your investment pot every month. Once you have set this up, you will very quickly adjust to your new financial reality. After you get used to it and you start seeing your pot grow, you might even consider upping the percentage to 12% or even 15% but 10% is a good number to start with. The more you invest, the faster you will become truly wealthy.

Whatever you manage to save, the upside of doing so over time is life changing and, due to the fundamental mathematical laws of compound interest we met earlier in the book, virtually guaranteed to make you a serious amount of money over time as long as you are doing the right thing with your money in the right kind of accounts.

---

9 For those of you who chose to subscribe to the Plain English Finance email / blog, I will be explaining the steps I take with my SIPP pot in the months and years ahead.

As long as you are saving less than the £940 per month we mentioned above you will be able to invest all of this money using an ISA wrapper (Individual Savings Account). Obviously this applies to the majority of people.

WHAT IS AN ISA?

An ISA account is simply a type of investment account within which the government lets you invest a certain amount of money each year. Crucially, any gains you make on that money are not subject to tax.

You can open an ISA account with a very large number of different companies in the UK, for example with the main high street banks and with a number of more specialist organisations such as stockbroking firms. To open an ISA account all you need to do is fill in a form or two and transfer some money into it, either a lump sum or a monthly payment. Most ISA providers will let you open an account with as little as £50-100 to begin with, some with even less.

CASH VS. STOCKS AND SHARES ISAS

At this stage I would like to highlight the existence of two broad categories of ISA account: The first is called a cash ISA. A cash ISA account is not that different from a current account. You open an account and put cash on deposit. The only difference is that you get a slightly higher interest rate, depending on who you open your cash ISA with and you do not have to pay tax on any interest you make.

A stocks and shares ISA is a slight misnomer in that it is simply a type of ISA account which enables you to invest any money in that account in a very wide variety of assets (if you have an account with a good quality provider). That is to say that you can buy products other than just stocks and shares such as bonds and commodities and can also keep your money in cash.

By now it should be clear that I would take a dim view of cash ISAs. With real inflation at the sort of levels it is at today you will most certainly be losing real wealth if you use a cash ISA product. The only beneficiary of a cash ISA product is the firm supplying it to you.

If you are to have any chance of making a real return on your money you need to open a stocks and shares ISA so that you have the flexibility to invest in things which have a chance of outperforming inflation and making you a real return. We will look in more detail at how you might do this and at the sort of investments you will put in the account in the next few chapters. For now it is enough for us to focus on ensuring you open an ISA account and do so with one of the best providers in the UK market so that you get the flexibility you need to succeed at the lowest possible cost.

As you might imagine, over the years, I have spent a great deal of time looking at the various different ISA providers in the UK market and have personally had accounts with no less than eight of them.[10] I have not named my favourite UK ISA providers here since this book is, by its very nature, a static information source. I am well aware of who I think the best ISA providers are at the time of writing but financial services companies are constantly launching new accounts and improved products.

As such, you will find information on the firms which I believe to be the very best in the UK market and an explanation as to why in the resources section of the www.plainenglishfinance.com website. Using this resource will ensure you know who is currently offering the best-value, best-quality ISA accounts.

AVOID THE HIGH STREET BANKS

I think it is worth noting explicitly that the high street banks are arguably a bad place to have an ISA. As we have seen, the ideal ISA account will enable you to buy a massive range of shares or funds and ensure that you can do so at low cost. If you open an ISA with any of the main high street banks you will generally only be able to choose from their limited range of in-house ISA funds. These tend to be expensive and limited in terms of what assets you can end up owning.

This is another key reason why so many people have a negative view of investing. If the only ISA or other investment you have ever owned is a high-cost, low-performance product from a high street bank you are very likely to have seen very little happen to your money over the years and have a pretty dim view of investment generally.

TAX FREE

The key thing about having an ISA is that you will not have to pay tax on the profits you make from any investments you make within that account. This is hugely beneficial to how quickly your money will grow.

As an example, I invested my 2010/2011 ISA in silver. I was lucky enough to sell my position for a 163% profit about eight months after my original purchase. This meant I had turned my original ISA allowance for that year of £10,200 into about £27,000. If I had done this outside of an ISA account, I would have owed the government nearly £5,000 worth of tax. Thanks to the ISA, I owed them no tax on those profits whatsoever.[11]

---

10 For what it is worth, over the years I have had accounts with: Fidelity, Newstar, Invesco, Selftrade, Williams de Broë, Hargreaves Lansdown, TD Direct and Killik & Co.

11 Please note that this was an exceptionally good "trade". In no way am I suggesting that you will regularly make these sorts of returns but it does show that they are possible .

So to conclude: You will want to open an ISA account with a top-quality provider. Please see the website for more details.

AND FINALLY: ANOTHER TYPE OF ACCOUNT TO CONSIDER - A SPREAD BETTING ACCOUNT

Before we finish this section on the various different types of financial account you might want to have, we should very briefly cover something called spread betting. Many people have not heard of spread betting but, for an individual who is prepared to put the time in, it can be one of the very best ways to make money from investing.

It is worth noting that there are relatively few countries in the world with a well developed spread betting industry: At the time of writing it is illegal in the US for example, which is a great shame for Americans.

So what is it and how does it work? The first thing to say is that spread betting is without doubt a method of investing that is only worth using if you are prepared to put in a decent amount of work. It is fairly complicated and if you don't know what you are doing it is possible to lose a large amount of money very quickly.

On the flipside, if you do spend the time to learn how it works, it is one of the most powerful tools for making money that is available today and we are very lucky that we have access to it as Brits.

For the time being, to give you a brief idea of what it is: If you have a spread betting account you are, quite simply, able to bet on the movement of a massive range of assets. Rather than betting on horses or dogs, you will be betting on shares, commodities and other investments. You do this by betting a certain monetary value "per point" on whatever asset you have a view on. Let us say you thought the gold price was going to go up. You would "go long" (buy) gold and decide how many pounds per point to bet.

At the time of writing, gold is trading at around $1600. As such, if you wanted to buy (or "go long") gold, you would decide how many pounds per point to bet. If you bet £1, you would end up theoretically owning £1,600 worth of gold. This would mean that if gold went up to $1800, you would make £200 (1800 – 1600 x 1). If you had bet £10 a point you would have made £2,000 and so on.

Two great aspects of spread betting are:

1. That you can end up with a theoretical exposure to whatever you are betting on that is worth far more than you have in your trading account. If you wanted to own £1,600 worth of gold as per the example above by actually buying some gold you would need to buy £1,600 worth. If, instead, you make a bet through your spread betting account you would only need a fraction of £1,600 and end up with the same theoretical exposure. This sounds rather complicated (to be fair it probably is) but if you understand what you are doing this can be extremely powerful: You can end up effectively "owning" thousands (or even millions) of pounds worth of an asset with a much smaller deposit.
2. You can bet on things going down as well as up. This means that if that thing falls in price you make money. This is called "shorting" and we shall look at it in more detail below.

So now we have looked at the various different financial accounts you can (and should) use to build wealth, let us look in more detail at the different kinds of financial vehicle available to you. Remember that one of the best things about investment in the year 2012 is that you are able to invest in a truly extraordinary range of things very cheaply and easily. This is very poorly understood by most people but is a serious string to your bow if you have even a basic grasp of what you are doing.

#8

THE TYPES OF INVESTMENT VEHICLE YOU WILL NEED TO USE

"Personal finance isn't that hard..."

– Ramit Sethi, Bestselling author and founder
of personal finance blog www.iwillteachyoutoberich.com.

In the last chapter we dealt with the bewildering array of financial accounts there are, now we need to deal with the bewildering array of financial products that exist. Once you have money in your ISA and pension accounts, you are ready to put that money to work by buying the right selection of financial products within those accounts. In order to do this, you need to understand a bit about what products are available and their relative merits.

CATEGORIES OF FINANCIAL PRODUCT / ASSET CLASSES

There are a number of different main categories of financial product, otherwise known as "asset classes" or "investment vehicles" with which you can store and (preferably) build wealth. Some of these are relatively well understood by people but I think it is fair to say that most of them are not. If you have never really known what a "bond" is or exactly what a "share" is, you have come to the right place.

The main types of individual investment vehicle we are interested in are:

1. Cash.
2. Property.
3. Bonds.
4. Shares.
5. Commodities.
6. Funds.
7. Insurance products.

...and to a lesser extent two further categories of interest to the more expert investor:

8. Foreign exchange, often called FOREX or FX.
9. Derivatives.

THE IMPORTANCE OF FUNDS

It is probably worth noting at this point that funds are arguably the most relevant of the above investment vehicles for the majority of private investors. This is quite simply because a fund allows you to own a large basket of any of the other products or even a mix of them from more than one of these categories.

As an investor in a single fund you can end up owning hundreds of shares for example. In certain other types of fund you could even end up owning a mixture of shares, bonds, property and commodities in the one fund. This is very important for a number of reasons which we will look at in more detail shortly.

AS EVER, DO NOT WORRY THAT THERE IS TOO MUCH TO LEARN

The above list might look quite daunting, with no less than nine categories of investment product to understand. Don't worry. It is true to say that you could read several hundred books on every single one of the categories above but you will be able to arrange your financial affairs very well without gaining an in-depth grasp of any of them. You really don't need to know in any great detail what a share or bond is or how commodities trade to make a huge positive difference to your financial affairs. That said, it is key to have a basic understanding of what they are, if only so you can best understand the suggestions that follow later in the book.

"ASSET ALLOCATION"

As we have seen briefly already, what is also of great importance is having an idea of what proportion of your wealth you should have in each of these categories. This last point, i.e. the mix of these different investment vehicles you own, is known as "asset allocation". Asset allocation is actually one of the most important things to be aware of when investing and something that far too few people understand or ever think about. It is also something that changes the older you get.

When you are young you want to be looking to grow your money. As you get older, however, you will want to ensure that you are investing more and more safely to preserve the pot you have made and derive a decent income from it. At the simplest level, this means that the older you are, the more of your wealth you should hold in bonds and cash and the younger you are the more in shares (equities).

A key thing to understand is that because of the huge obsession with property in recent years, most people in the western world tend to have nearly all of their wealth in property (assuming the equity in their property exceeds their mortgage at least). In the long run this is inadvisable. As we shall see, over time it is actually best that you own all of the above types of financial vehicle. If all you have is property, there is a surprisingly high risk you will fail to become wealthy in your lifetime.[1] To give yourself the best chance of becoming truly wealthy you need to ensure that you are aware of and exposed to the other asset classes and shares, bonds and commodities in particular.

GENERAL CONSIDERATIONS COMMON TO ALL ASSET CLASSES

Each of the above types of investment vehicle has certain individual characteristics but the two most important considerations when we look at any of them are:

1. How safe your money is when invested in that asset class.
2. What sort of percentage return you might expect to make.

Put another way, when we consider the relative merits of an investment vehicle or financial product, we are concerned with the return *of* our money and the return *on* our money. As I have already said, it is not necessary for you to have an in-depth understanding of each of the types of financial products listed above. All you need is to understand a little about what they are, how safe they are and what sort of return they might give you. So let us look very quickly at each in turn with this in mind:

1. CASH

First, let us just be clear that for the purposes of this discussion "cash" means money on deposit at a financial institution such as a bank or building society. Cash is also quite obviously the word we use to describe what you have in your pocket, wallet or purse but we are looking at the merits of cash as an investment vehicle here and you don't get paid interest on what you carry around with you (sadly).

Obviously the great thing about cash in a bank account is that it is basically "safe". Barring a financial crisis, massive natural disaster or revolution,[2] you should always have access to money you have in a bank account and the amount of money you have in that account will not suddenly be less one day than it was the day before because "the market has crashed".

---

1 If you think I am being too negative about property, track down someone who bought a house in California, Arizona, Florida, Dubai or any number of other places in 2005 – 2007. Sadly many of these people will quite possibly never recover financially from that one decision.

2 All of which have obviously happened before.

As such, cash is seen as very safe and the percentage return you can make on cash (interest rate) tends to be low as a result. When you are a saver and have money on deposit at a bank or building society, they will pay you an interest rate as a thank you for providing them with money they can lend out to borrowers. They will then charge borrowers a higher interest rate than they pay you, which is how banks make their money or at least how they used to.

AS ALWAYS, WE MUST NOT FORGET INFLATION

That is pretty much all we need to know about cash as an investible asset: It's all about the interest rate. Before we move on to the next section, however, there is a key factor we need to be aware of when thinking about cash: Inflation. When considering how "safe" your money is on deposit at a bank or building society you must understand the difference between the interest rate your bank is paying you, called the nominal rate, and the interest rate your money is actually earning, called the real rate. The difference is inflation.

A few pages earlier when talking about current accounts I mentioned an account at a major high street bank paying 1.8% interest and how this equates to 1.44% for a basic rate taxpayer. We have already seen how official UK government inflation numbers have been at about 4-5% but how real inflation based on more honest methods of calculation is at more like 10%.

Using these numbers, if you have your money on deposit earning 1.44% when inflation is running at around 10% you are losing more than 8.5% of your wealth every year in *real* terms. It is for this reason that I said in the introduction that believing "cash is king" can be a dangerous way of looking at the world.

Losing 8.5% of your wealth in a year does not sound very "safe" to me. When inflation is high and interest rates are low, real interest rates are negative. The calculation is very simple:

REAL interest (return on cash) = NOMINAL interest (what your bank is paying you) − INFLATION.[3]

It is important for your long-term financial success to keep as much of your wealth as possible in assets whose real return is positive. As such, when real interest rates are negative as they are now, you should look to have only as much cash as you need to pay for things in the short-term. It is perhaps easiest to think about "the short-term" as less than one year.

---

3 Some of you may be aware that the actual accurate method of calculating real return is a tiny bit more complicated: It is $((1+r / 1+inf)-1) \times 100$ where r = nominal interest rate and inf = inflation. So in this example: $((1.0144/1.1) - 1) \times 100 = -7.8\%$. The simple method above makes the same point and is obviously much easier to calculate.

Think about what you need to live on each month, add any other purchases or expenses you think you will need for this year (holiday, car, university tuition), add a margin of error for safety and invest everything else in assets other than cash. So let us turn to those other assets now:

2. PROPERTY

We looked at property in some detail in chapter six when we looked at creating financial surplus. When we consider the return of our money, property is obviously one of the better asset classes. A house or flat will always have some value given there is always demand for places to live and is almost certainly never going to be worth nothing at all as can be the case with a share.[4]

That said, as with so many investments, it is important to understand how to value property to give ourselves a fighting chance of buying it at a good level over time. We looked at the ideas of rental yield, capital gain and property prices as a multiple of salary in chapter six so there is no point in going over those ideas again but it is worth remembering that these metrics enable us to compare property as an investment to all the others.

There are a couple of additional points that it is probably worth making: As we have said, many people in the Anglo-Saxon world have a very high percentage of their net worth, in many cases all of it, tied up in their primary property.

We have seen that in the long run one of the most important things you need to bear in mind if you wish to grow your wealth in the safest way possible is asset allocation. As such, if you already have a huge percentage of all of your net worth tied up in property you should probably focus on investing in other asset classes before you consider another property investment such as a buy to let flat for example. Obviously this will depend on the returns you think you can achieve after inflation when you compare the various different options as we have already discussed.

There are, however, two other categories of property investment to think about over and above where you live: Commercial property and foreign or overseas property (and overseas commercial property for that matter). It is often the case that there will be very interesting opportunities in either or both of these categories that are worth considering even if you already have a large percentage of your wealth in UK residential property via your primary residence.

---

4 Although as anyone who owns a house in Detroit or the flood-ravaged parts of New Orleans can tell you, this isn't always true.

One of the ways of getting exposure to overseas and / or commercial property will be through owning a fund and this may be worth considering. We shall look in more detail at the idea of "funds" shortly.

PROPERTY AND BORROWING MONEY: A KEY POINT

I would like to make one final important point about property as an asset class: Unlike any of the other main asset classes, private individuals have traditionally been able to borrow reasonably large sums of money in order to invest in property. To a great extent this is a unique feature of the property market. Most private individuals are not able to borrow money to invest in shares or commodities for example. There are exceptions, usually for wealthy individuals with a track record and a private banking relationship and for those that use spread betting but these are relatively rare.

Mortgages enable individuals to control an asset with a value significantly more than the deposit they have saved. In a strong market this is obviously great news for the investor: For the last several years it was common practice to be able to buy a property with only a 5-10% deposit. Lenders such as Northern Rock were even offering 110% mortgages, thus effectively lending buyers their deposit.

In a strong market, this is obviously very good news for property investors. If you could put down £25,000 or even less to control a £250,000 property, for example, and that asset then increased in value sufficiently quickly, you could build real wealth very quickly. However, using debt (otherwise known as leverage or gearing) to buy any asset is a double-edged sword. In a bull market, you are able to use other people's money to grow your wealth. This is very powerful and has benefited many people in the English-speaking world over the last few decades, at least the ones who then sold out of those properties at the peak of the market.

That said, if you have borrowed to purchase an asset and that asset then falls in value, you will end up with nothing to repay your loan. We have already discussed this briefly when we looked at negative equity earlier. This can be very painful which is one of the reasons why I said in the introduction to the book that people can go very wrong with property investment.

As a general rule, the fact that you can borrow money to buy a property means there are opportunities for the smart investor to make great money doing so. It is crucial, however, to make sensible assumptions about what might happen to the value of what you buy and the cost of the money you borrow. The sub-prime crisis in the US came about primarily because thousands of people assumed US property would always appreciate in value and only thought about their monthly payment today rather than what might happen to that monthly payment in the years ahead. I would hope that the points made earlier in the book will help you to ensure you don't make the same mistake.

3. BONDS

Many of us are familiar with the idea of a loan: Quite simply a bank will lend you a certain amount of money in return for which, after a given amount of time you will pay them the money back plus an agreed amount of interest to compensate them for being without that money for that time. This is why it is helpful to understand interest rates as the "cost" or "price" of money. Arguably, less people are familiar with what a bond is but it is simply…

…A loan divided into many pieces so that it can be made by lots of people.

To explain: Imagine a big oil company plans to build a new refinery and needs £1 billion to do so. They might go to a big bank and ask for a £1 billion loan. If the bank was particularly relaxed about the strength of that oil company they may well simply lend them the money and ask for an appropriate interest rate. More likely, however, they would feel that £1 billion is too large a sum to be owed to them by one company and that the deal is too risky for them to do by themselves. This being the case they might do one of two things:

1. Approach some other banks to ask them if they would be interested in lending some of the £1 billion. Let us say that they actually do find nine other banks who are happy to lend £100 million each or four other banks who were happy to lend £200 million each. This would then be known as a syndicated loan – i.e. – a group (or syndicate) of banks has clubbed together to reduce their exposure (known as credit risk) but ensure that the deal still gets done. In this example, not only would the original bank receive interest on its loan, it would also charge a fee for organising the syndicate. This is one of the things an investment bank does.

2. The other option for that bank would be to print many pieces of paper, each one of which would represent a small fraction of the value of the £1 billion loan and offer those pieces of paper for sale to anyone who was interested in providing that fraction of the loan and receiving interest as compensation. This is essentially exactly the same process as with the syndicated loan above except that the pieces of paper are called "bonds" and their existence means that the loan can be "syndicated" (spread) to hundreds or even thousands of potential investors all over the world rather than to just a small group of banks.

So, in this example, let's say the bank prints one million bonds, each of which is worth £1000 and the oil company is committed to paying 5% interest on those bonds. When that bank offers these bonds for sale, potential investors can buy as many or as few of them as they like. For each one that they buy they will now be owed £1000 and 5% interest on that money by the oil company. Note that the interest paid by a bond is referred to as its "coupon". This is because in the past when a bond was literally a piece of paper it had a detachable "coupon" for every interest payment the owner would be entitled to receive.[5]

If you bought a bond that would be redeemed in three years time and which paid 5% interest by paying the holder 2.5% twice a year, there would have been six coupons. When bonds were originally invented, the bondholder would literally have taken those coupons to the bank every six months and exchanged them for a cheque or cash equivalent to 2.5% of the face value of the bond. Today these payments tend to be automated.

I should clarify that another feature of bonds concerns how long the buyer is lending the seller money for. A bond may entitle its owner to 5% a year and their original money back in three years or five years or even longer. Some government bonds last as long as fifty years. As you can imagine, a bond which promises to pay you 5% a year for ten years will tend to cost more than one which pays you 5% a year for two years, all other things being equal.

BONDS HAVE A SECONDARY MARKET

A further crucial aspect of bonds is the existence of a secondary market in them. This just means that, say you had purchased £10,000 worth of the oil company bonds we have just been discussing when they were offered by the investment bank: A month later you read that the oil company is in financial trouble or perhaps you just need your money back suddenly. You might decide you would rather get your money back than hold on to the bonds and collect your interest payments. Luckily for you, somewhere out there in the world is very likely to be someone who still thinks the oil company is a good bet and would like to own your bonds and collect the interest. As a result you will be able to sell your bonds to them via an intermediary, such as an investment bank or stockbroker.[6]

One important thing to bear in mind at this point is that it is pretty unusual for a private or "retail" investor (you) to buy bonds directly. Most bonds, whether issued by a company or a government, trade in amounts that are generally too big for the average private investor (but small enough for someone very rich, another of our reasons why the rich stay rich). For this reason, we would usually look to get exposure to bonds by owning a fund, which we will look at in more detail shortly.

5 If you google "bond coupons" and look at the images you will get a good idea of how this worked.

6 Again, this is one of the main jobs an investment bank does.

GOVERNMENT BONDS

The next very important thing for us to understand about bonds and the bond market is that it is the main source of money for governments other than taxation. It is vital that we understand something about this in order to fully appreciate what is happening today and further strengthen our understanding of what to do about it.

Governments all over the world have essentially only two ways of raising money to pay for the vast array of things they want to fund: First, taxation. This is reasonably well understood by most of us. We all pay tax in a wide variety of obvious and not so obvious ways and the companies we all work for and from whom we buy products and services do too.

Since their creation, however, very few governments have been able to survive on less than what they took in tax. This has been true for thousands of years. Throughout history, the primary reasons for the failure of political elites to survive on tax revenues has been the cost of war. In times of war the costs borne by government skyrocket. Ships must be built, soldiers must be paid and supplied. We only really need to understand this because it was this reality that lead to the creation of the bond market.

For the last several centuries, therefore, in times of emergency or war, governments have been forced to spend significantly more than they have earned in taxation. They have made up the difference by selling bonds to their population and, more recently, to foreign investors.

There is basically no other way for a government to raise money other than from taxation or from selling bonds to investors.[7] Sadly, even though most have enjoyed unprecedented peace since the end of the Second World War, nearly all western governments have still made a very regular habit of spending far more than they have been able to raise from taxation.[8]

They have made up the shortfall by selling bonds, that is to say raising debt. Remember that a bond is just a loan divided into lots of little pieces so it can be made by many different people or organisations.

---

7 One exception to this would be where a government sells assets such as land, gold reserves or foreign embassy buildings or military bases for example. These sales are obviously not a recurring income stream and tend, as a result, only to be used in emergencies or when those in power feel markets are at a particularly advantageous level. Governments can be pretty bad at this as we saw when Gordon Brown sold the UK's gold reserves close to a record low.

8 We have already seen this in the graphs of US and UK government debt in an earlier chapter. The only real exceptions have been small economies with a huge natural resource endowment per capita and decent political leadership such as Norway.

You might be surprised to learn that for a long time this policy was entirely sustainable. Banks offering mortgages, loans and credit cards are obviously comfortable offering such debt products to wealthy individuals who enjoy high annual earnings. There is a very good chance that individual will pay back their debt.

In the same way, investors all over the world were comfortable lending money to the governments of countries with high and usually rising annual "earnings" by buying their bonds. Translated into the language of the bond market: Investors were happy to buy the government bonds of countries with a high and growing GDP (Gross Domestic Product).

"RISK FREE"
Financial theory then assumed, until very recently, that lending money to the government of a modern country such as the US, UK or France was "risk free". If you were to buy $10,000 of bonds from the US government for your pension, you assumed there was no chance at all that you would not get your money back plus the interest promised.

The US government was deemed to be so big and rich that no one even considered for a moment the idea they wouldn't be able to fulfil their obligations and pay you back. Even if some incredible catastrophe were to occur, the US government would still be able to print as many dollars as it liked in order to pay back the money they owed you.

In fact, this is precisely what they are doing today. They can no longer afford to pay bond investors the interest and principal on their bonds without inventing "science-fiction" new money to do so. The trouble with inventing lots of new money (e.g. QE) is that it devalues that money as we have discussed above in the sections on inflation.

Whilst investors all over the world continued to believe the bonds of wealthy nations were essentially risk free, it should be intuitively obvious that they were prepared to earn pretty low returns on those bonds. With a choice of places to invest your money, you are willing to accept a lower return on "risk free" money, which you feel you are guaranteed to get back than you are on a riskier investment where you worry you may not. Part of the whole crisis of the last few years is that, increasingly, investors all over the world do not see the bonds of many developed countries as "risk free". This is another part of the paradigm shift I mentioned right at the beginning of the book. This is very important as it impacts interest rates and inflation. Let us look quickly at why this is:

GOVERNMENT BOND PRICES AND INTEREST RATES

At this stage, I would like to briefly explain the relationship between bond prices and interest rates: Imagine that the US government is selling a one-year bond worth $100 and offering to pay $5 of interest. This means that if you buy the bond, you are entitled to $100 of capital and $5 of interest at the end of the year.

If you pay $100 for this bond, your return on that investment will be 5%. This should hopefully be reasonably easy to understand. You pay $100 and after a year you get $105 back. A simple percentage return calculation shows us that this is 5%.[9]

However, in the "secondary market" that we talked about earlier, bond prices constantly move depending on what investors all over the world feel about the country or company who issued the bonds. As such, you can end up paying more or less than $100 for $100 "worth" of bonds.[10] In the above example, if you were to pay $101 for the bond, your return would end up being about 3.95%. This is because you are now losing 1% of your capital (you paid more than $100 for the bond but only get $100 of capital back at the end of the year) and your percentage return on the $5 of interest is a tiny bit lower than before (5/101 instead of 5/100).

Similarly if you were to pay $99 for it, your return would be about 6.05%. This is the same point in reverse. This time you are making a tiny bit more than 1% on your capital (you paid $99 but receive $100 back at the end of the year) and your $5 of interest represents a slightly higher fraction of $99 than it does of $100.

In a nutshell:

Lower bond prices mean higher interest rates and vice versa. They are two sides of the same coin...

This is important to understand. As explained above, governments who need to raise money to pay for all the things their tax revenue can't cover, must sell bonds to investors at home and abroad to make up the difference. If those investors are less confident about the financial strength of that government they will be prepared to pay less for those bonds. This will mean the price of their bonds fall. Lower bond prices mean higher interest rates. More accurately lower bond prices *are* higher interest rates.

---

9 Without wanting to get bogged down in maths, I like to think of percentage return as: "%age return = ((Number going to / number coming from)-1) x 100." So in this example: ((105/100)-1) x 100 = 5%.

10 This is one of those moments where you do not need to understand what we are discussing in detail, just the main points we are making.

THE BOND MARKET DRIVES INTEREST RATES (NOT GOVERNMENTS)

This is exactly what is happening all over Europe at the time of writing. Investors from all over the world are less and less willing to buy the bonds of countries such as Greece, Italy, Spain, France, Portugal and Ireland. These countries can only sell their bonds to raise money at lower and lower prices, which is the same as saying higher and higher interest rates. This has pushed interest rates in those countries up by a huge margin and shows us that the massive global bond market (thousands of investors from all over the world with trillions of dollars, pounds, euros, yen et al.) is more powerful than pretty much every single country in the world when it comes to setting interest rates, even the US. These countries have less and less control over their own interest rates. Governments have far less power to set interest rates than you might think.

In fact, the only difference between the troubled European countries and the US and UK is that both the US and UK can invent new money to buy their own bonds (QE). This keeps bond prices up (interest rates down) but creates inflation (devalues the dollar and the pound) so the effect is still negative.

As you might imagine, falling bond prices are also something of a vicious spiral: As interest rates rise in those countries, the government needs to pay more to borrow money, making investors even less willing to invest in those bonds.

You may already be aware that rising interest rates put a big brake on an economy for the following reasons:

1. People are less inclined to take out a mortgage or other loan or form of credit. This depresses the housing market and the retail sector.
2. Those who have a variable rate mortgage see their monthly payments go up and have less to spend in the rest of the economy as a result. If interest rates increase too much, they may even end up being forced to sell their home.
3. Companies are less likely to make investments in hiring people or in a new factory or piece of equipment as their cost of capital has increased: If they have to pay more to borrow money to invest, then they will make fewer investments.

All of these slow the economy down. Any government that has mismanaged its financial affairs finds itself having to drop the prices of its bonds in order to sell them to raise money. This results in the extremely unpopular and economically damaging reality of higher interest rates: They are stuck with the devil's alternative of either not being able to raise money on the bond markets or raising money but forcing interest rates up.

Given neither of these options is a vote winner, plenty of governments throughout history have come up with the alternative option that we have just mentioned: Inventing money out of thin air to buy their own bonds. This is what the UK and the US have been doing for the last few years and what the Europeans are having a massive argument about as I write. The Italians, Irish, Spanish, Portuguese et al. need to "invent" money to deal with their enormous debts. German politicians, however, are reluctant to let them do this given their more prudent approach to economics. Germany suffered brutal hyperinflation[11] in the 1920s as a result of inventing money and fear of inflation is very much ingrained in the national psyche as a result.

"Inventing" money has been tried dozens of times throughout history and been described in various different ways (debasing coins, printing money, quantitative easing). It has almost always resulted in economic disaster for the country or society involved (ancient Rome, Weimar Germany in the 1920s, Argentina and many other Latin American countries in the 1980s and 2000s, and most recently, Zimbabwe).

For most of history, neither the UK nor the US played this game. They were strong enough to pay back their debts with real money and for bond market investors to be happy buying their bonds at low interest rates. Sadly, this is no longer the case. In the last three years both the US and UK have had to resort to inventing money to buy their own bonds to keep interest rates artificially low.

The UK and US authorities have chosen to call this money inventing exercise "Quantitative Easing" (QE). I know I said there are only two ways to raise money and I stick to that statement because this third way is not a way of raising real money at all. Let me explain:

In a nutshell, QE is when the Government simply invents some "money" in a computer and uses it to buy those bonds that it couldn't sell at the more expensive lower yielding level because normal, professional investors wouldn't pay. At the time of writing the US Federal Reserve is buying up to 80% of all new bond issuance and the UK authorities about 50%. That is to say, they are buying 50-80% of their own bonds. This is an extraordinary case of "robbing Peter to pay Paul".

As we have already seen, if you invent money, the effect is inflationary: We have made the point before but if you have basically the same amount of "stuff" in an economy and the quantity of paper money doubles, the price of that "stuff" will double with a certain time lag. This is because inventing money does not

---

11 See: http://en.wikipedia.org/wiki/Hyperinflation_in_the_Weimar_Republic . Hyperinflation in 1920s society destroyed the German middle class and many argue was a crucial factor in Hitler's rise to power. Also see "When Money Dies" by Adam Fergusson in the bibliography.

cause any more stuff to be created: More oil to be found or wheat to be grown, for example: The supply of "stuff" remains the same but the amount of money everyone has to pay for that stuff increases.

If the government doubles the amount of money in existence in order to buy its own bonds and avoid dealing with the consequences of its previous actions...

...you will need your employer to double your salary just to stand still financially...

Do you anticipate this being a possibility? I didn't think so. We have already seen the following John Maynard Keynes quote but it bears repeating yet again to really make the point:

"By a continuing process of inflation, government can confiscate, secretly and unobserved, an important part of the wealth of their citizens..."

This is exactly what is happening right now. If you think that my example of the government doubling the money supply is far-fetched, think again. As you have already seen above, the US money supply has more than tripled in the last few years. Best-selling economic writer and pundit, Bill Bonner, notes: "It took 95 years to get the Fed's holdings to $600bn. In the space of three years it has added $1.4 trillion more..." It is worth noting that this is the growth in the money supply using official numbers. There are many smart analysts out there whose numbers suggest the real situation is far worse.

As we have seen, at the same time that the US and British governments are doubling and tripling their money supplies (or worse), they keep a lid on people's understanding of how inflationary this is and, therefore, how bad for their wealth by using science fiction inflation numbers.

CRUCIALLY, MANY POLITICIANS REALLY DON'T UNDERSTAND THIS STUFF

Perhaps even more worrying than these inflation numbers, however, is the fact that many of our lawmakers simply do not understand these issues which means they are highly unlikely to be resolved any time soon. I was reading a story recently about a US Congressman[12] who was sitting on a key finance committee in the US Government listening to arguments from academics and finance professionals. After an hour or so he put his hand up and asked: "Sorry, but what is this 'QE' you keep talking about?"

---

12 A Congressman is the US equivalent of an MP. As I mentioned earlier, my first job was working for a Congressman in Washington DC.

The fact that an elected politician, sitting in the US Government and partly responsible for making US financial policy asked this question is absolutely shocking and goes some way towards helping us understand why we are in the state we are in: As crazy as it sounds, large numbers of the people in charge on both sides of the Atlantic have no idea what they are doing. They just don't understand the economics. This is abundantly obvious to me day in day out as I listen to journalists and politicians being interviewed on the radio, for example. Whilst making my lunch and listening to the radio, I narrowly avoid throwing things around my kitchen on a regular basis. Once you have finished reading this book you will, without exaggeration, quite possibly understand more about economics than many US and UK politicians.

A US Congressman or MP working on economic policy should not be forgiven for being unfamiliar with the term QE but I think it is entirely fair that you might not have fully understood what it was before reading the above. As ever, understanding this concept is another string to your bow in terms of being able to improve your financial situation. To paraphrase an earlier quote in the section about compound interest: Those who understand QE are destined to make money from it and those who don't are destined to suffer.

One final aspect of bonds which is important to understand is that, unless the company or country that issues them goes bankrupt, they are legally obliged to pay the bondholder their interest and their money back. If a company or government cannot pay this money back due to bankruptcy this is known as "default." Default in the bond market has been relatively rare.

Given the relative rarity of default, bonds have traditionally been viewed as the safest financial investment you can make, similar to simply keeping your money in a deposit account: You are almost certain to get back your original money plus the agreed interest. The downside is that the return you make is small. You might be paid 2-3% on your holdings in bonds. Don't forget that you need to account for inflation when considering what your real return is. If inflation is running at five or ten percent you will be losing real wealth if you own bonds.

For bigger returns we have to look elsewhere. The first place to look for higher returns is stocks and shares, otherwise known as equities and our next section:

4. SHARES / EQUITIES / STOCKS

Many people are aware of the existence of "stocks and shares" but in my experience very few really understand what they are, including a large number of folk who invest in them. This is clearly bad news for them and another reason why people think investment is "risky". Perhaps the best way for us to grasp them at a fundamental level is to have a quick look at history and see how they developed.

Along with the debt market and bonds, shares were an extremely important development in history. It is not an exaggeration to say that without their invention the industrial revolution and the enormous technological and social developments of the last few centuries that made us all substantially wealthier would have been impossible. Why?

Because their creation enabled large groups of people to pool resources and spread risk like never before. The joint-stock company came into existence in Holland and Britain at roughly the same time in the early seventeenth century to fund the exploration and exploitation of the East Indies.

People in Europe had acquired a taste for all things Eastern but getting there and back was extremely risky. A voyage could take as long as two years and there was always the risk that an entire fleet of ships might be lost on the way. It quickly became clear that even the aristocrats and royal families of Europe could not afford to fund such voyages by themselves. Fleets of ships were incredibly expensive back then.

The solution was the creation of a company and selling "shares" in that company to anyone who was interested in investing. Essentially this meant that an investor who contributed, say, 1% of the costs associated with a voyage would be given a piece of paper which recorded their entitlement to a share of 1% of any profits made.

The difference between this and a bond was that the share investor had no guarantee of a return. Someone buying a bond was essentially guaranteed to get his or her money back with the agreed interest unless the bond issuer went bankrupt (defaulted). Someone buying a share would only be entitled to that percentage share of any profits made: If the voyage lost a minimal number of ships and came back to Amsterdam or London with lucrative cargo the shareholder would have made their fortune. If, on the other hand, the fleet had been decimated by storms or piracy the investor might find they had lost all of their original investment.

Not much has changed to this day except that you can now buy yourself a share in far more things than a risky sea-voyage to the East Indies. Today, more than ever, you can own a share in a fantastic diversity of human activities from all over the world. Some of these, like the seventeenth century voyages of the Dutch and British, carry with them a high degree of risk and potential reward. Others are inherently much safer.

When you buy a share in a company, otherwise known as a "stock" or "equity", you quite literally become a part owner of that company. This means you are then entitled to your proportional share in the profits of that company. If you think about it this is a very exciting invention. By owning a share in a business you can benefit from the work of everyone involved in it.

This is how you should always think about shares: That you are becoming a part owner of that business. As such, when anyone considers whether to buy a share in something or not, they should think about two key things:

1.   Is this a good business (preferably a very good business)?
2.   Am I paying the correct amount for my slice of this business?

One of the biggest mistakes I encounter when I speak to people about investing in shares is that they tell me with great enthusiasm about the great companies they have invested in but have not stopped for minute to consider what price they paid for those companies in real terms. It is arguably not that controversial to say that Tesco, Marks & Spencer and Shell are three fantastic companies (or Microsoft, Intel and Coca Cola in the US for that matter). I would completely agree with these statements. But finding a great company is only the first job. Working out what to pay for that company is the next and fundamentally more important one.

Let us take Tesco as an example: In the last ten years you could have bought Tesco shares for as little as around 160p and as much as around 485p. At the time of writing they are about 328p. At all three prices Tesco has basically been the same excellent retail company but you can see that people who purchased their shares at or close to 160p are on their way to a happy early retirement and those who bought theirs at 485p have lost around a third of their money.

HOW TO VALUE A SHARE

So how can an investor work out when a price is good or bad? "Hindsight is 20/20" as they say but how might we have known that 160p was a good price for Tesco and 485p a bad one at the time? As ever, the books written in a bid to answer that question would fill an enormous warehouse but we can do our best to draw out the key ideas in "Plain English".

The important thing to realise goes back to our point that when you buy a share you become a part owner of the business. This means that you are entitled to a share in any profits the business makes, just like the 17th century investors from London and Amsterdam who were entitled to the fruits of a successful expedition to the East Indies. What you need to work out is how much you are paying for your share. Annoyingly enough and as counter-intuitive as this sounds the share price alone does not give you this information.

To work out how much you are paying for a share in real terms you must think about how much profit a given company is making and might make in the future and compare how much you might have to pay for your share of that profit to how much you might pay for the same share of another company's profits. This is actually much simpler than it sounds. Let us look at a quick example:

Imagine you were thinking of investing in one of two companies that did basically the same thing. As we were using Tesco earlier, let us use Tesco and Sainsbury's for this example. Now imagine that both companies are going to make £100 million of profit this year.[13] Imagine too that there are 100 million shares in existence for both companies.

Remember that in essence a share entitles you to your percentage of the profits in a company. If you own 5% of a company, you effectively own 5% of that company's profits (and its assets).

Hopefully you can see that in our example each Tesco or Sainsbury's share "owns" £1 of profit. We call this number Earnings Per Share (EPS). Both of these companies are making £100 million of profit this year and there are 100 million shares of each. Each share "owns" £1 of profit. If you owned 1000 shares, you would "own" £1000 worth of profit. Simple enough.

THE PRICE / EARNINGS RATIO (P/E)
Now here comes the genius part where you will hopefully realise that you are perfectly capable of understanding shares. Imagine that Tesco shares currently cost £10 each and Sainsbury's shares cost £8. Can you see that if you buy a Tesco share, you pay £10 to own £1 of profit but if you buy Sainsbury's shares you pay £8 to own £1 of profit?

The price of a Tesco share is ten times the earnings per share and the price of a Sainsbury's share is eight times the earnings per share. This is a ratio that we call the price to earnings ratio or p/e for short.

All other things being equal, you can see that Sainsbury's shares are "cheaper" than Tesco shares. A lower p/e ratio means that you are paying less for the same entitlement to profit. Crucially a lower share price does not give you the same information (without thinking about earnings). Let us introduce a third company into the equation to clarify this point. Let us look at Morrisons as well.

Imagine that Morrisons are also going to make £100 million of profit this year but

---

13 The numbers I will use in this example bear no relation at all to the real world numbers but will make things easier to understand.

there are 200 million Morrisons shares in existence, rather than 100 million. We can see immediately that for each Morrisons share you own, you are entitled to only 50p of profit, rather than the £1 your Tesco or Sainsbury's shares would get you since there are twice as many shares with claims on that profit.

Now let us say that Morrisons shares cost £6 at the moment. Are they "cheaper" or "more expensive" than Tesco and Sainsbury's shares which are trading at £10 and £8 respectively? Hopefully you can see straight away that even though the Morrisons share price is less than the other two, for every £1 you spend on a Morrisons share, you only get 50p of earnings (profit), rather than £1 because there are twice as many shares to split those profits with. This means that in this example, Morrisons shares at £6 have a price to earnings ratio (p/e) of 12x (600p / 50p).

Here is a quick summary table:

Supermarket share prices					
Company	Profit	No. of Shares	Price (£)	Earnings / Share (£)	p/e multiple
Tesco	£100m	100m	10	1	10
Sainsbury's	£100m	100m	8	1	8
Morrisons	£100m	200m	6	0.5	12

This is arguably the single most important thing you will ever learn about shares. It is frightening the number of people who still think that a share that costs £5 is "cheaper" than a share that costs £10. The share price tells you nothing about how fundamentally expensive or cheap a share is, it is all about the multiple of profits that each share costs. If you are now incredibly confused please go back and read the last page again. As soon as you understand this concept you will know more about shares than a large number of people and will have taken your first step towards being able to invest in them successfully.

So, to establish whether a share is truly cheap or expensive you have to work out what you are paying for the profits you are entitled to and for any other value in the business. If a share that costs £5 is entitled to half the profits of a share which costs £10, they are actually worth exactly the same, all other things being equal. The p/e multiple that you have just looked at is widely available online and in the financial press and is your first step to understanding whether a share is expensive or cheap.

EARNINGS YIELD

The next great thing to think about is what we call "earnings yield". If you think about Tesco above, you are paying £10 for the right to £1 of profit this year. If you think about it, this means you are making a 10% annual return on your £10. Assume that you invest £10 today and Tesco continues to make £100 million of profit every year for the next ten years. You will make £1 of profit for each of your shares every year. You have paid £10 and you get £1 back each year, i.e. 10%. This is what we call the earnings yield and it is easily calculated by simply dividing the p/e ratio into 1. In the above example, Sainsbury's has an earnings yield of 12.5% (1/8) and Morrisons of 8.3% (1/12).

WHY DO DIFFERENT SHARES HAVE DIFFERENT P/E RATIOS AND EARNINGS YIELD?

The next thing to think about is why one share might have a higher p/e ratio (lower earnings yield) than another one. In the above example, Sainsbury's and Tesco should theoretically have the same price as each other and Morrisons shares should actually trade at exactly half that price since they are all making £100 million of profit but Morrisons has twice the number of shares to split that profit with.

Why might Tesco cost more than Sainsbury's? Again, thousands of books have been written on the subject but there are broadly two reasons:

1. Expectations of future profits.
2. Value in the business other than profit.

So far we have only looked at the value in these businesses in terms of their profitability. One reason that you might be willing to pay more for one share than another would be if you expected that company's profit to be higher in the future than the other company's profit will be. Let us say that we expect Tesco to make £120 million next year but Sainsbury's to only make £90m. If this were the case, we would most likely be willing to pay more for Tesco shares than Sainsbury's shares. Hopefully this makes sense to you.

The other basic reason we might be willing to pay more for Tesco than Sainsbury's could be that there is more value in Tesco than in Sainsbury's for reasons other than the profits they might make. You might have already worked this out, but imagine that Tesco owns £1 billion worth of property and Sainsbury's only owns £500 million worth. In this example, imagine they both make the same profit this year and are very likely to make the same profit next year.

You would be willing to pay more for Tesco than you would for Sainsbury's because, remember, as a shareholder you are a part owner of the business and, all other things being equal, you would rather have a share in £1 billion worth of property and £100 million of profit than in £500 million of property and £100 million of profit. This brings us to our next simple valuation tool, book value:

BOOK VALUE

This is simply the value of all the assets a business owns added up by the accountants and another way we might compare the value of one share to another. Imagine if Tesco have lots of property and lots of cash in the bank. If you own a share in Tesco, you effectively own a share in those assets as well as a share of any profits the company makes. This number can be divided by the number of shares to give an idea of the value of existing assets each share is entitled to. This ratio is called price to book.

A fascinating thing to be aware of is that it is entirely possible for some shares to be trading at less than book value. That is to say that if you bought that share and the company was then wound up (closed down), you would be entitled to more money back than you spent on your shares. When a company is in this situation you can have a fair measure of security that you are investing when the company is cheap. It might be cheap for a reason such as falling profits but you will literally quite possibly be paying 80p to own 100p worth of intrinsic value.

The whole point here is that if you have a basic grasp of some of these valuation metrics (ways of understanding the value of a share) you give yourself a decent chance of buying a share when it is good value and this will vastly increase your chances of making a decent return. In my experience many people investing in shares do not have such a grasp which is one of the main reasons they lose money.

DIVIDENDS AND DIVIDEND YIELD

Dividends are another very important aspect of shares you will want to be aware of. We have already dealt with the idea of earnings yield above. As a reminder, the earnings yield is basically the amount of profit you are entitled to each year expressed as a percentage of what you paid for your shares. As you might imagine, however, most companies do not pay all of their profit out to their shareholders each year. A company will usually have lots of interesting things to spend those profits on if it wishes to continue growing. As such, each year, the management of a company will decide how much of the profit to keep (this is called retained earnings) and how much to pay out to shareholders.

What gets paid out to shareholders is called the dividend. Just as with earnings yield, dividend yield is simply the percentage return you get if you divide the money you get from your dividend into the money you have invested in your shares. When you look at a company, it is important to look at how much that company has traditionally paid out in dividends and what analysts think it might pay out in the future.

LOOKING AT THE WHOLE MARKET

We have looked very briefly at some of the fundamental ways of understanding the value in a share and I hope that, as with most of this book, the above has made you feel as if you are perfectly capable of understanding these things. The key things you need to learn about finance just aren't that difficult.

Before we move on, I want to make one final point about shares, which is to say that all of the above metrics can be applied to the stock market as a whole. This means that at any given time we can have a think about what the p/e ratio, book value or dividend yield of the entire stock market is and compare it to other stock markets (e.g., compare the UK to the US or Japan) and to other times in history. If we know that the p/e ratio or book value of a market is historically low, we have a much higher chance of making a great return on our money in the next few years than we would if those ratios were historically high.

Obviously, things are complicated in the real world. One of the issues we will confront when trying to do this analysis is how reliable the numbers are. It is also true that a cheap market can get even cheaper, meaning that if you buy it, you could lose money for a while and an expensive one can get even more expensive, meaning that you might have avoided buying it and would then miss out on more upside. Nevertheless, just as we said when considering property in chapter six, over the long run or your lifetime, if you are aware of key valuation metrics when considering any market for investment such as those outlined above, you stand a far better chance of buying and selling at sensible levels than the vast majority of the population who are investing without this knowledge.

We will look at equities in a little more detail in chapter twelve for those of you who are interested but for now we shall move on to our next topic, commodities:

5. COMMODITIES

Many people are well aware of what a "commodity" is but it is perhaps still worth clarifying precisely: Wikipedia describes a commodity as: "…a good for which there is demand but which is supplied without qualitative differentiation across a market…"

That is to say that oil is basically the same whether it is supplied by Nigeria, Russia or Venezuela and wheat is basically the same whether it comes from Russia, Germany or Canada (within reason). Compare this to something like a car, the value and price of which will be based on a large number of differentiating variables such as brand, top speed, engine size or finish quality for example.

Commodities have been used as a store of value since the beginning of recorded history. Throughout human history many commodities have also been used as money. Everything which follows is relevant to all commodities but it is worth noting at this point that it is useful to think of the precious or monetary metals (gold and silver) as a separate category of commodity to all others given their long accepted role as money. This role has not been shared by any other commodities for several hundred years. We will discuss this important differentiation in more detail below as understanding it can make us wealthy in the years ahead.

As a general comment, I would stress that we should be particularly interested in commodities today. One of the world's best ever investors, Jim Rogers, starts his excellent book "Hot Commodities" by saying: "Too many so-called smart investors consider themselves diversified if they have money in stocks, bonds, real estate and maybe, for the sophisticates, some currencies or timber. But commodities rarely, if ever, hit the radar screen…"[14]

A key part of the message of this book is that you must not fall into this trap. For a wide variety of reasons it is absolutely essential that you think about and have exposure to commodities if you want to grow your wealth in the next few decades. Let us see why:

1. THERE IS A HUGE GROWTH IN THE DEMAND FOR COMMODITIES

Given the media coverage this news received, many people will be aware that the seven billionth human being was born in October 2011. We have already discussed the world's rising population in the section on global growth above but it is perhaps worth repeating: The world's population continues to grow by seventy five million or more people per year or just over two hundred thousand per day and this is set to accelerate for the next few years.

Just as important as this incredible growth in population is the fact that increasing numbers of these people are getting wealthier. Twenty years ago hardly anyone in China had a car, there were no high-speed trains and hardly any skyscrapers. As we have seen, today the Chinese buy more cars per year than the Americans, have more miles of high speed train track than anywhere else in the world and have hundreds of skyscrapers and many more planned or in construction. This has obviously has a huge impact on the market for all commodities, particularly those used in the automotive, rail and construction sectors.

Until very recently, most people in the developing world also survived on a very simple diet and could afford very little meat. Today millions more Chinese, Brazilians, Indians and so on consume chicken, fish, pork and beef than previously.

14 "Hot Commodities" by Jim Rogers.

This ongoing trend has very serious implications for global agriculture and water supplies. We must not underestimate that as millions of new consumers grow up and become richer all over the world the overall demand for all commodities will grow at a rate never before seen in history.

2. THE WORLD HAS SOME SERIOUS ISSUES WITH THE SUPPLY OF COMMODITIES

At the same time that there is this significant and ongoing structural increase in the demand for commodities, the world is beginning to encounter serious supply constraints for many of them. For example, as an illustration, the volume of rock a mining company has to dig through to find one ounce of gold today is a multiple of what it was only a few years ago: Today a miner creates more than twenty tonnes of waste just to produce one wedding ring.

Most of the biggest gold mines in the world, many based in South Africa, are seeing supply dry up. Hardly surprising when you consider they have already been dug to a depth of between three and four kilometres.

This phenomenon is true of nearly every metal we use: Copper, zinc, platinum, gold, silver and so on.[15] We are finding it harder and harder to find new supplies of all of these things. The same is true in the oil market, where companies are having to go to extraordinary lengths to find new oil and many energy experts believe that the "cheap", which is to say relatively easily accessible oil is now essentially gone.

We are also inevitably running into supply constraints with "soft" commodities (things that grow) as the world exhausts its supplies of arable land, fish and fresh water in a bid to feed so many billion people. This will only get worse as people in the developing world acquire a taste for more meat since livestock farming leads to far higher water consumption than growing crops.

DEMAND UP, SUPPLY DOWN EQUALS PRICE UP

Basic economics tells us that where demand for something is increasing and supply is decreasing or fixed the price of that something will go up. This should be fairly obvious. If more people want something but there is less of it available they will have to offer more money than the next person to get hold of it. This goes some of the way towards explaining why virtually every commodity in the world has seen a significant increase in its price in the last decade or so. This being the case, we can conclude that the fundamental, structural (inherent) trend in commodities will be for their prices to increase given points one and two above. There is, however, another reason why commodity prices (in terms of paper currency) look set to carry on rising. I would argue this is an even more important driver:

---

15 There are some serious analysts who have predicted silver will completely run out by 2020.

3. THE SUPPLY OF PAPER MONEY

As we have mentioned several times already, in recent years governments all over the world have been "inventing" vast quantities of new money. The Americans have more than tripled the outstanding supply of US dollars in the last three years.[16] If you triple the supply of money but the supply of things is basically fixed then all other things being equal, the price of those things should triple, albeit with a time lag.

This is another reason why the dollar (and Yen and Euro) price of nearly all "stuff" has increased rapidly in the last few years. Whilst governments all over the world continue to pursue a policy of money printing (or "inventing" as I prefer to call it), all other things being equal commodity prices, priced in those currencies, will generally trend up strongly.

It should be obvious that this is very bad news for your standard of living if your salary in paper currency is basically fixed, which is the case for most people. If your salary this year is the same as last year but bread, eggs, milk, petrol and so on have increased in price by more like 20% it should be clear that you will suffer a reduction in your real standard of living and this is precisely what is happening all over the world at the moment. The great news is that there is something you can do about it: You can own commodities. I describe this as "owning inflation".

Luckily for us, developments in financial products in the last few years have made owning commodities easier and cheaper than ever before. As already discussed, it wasn't that long ago that it was actually very hard to buy financial exposure to commodities. You had to have a reasonably large sum of money and a private banker. This is no longer the case which is extremely good news.

One of the main reasons we can now own commodities is thanks to the development of our next and arguably most important category of investment vehicle: Funds…

6. FUNDS… (PERHAPS THE MOST IMPORTANT CATEGORY FOR OUR PURPOSES).

For the large majority of people funds are the most relevant investment vehicle. This is because a fund enables you to own a large basket of many of the other products discussed in this chapter. This tends to be the most appropriate investment vehicle for the average investor. Buying the right funds at the right

16 This is according to official numbers. The reality is almost certainly worse. Have a look at this video: http://www.youtube.com/watch?v=3dl1y-zBAFg

price will make a huge difference to your life. So what are funds and more importantly what are the "right" ones?

Funds were created several decades ago for a very logical reason: We have already referred to the term "diversification". This is simply the investor's version of "not putting all of your eggs in one basket." Since very early on in the creation of financial assets, particularly shares, it was clear to anyone with common sense and has been shown academically many times that splitting your money between several investments was inherently less risky than having all of your money in one investment. This should make sense to you intuitively.

It was also the case that many potential investors were excited about investing in more than just one business area or "sector". Why restrict yourself to owning one oil company if you could invest in several oil companies and a number of tobacco companies, railway companies, pharmaceuticals, defence contractors and so on at the same time? Equally, as we have already suggested, why restrict yourself to assets from only one region of the world?

By owning a wide variety of companies from a wide variety of countries, not only would you spread your risk, you would also give yourself exposure to as many exciting parts of the world economy as possible.

It is clear then that many people with money to invest were interested in owning a large number of shares in a large number of sectors and countries. The only problem for most people was that there was usually a reasonably large minimum investment required to buy any given share. This meant that in the early days of the stock market, only very rich people were able to own a large number of shares in a large number of sectors, yet another reason the rich found it relatively easy to stay rich.

If you had to invest a minimum of $1,000 in each share, for example, you would obviously have needed $10,000 to invest in ten shares or $30,000 to own each of the thirty stocks in the Dow Jones, an "index" of thirty of the biggest companies in America. We will say more about what an index is below. In the early days of the stock market this was a huge amount of money for one person to invest.

THE GENIUS OF FUNDS

It was to solve this problem that investment funds were created. The idea was simply to pool money from many investors, who were each interested in owning a large cross-section of investments. This large pool of money would then be able to invest in just such a large cross-section of investments. If ten thousand people invested an average of ten thousand dollars, for example, you had a fund of $100 million, which could then buy dozens or even hundreds of different shares.

Everyone who had bought shares in that fund would then nominally (theoretically) own that proportion of all of the shares owned by the fund even if that theoretical investment in each share was far less than the minimum amount they would ordinarily be permitted to own directly.

The other advantage was that the company offering the fund for sale would have to take care of the administrative burden of owning dozens or hundreds of shares. This was obviously preferable to doing it yourself.

FUND MANAGEMENT COMPANIES

As you can imagine, given the many advantages in terms of diversification and administration that funds gave investors, the idea caught on. Today there are hundreds of companies offering thousands of different funds. Companies that offer a range of funds are called Fund Managers, Asset Managers, Investment Managers or Hedge Funds. These terms all mean basically the same thing (although hedge funds are slightly different).

You may or may not have heard of companies such as: BlackRock, Jupiter, Fidelity, Hendersons, Invesco, Gartmore, Aberdeen Asset Management and so on, or seen them advertising. There are literally hundreds of these companies in the UK market.

Over the years two important over-arching categories of fund developed: Active and passive.

ACTIVE FUNDS

These are funds where an individual (known as a fund manager) tries to use his or her skill to pick the best shares or other assets such as bonds or commodities to make the best return possible for investors in that fund. A fund of this type will usually be limited to investing in a certain type of asset class: For example, it might be a "European equities fund", in which case the fund manager would be limited to buying European shares and would do his or her best to pick the best performing European shares.

This limitation on what the fund manager can invest in is called a "mandate". The "mandate" any given fund has describes the type of assets in which that fund manager can invest. This is something I don't like about many active funds as it means that if the asset class it is limited to has a bad year, the fund manager is basically unable to get out of those assets and put your money into something safer. Active funds also tend to be relatively expensive, as you will have to pay for the "clever" well paid fund manager to invest in the "right" shares, bonds or commodities depending on what type of fund you have purchased.

As we have seen right at the beginning of the book, some fund managers are excellent and are well worth this premium, however there is a wealth of research that says that on average over the long run passive funds outperform active (after accounting for costs). So what are passive funds?

PASSIVE FUNDS

This is where a fund management company copies the performance of an index (see below). These funds are also sometimes called "tracker" or "index" funds (because they "track" an index). A good example would be a tracker on the FTSE 100. If you were to buy into such a fund it would aim to replicate as closely as possible the performance of the FTSE 100 index. If you were to invest in a "FTSE tracker" your money would essentially be divided between the 100 shares in the FTSE index. This is a crucial advantage of being in a fund as you yourself would not be able to own all 100 stocks in the FTSE index unless you had a great deal of money and a great deal of time to devote to investment.

These days even the super rich will tend to use a tracker to own the FTSE 100 stocks as they would see too much of their potential return eaten up in fees if they actually bought all of the stocks in the FTSE 100 index individually. Paying for one hundred separate transactions in order to end up owning all of the companies is clearly not ideal when instead you can pay once to own a tracker fund and have basically the same exposure. It is also much more work, as you can imagine.

Passive funds are a cheaper way to invest than active funds and obviously a much cheaper way to get exposure to a large number of shares than buying those shares individually.

INDICES

At this point it is important to explain what an index is, the plural of which is "indices". An index is simply a method of measuring a stock market in some way. You will most likely have heard of the FTSE 100 we mentioned above, since it is referenced by most of the British press every day. The FTSE 100 is an index. It is simply an invention of the London stock market which adds up the price and size of the biggest 100 companies in the UK to generate a number, known as the "level" of the FTSE 100.

The point of doing this is that it gives investors all over the world a very quick snap-shot of how well the British stock market is doing and, to a certain extent, how well the British economy is doing. The FTSE 100 does not represent the entire British economy but is a good proxy on how it is doing since the top 100 companies tend to represent about 80% of the entire value of the UK stock market and a reasonably large percentage of the value of the UK economy as a whole.

The FTSE 100 index does not tell the whole story about the British economy because there are hundreds of smaller companies listed on the London stock market and there are also thousands of other "private" companies operating in Britain. These are companies that are not listed on the stock market. The UK's top 100 companies also do a great deal of their business overseas. Nevertheless, it is still a useful proxy for the UK economy.

Every country in the world that has a stock market has several stock market indices. These were originally created and managed by the companies in charge of those stock markets, for example the New York Stock Exchange in America or Deutsche Börse in Germany. Examples you may know include: The Dow Jones 30 in the US, which is made up of a selection of thirty of the largest companies in the US. The US also has the NASDAQ and S&P 500 indices both of which have a much broader composition than the Dow Jones. The S&P has no less than 470 more stocks in it than the Dow 30 as its name suggests. In Japan there is the Nikkei 225, in Hong Kong the Hang Seng 45, in Germany the DAX 30, in France the CAC40 and so on.

It is important to realise that indices are somewhat arbitrary constructs. Each stock exchange chooses to include different numbers of stocks in their main index and then cut their market up in a variety of different ways, providing other additional indices for the investor to look at.

Despite being "arbitrary", indices are very useful: If you want to make sure that you own the hundred biggest companies in the UK, thirty of the most important companies in the US or the forty largest companies in France, you need look no further than those indices to find out which companies you need to own: There will then be a tracker (or passive) fund of that index available to buy which will leave you the proud owner of all of those companies for one transaction fee. I hope you can see that these funds are potentially exciting investment vehicles and a great financial innovation.

SMALLER COMPANY INDICES

You might also be interested in owning a number of smaller companies from the countries above. As you might imagine, smaller companies tend to be faster growing than large ones. It should strike you as common sense that it is generally easier for a company with £100 million of sales or profits to grow that number by 10% than it is for a company with £10 billion of sales and certainly easier for them to grow at 50%.

All other things being equal, faster growing companies often have faster growing share prices. This means you may have the chance to make higher returns in successful smaller companies than you do in very large companies. For this reason, many investors like to have exposure to smaller companies as well as larger ones. Most countries, therefore, provide a smaller company index as well as the larger one. This is why we have FTSE 250 and FTSE Small Cap indices in the UK market and why there are similar mid and small cap indices in other countries. The FTSE 250 includes the next 250 companies after the biggest 100 companies found in the FTSE 100 index. Collectively all 350 companies are called the FTSE 350. Pretty simple stuff.

In recent decades there has been an explosion in indices across the world. In the past, the long standing, well known, indices were originally calculated and supplied by the information divisions of the various national stock markets as explained above. In recent years, independent financial information firms such as Reuters and Bloomberg and divisions of investment banks like Barclays and Goldman Sachs have created their own indices on a very wide variety of assets. What this means is that you can now find indices and related funds on pretty much any asset or country in the world: Bonds, commodities, big companies, small companies and stock market sectors such as banks, telecoms or pharmaceutical companies for example.

The reason this is important for our purposes is that, increasingly as a private investor you are able to "buy" these indices in an index or passive fund as explained above. There has been an explosion in the choice available for the private investor in recent years. Today, if you have a strong view on the UK Economy you can buy a FTSE 100 index fund. Equally, if you think biotechnology companies are likely to have a good time you can own them through a biotech index. If you feel that Singapore has a bright future you can "own" Singapore or Vietnam and so on.

Within reason, you can own almost anything that occurs to you. If you read an article explaining why something has a bright future (graphene, thorium, tungsten, water, Bangladeshi coal mining, Brazilian oil, property in Montenegro, diamonds, the list is very, very long) you will be able to buy something that makes you money if this turns out to be true. Don't forget, however, that you will also need to buy into that something at the right price.

SHORTING: YOU CAN ALSO MAKE MONEY WHEN THINGS GO DOWN

Another thing to be aware of is that if you think something will fall in value, as counter-intuitive as it might seem, today you are often able to make money out of that too. This is called "shorting". It really isn't any more complicated a concept than the idea that you are able to own a financial product which is a bet that something goes down instead of up and will make money if you are correct.

For example, if you believe the German stock market will suffer due to the current Eurozone crisis, you can short it. That is to say that you can buy a product that will make you money if the German stock market falls. Shorting is another great thing to be aware of. Many people have never heard of it and most have no idea that anyone can do it. You just need to know how.

The great thing about indices and the funds that are based on them is that you are able to own or short hundreds of different shares even if you only have a small amount of money to invest and you are able to do so with low fees.

AN ANNOYING COMPLEXITY OF FUND NAMES ESPECIALLY DESIGNED TO CONFUSE?

The distinction between passive and active funds is probably the most important thing to understand about funds generally. As you start to look into investing your money in funds, however, you will encounter a bewildering array of names to describe different types of them over and above the idea of passive and active. These include: Open-ended vs. closed-ended funds and within these categories terms such as Open Ended Investment Companies (OEICs, pronounced "oiks"), Unit Trusts (UTs), Mutual Funds, Investment Trusts (ITs) and Exchange Traded Funds (ETFs).

It is not necessary to have an in depth understanding of precisely what all of these terms mean and it is certainly not worth getting confused. There is a fair amount of overlap between the different types and the specific differences can get rather confusing. It is enough simply to understand that there are a number of different types of fund that have grown up for historical and legal reasons.

HOW TO BUY FUNDS AND WHAT YOU PAY

What is important about these different types of fund, however, is to understand how they are bought and sold and what you will pay to buy and sell them. Different types of fund are traded and charged for in different ways and this is the main thing you need to think about. As you will recall from our examination of compound interest above, the cost of owning something is key as small percentage changes can mean large differences to your cash pot over time. So let us look at the two main ways we can own funds. Funds are, basically, either traded on the stock market, like a share, or not. Let us look at this reality in more detail:

EXCHANGE TRADED OR NOT – CHARGES FOR FUNDS ARE KEY

Probably the most important distinction in terms of what you pay to own a fund is between funds that trade on the stock market like a share, and those that do not. We need to understand these two broad categories because the way they are traded and charged for differs.

Once you have an ISA or SIPP account with a good stockbroking firm, you are able to invest any money that you have paid into that account in a huge variety of different things. This includes thousands of shares from stock markets all over the world and thousands of different funds both active and passive.[17]

---

17 It is worth reiterating that if you have an ISA account at most high street banks you will most likely not enjoy this flexibility and choice.

When you buy or sell a share in your ISA or SIPP account through a stockbroker, that broker will charge you a commission. In the old days this commission was usually a percentage of the money you invested and could often be as much as 1.5% of the value of what you were buying or selling, usually with a minimum charge, such as £50.

As an example, if you called your broker and instructed them to buy £1,000 worth of a share, you would have ended up with £950 worth of that share and paid the broker £50 as their commission for performing the transaction for you.[18] If, however, you had purchased £5,000 worth of that share you would have paid £75 commission and ended up with £4,925 worth of stock and so on.[19]

You can see that if you had a large amount to invest, commission charged as a percentage quickly became an annoyingly significant amount of money. Imagine someone selling £50,000 worth of shares (as you will be doing in a few years time). At 1.5%, that person would be paying a commission of £750. It is also worth understanding that with 1.5% charged to buy and sell the share, the investor would need to see at least a 3% return before they started to make any real money. Actually, as many of you will now realise, in an environment with 5% or more inflation the investor would need to see that share appreciate by at least 8% before they were making a real return. Again this shows us how important fees are.

To a great extent it is no harder for a stockbroker to buy or sell £100,000 worth of a stock for someone than £1,000.[20] Unsurprisingly, many of their customers felt pretty hard done by paying such large commissions in order to execute their trades.

As the financial services industry became more competitive, the more forward-thinking broking firms started offering their customers better terms to trade such as commission rates with an upper cap. The advent of online trading in the 1990s then enabled the very best broking firms to start offering their clients even more competitive commission rates given that the cost to them of offering a computer based online service was much lower than having to pay large numbers of staff to service clients over the phone. Today it is possible to buy and sell shares online for as little as £5.95 or even £1.50 per trade, a vast improvement over several hundred pounds.

High percentage commissions still exist if you wish to phone up a broker and instruct them to buy or sell shares for you over the phone but it is only really

18 1.5% x £1,000 is only £15 but remember the broker has a £50 minimum charge.

19 1.5% x £5,000 = £75.

20 It is harder for a stockbroker to sell very large quantities of a share but very few private individuals would have enough to buy or sell to cause problems.

older, technologically limited clients or very wealthy individuals who have large numbers of shares to trade who persist in doing this given just how much more expensive it is.

So, if you want to buy a share or anything that trades on the stock exchange in the same way a share does, you will pay whatever commission rate your stockbroking firm charges. With costs to do this as low as they are today, this is great news.

As explained above, certain types of fund trade on the stock exchange like shares. The main ones you need to know about are called Exchange Traded Funds (ETFs) and Investment Trusts (ITs). ETFs are almost all passive funds. You can buy an ETF based on the FTSE 100, on gold, on the Australian Dollar, on the CAC40 and on and on. There are thousands of ETFs based on thousands of assets. Investment Trusts tend to be active funds run by a fund manager with a particular focus, such as UK smaller companies or Japanese equities (Japanese shares) and so on.

BUYING AN EXCHANGE TRADED FUND IS OFTEN A GOOD VALUE OPTION
This means, that whether you want to own all 100 of the largest UK companies, a basket of shares from all over the world, a portfolio of commercial property assets, or a fund that specialises in American technology shares, in fact almost anything you can think of, you can get that exposure and often only pay the commission on buying a share.

As explained above, today if you are with a good stockbroking firm you will buy and sell shares and funds which trade like shares for as little as £5.95 to about £15 per transaction. In fact there are a number of firms in the UK market with whom you will only have to pay £1.50 per transaction if you set up a regular monthly payment into certain funds or shares.[21] The UK market has come a very long way in the last few years in this respect, something that only a tiny percentage of the population are taking advantage of.

HENCE WHY I SAY "FINANCIAL PRODUCTS TODAY ARE BETTER THAN EVER BEFORE"
Investors from the 1980s would find it hard to believe that today it is possible to buy and sell shares for as little as £1.50 and this reality is part of the whole Plain English Finance world view as outlined in part two of chapter four: "Today's financial products are better than ever before." If you know where to go, the difference between the best financial accounts and products available today and those of only a few years ago is like the difference between a sports car and a horse and cart. Sadly, many financial services company in the UK and certainly most of the high street banks continue to sell "horse and cart" type products because many people don't know where to find the "sports cars". This is another reason it

---

21 You can find out who these firms are in the resources section of the site.

is perhaps understandable that so many people think investment is a mug's game.

One final thing to be aware of in terms of how many Exchange Traded Funds and Investment Trusts are priced is that there is sometimes also an annual management fee[22] on top of the commission you pay. This is incorporated into the price of the fund you are buying so you will generally not see it explicitly but it will be detailed on the website of whomever you are buying that fund from. As an example, the gold fund I own has an Annual Management Charge of 0.4%. So, if I want to own some gold it costs me the dealing commission of about £10 plus another 0.4% of the amount I'm investing each year.

This is cheaper than buying actual physical gold through a specialist bullion dealer and I don't have to worry about storing it or security. More generally as we will now see, 0.4% plus a dealing commission is a lower cost way to invest in something than what you might pay if you buy funds which are not traded on the stock exchange. Let us look at them now:

FUNDS THAT DO NOT TRADE LIKE SHARES
We are now aware that there is a huge range of funds that trade like shares. There are also many thousands of other funds that do not trade like shares. These funds are usually what are called Open Ended Investment Companies (OEICs, pronounced "oiks") or Unit Trusts.

Just as with funds that trade like a share, you can buy an OEIC or a Unit Trust on an incredible range of investments. There are funds which give you exposure to UK shares, UK bonds, European smaller companies, commodities, Russian shares, Latin American shares and so on. The main thing we are concerned with, however, is how much we end up paying to own one of these funds. We will worry about what kind of investment we would like exposure to later, for now let us look at what the cost of owning an unlisted fund is (one that does not trade like a share).

Again, one of the key reasons so many people have had a bad experience of investing is that they have bought products without understanding what percentage of their money they are paying away in fees and charges.

TYPES OF FEE YOU WILL WANT TO UNDERSTAND
There are basically three types of fee or charge you will need to be aware of when considering whether or not to buy an unlisted fund: The Initial Charge, the Annual Management Charge (AMC) and the Total Expense Ratio (TER). It is crucial that you understand these and know how to find out what they are before you invest in something. This way you can minimise the proportion of your hard-

---

22 Annual charges on funds are called the AMC = Annual Management Charge.

earned cash that gets eaten up by fees. As ever, many people have no idea what these fees are when they walk into their high street bank and ask to see a financial adviser and it is for this reason that they can end up paying too much in fees and struggling to make a good return on their money.

INITIAL CHARGE

Traditionally companies offering Unit Trusts and OEICs would charge you a percentage of your money when you originally bought the fund. For a long time this could be as much as 5% of what you wanted to invest and sometimes even more than that (especially for a "hot" sector. There were many internet and technology funds in the dot.com boom that charged very high fees up front with financial professionals "making hay whilst the sun was shining").

This means that, say you were lucky enough to have your full ISA allowance of over £10,000 to invest and decided to buy one of these funds, you could pay more than £500 for the privilege. In addition, if you were using a financial adviser to decide which fund to buy, you would have paid their fees too. Contrast this with what you would have to pay if you make your own decision about which fund to buy and had put that money into an Exchange Traded Fund as described above: Through a good stockbroker you could pay as little as around £10, i.e. just the dealing commission or even only £1.50. At worst you would pay that £10, plus the Annual Management fee that some stock-exchange listed funds have, which will generally not be more than 0.5%.

On £10,000 the difference, therefore, would be as much as £800 or 8% of your money.[23]

Without wanting to labour the point, if you pay away 8% more of your money than you need to in fees and assume inflation is at least 5%, you will need whichever investment you have chosen to return 13% before you see any real return. This disastrous reality is one of the reasons so few people see a real return on their money. Remember that real inflation is also higher than 5%. That is to say that the reality is even worse than this example.

Many funds still charge these onerous initial fees but if you have an account with a good quality stockbroker, you will usually be able to buy an unlisted fund with a 0% initial fee because they will waive it. There will be charges for some of the more popular funds, even at a good stockbroking firm but the fee will be significantly lower than the sort of fees you are likely to be charged by other providers, especially the high street banks. If you have made your own decision about which fund to invest you will also have removed the layer of fees levied by a financial adviser. Taken together, this will have a meaningful impact on your

---

23 For the sake of argument: 4% to a financial adviser and 4% to the fund manager.

returns.

ANNUAL MANAGEMENT CHARGE (AMC)
In addition to the initial charge on a fund, nearly all funds will charge you an annual fee, ostensibly to cover their costs of administrating the fund. This number will be quoted in the fund's literature. Crucially, the AMC does not tell the whole story. When you are considering the purchase of a fund, you should ask for or find the…

TOTAL EXPENSE RATIO (TER)
This number includes a few additional costs that the AMC does not. Many fund management groups do an impressive job at keeping the TER in the smallest of small print. In fact, during a recent visit I made to a UK high street bank, the financial adviser struggled to even find the TER for a fund my friend owned. I found this quite outrageous and further evidence of just how few people in the UK market understand what they are paying when they buy a financial product.[24] There is no need to understand in detail what goes into the TER, you just need to know what percentage it is so you know how much of your money will be eaten up every year. Obviously the lower it is the better.

EXIT AND PERFORMANCE CHARGES
There are two other charges you may encounter although they are both relatively rare. An exit charge is what it sounds like: i.e. the fee you will pay when you sell a fund. Thankfully they aren't very common for funds these days, although many mortgage products still have them.

Performance charges are something that tend to be found in the hedge fund industry and at the racier end of the fund universe. Quite simply, a performance charge is an extra percentage of your money that will be paid to the fund manager if your fund goes up by more than a certain percentage.

There is nothing wrong with a performance charge as long as the return which triggers it is sufficiently high and it is sufficiently low. This is common sense stuff, but you can obviously see that it is perhaps worth paying another 2% in fees if your fund increases by more than 12% for example. Be careful, however. Remember that you need to take account of inflation when working out your real return on a fund. In the example above, if the TER of this fund was 2% and the performance charge 2%, if the fund returned over 12% then the real return would still be 0% if inflation was 8%.[25] You would have been better off owning a Gold ETF with a 0.4% annual fee and +13% performance for example.

---

24 He got there eventually but it took him at least ten minutes. It was obvious that I was the first person who had ever asked him for a TER.

25 Total Real Return = %age gain – fees – inflation. So here 12% - 4% - 8% = 0%.

A REMINDER ON FINANCIAL ADVISERS

We have just looked at the various costs associated with putting your money to work in different types of fund.

Remember: If you are able to make your own decisions about which fund or funds you invest in, you will not have to use the services of a financial adviser. This will save you a great deal of money, particularly over time...

ACCUMULATION AND INCOME FUNDS

One final aspect of funds to be aware of is the difference between accumulation and income funds. Shares often pay a dividend. If you own shares in a company, that company will pay out a proportion of its profits to its shareholders, usually twice a year. This is the dividend. Bonds also pay a percentage return, known as a coupon. Dividends and coupons are collectively described as "income".

If you own a fund which generates income from dividends or coupons you can chose to have that income paid out to you in cash as would be the case in an income fund or you can elect for that money to be ploughed back into units in the fund you own. This is called accumulation.

Very often you will be able to own either income or accumulation versions of the same fund. Unless you need the money, for example if you are retired, it is best to chose to own the accumulation fund. Ploughing the income earned back into your fund will maximize the effect of compounding on how your money grows.

We have nearly finished our brief explanation of the various different types of investment available to private investors and are going to move on to a more precise outline of what to do in the next chapter. Before we do, however, for the sake of completeness we will just look very briefly at three final categories you may recall from the beginning of this chapter: Insurance products, Foreign Exchange and Derivatives.

7. "INSURANCE" PRODUCTS

I would describe another category of investment product as "insurance products". These include a range of different products which are usually structured by insurance companies and then sold by them to the public directly through their own sales network or via third parties such as high street banks, building societies and financial advisers.

Within this category I include the type of "endowment" product sold to large numbers of people in recent years as a way of building money to pay off their mortgage. The nomenclature here is slightly confusing because the word "endowment" also describes money left to a non-profit institution like a university or charity, usually by a wealthy individual in their will. Here we are concerned with the mortgage product.

The other main category is "investment bonds" of which there are several types you may have heard of: These include, "with profits bonds", "distribution bonds", "guaranteed income and growth bonds", "stock market bonds" and "property bonds".

The point here is that these products are very similar to funds, as discussed above, with the main difference being their tax treatment and the costs you are likely to pay to own them. Because these products are considered to be insurance products the government taxes them differently to funds.

Depending on your tax situation, this can be advantageous, however, I would argue that unless you are wealthy enough to be saving/investing more than your monthly ISA allowance you are generally best off avoiding these products.

First, these products tend to give you far less flexibility in terms of what you will end up owning than you can achieve with funds or many of the other investment categories discussed in this chapter which you can own in your ISA account. To quote the CISI again as we did in chapter two: "Nowadays almost all of the funds offered within investment bonds can be bought directly as Unit Trusts or OEICS which are much more flexible. Money can be withdrawn from a unit trust or OEIC at any time without penalty..."[26]

Secondly, to return to what I hope by now is a familiar theme, these products tend to be expensive and their costs rather opaque. Again, the CISI themselves say: "Charges applicable to investment bonds are not always easy to understand... IFAs... who sell investment bonds can receive up to 6-7% or even 8% initial commission. These high initial commissions are seen as the primary reason why some unscrupulous advisers might recommend investment bonds when an alternative investment product may be just as good or better..."[27]

I have had personal experience of this reality: I was lucky enough to buy a flat in central London in my mid-twenties. When I went to see an IFA to help me with my mortgage situation, not only did he suggest one of these products with, what I deemed to be excessive commission charges, he wanted to charge me an additional £500 for having suggested the product in the first place. I flatly refused

26 From the CISI "Securities" work book p. 356.

27 As above, also p. 356.

to take his advice and made my own arrangements. Again, it is not my intention to disparage all financial advisers by any means and I acknowledge that this is anecdotal but you can obviously avoid these sorts of charges and very likely do a better job with your financial situation as a result if you are willing to take a little time to understand what the other, better options are.

8. CURRENCY OR FOREIGN EXCHANGE (FOREX OR FX):

Many of you reading this book will have heard of the foreign exchange or "FOREX / FX" market. It is quite simply the global market in different currencies. You will have encountered the "retail"[28] FOREX market every time you have gone on holiday and needed to buy euros, dollars, Indian rupees or whatever else you might have needed for your travels.

As you can imagine, there is a huge need globally for companies, governments and all sorts of other organisations and individuals to change money in order to be able to buy and sell things across borders. Because of this, the FOREX market is by far the biggest market in the world. The latest number given on Wikipedia is that around $4 trillion a day is traded. This is unsurprising when you think that nearly every single good (oil, cars, agricultural products) or service (telecommunication, banking, legal) which crosses a border necessitates a foreign exchange transaction. In addition there is an enormous amount of trade in foreign currencies for purely speculative (financial) reasons.

As with any other market, the prices of the assets involved move around a fair bit. In the FOREX market these "assets" are the currencies of hundreds of countries. A country's currency will lose or gain value against other currencies based on a combination of what is happening in that country and what FOREX traders expect to happen to that country in the future, just like a share will move around based on what people think the company is doing and will do in the future.

A share will tend to go up in value if the company is doing well and if people believe that it will continue to do so. A currency will do just the same if people feel the same about the country behind it. A great recent example of this is the strength against nearly every other world currency of the Australian (AUD) and Canadian dollars (CAD). Anyone lucky enough to visit Australia in 2007 and then again in the last year or so will have seen the incredible change in the value of the Australian dollar. In 2007 a British tourist would have received around

---

28 The word "retail" in finance is used when describing a financial service provided to the private individual rather than a company. "Retail" banking is what you experience at Lloyds or HSBC. "Corporate", "investment" or, less in use these days "merchant" banking is the service that a big company or big investment company gets from someone like Goldman Sachs (although many banks do both retail and investment banking, HSBC being a good example).

AUD 2.5 for every one of his pounds, at the time of writing he or she would get about AUD 1.5.

Put another way, if a British tourist had purchased a large number of Australian Dollars in 2007, held on to them and then converted them back to pounds this year he or she would have made around 40%. This would have been a far better investment than owning the UK stock market by which we mean the FTSE100, or nearly all UK property over the same time period. Investing in Australian dollars in early 2007 would have beaten the UK stock market by about 55% at the time of writing.

"THERE IS ALWAYS A BULL MARKET SOMEWHERE"

The same sort of return could have been made in a large number of other currencies. The great thing about the foreign exchange markets is that "there is always a bull market somewhere". One currency's strength is, inherently, another currency's weakness so, no matter what is happening in the world economically there is always the chance to make money in the FOREX market if you know what you are doing.

As such, you can hopefully see that investing in other countries' money can be another useful string to your bow financially. Just as we have already seen with other investments, another superb thing about the FOREX market today is that there are ways for the private investor to participate in it which did not exist until quite recently.

One of the main ways that private individuals can invest in the FOREX market is by using spread betting, which we mentioned above. There are also Exchange Traded Funds available for a large number of currencies which is perhaps a simpler way for the "average punter" to get exposure. That said, trading foreign exchange can be quite complicated and is not for the faint hearted. For the majority of people reading this, simply owning assets from all over the world will give you a useful exposure to a large number of the world's currencies without your having to worry about learning the "black magic" of FOREX. We will look at how to do this in the next few chapters.

9. DERIVATIVES:

The final category of financial product for us to address is derivatives. These are without question the most complex and "professional" of investment products and arguably not appropriate for the vast majority of individuals as a result. One of the main reasons for this is that with derivatives it is possible to lose a great deal more money than you start with.[29] This is one of the reasons that famous investor, Warren Buffett, has described them as "...weapons of financial mass destruction."[30]

The term "derivatives" encompasses a large number of different products, most especially futures and options. It is perhaps easiest to think of a derivative as quite simply a bet between two people about what the price of something will do in the future.

The oldest derivatives in the world are agricultural futures. Merchants and farmers of rice in Japan and wheat and other similar crops in Europe and the US came up with the clever idea to agree a fixed price for an agreed quantity of a crop at some time in the future. This helped the farmer to budget given that he was then guaranteed a certain amount of money no matter what happened to the price of his crop throughout the year and it helped the merchant to manage his inventory because he or she knew what price he would pay for what quantity from the farmers he was trading with.

The derivatives market has come a long way since agricultural futures and is now a complicated and sophisticated market within which you can make bets on a vast number of financial instruments, commodities and even more left-field things such as who will win the US Presidential election. Because of their complexity and the high risk associated with them very few people should get involved in buying and selling derivatives, at least until they have spent a good amount of time learning about financial markets generally and derivatives specifically.

That said, arguably more than any other type of financial instrument, it is possible to make a very large amount of money in a short space of time if you trade derivatives successfully. For those who are interested in getting involved with the derivatives market, the best way to trade them as a UK based individual is using a spread betting account. We will look at how to do this in more detail in a couple of chapters time.

---

29 This can actually easily be avoided by using something called a "stop loss" but the point still stands that it is entirely possible to lose a vast amount of money and more than you started with if you get involved with derivatives.

30 Warren Buffett's concern about derivatives is also because he seems them potentially threatening the entire global economic system.

IN CONCLUSION

Having read this chapter, I would hope that you now feel more confident about what financial products are out there in the world. I would repeat that you do not need to have an extremely detailed understanding of financial products but a basic grasp will be hugely helpful. Now you have that basic grasp we can move on to the next section where we will look in more detail at the precise steps you will want to take to get your finances humming...

SECTION THREE

WORKING OUT WHAT TO INVEST IN...

#9

WHERE DO WE GO FROM HERE?

So far we have:

1. ...looked at why you need to take action with your finances...
2. ...seen how this is easier than you thought, thanks to compound interest, great financial products, ongoing global growth and high real inflation...
3. ...seen how you might free up some money to invest...
4. ... looked at which accounts you will want to have to ensure quality and cost...
5. ...looked at the range of financial products you need to understand a little about...
6. ...understood how to keep your costs low by using the right accounts and products and why this is so important for your long term financial success...

Having covered this ground, we are now ready to look in more detail at what you might own and how you might own it in order to really kick your finances in to gear. The next three chapters, then, are going to look at three fundamentally important topics.

CHAPTER TEN: "MAKING A PLAN: YOU CAN'T GET TO YOUR DESTINATION UNLESS YOU KNOW WHERE IT IS..."

In chapter ten we are going to look at working out how much you need to live on. As with many things in life, if you don't have a specific target to aim at, then you are unlikely to hit anything. The budgeting process we will look at isn't that complicated but it is arguably the first step towards achieving financial freedom and an important process to go through as a result.

Chapters eleven and twelve, however, are probably the most important in the whole book. Each of them will look at a different basic approach to investment that you might take from here:

CHAPTER ELEVEN: "KEEPING IT SIMPLE:"

Many of you will have read this far and will hopefully be keen to get your money to work as a result. Nevertheless, you will not be particularly interested in spending much more time learning about money and finance. This book may well have been the limit!

You want to invest the money you have managed to free up for your ISA account but you don't want to have to spend time each week keeping up with finance and current affairs, read any more books on the subject or learn in any more detail about things like shares, bonds or commodities.

If this describes you then you will want a simple plan that you can set up and maintain with the minimum of fuss and effort but which still does a very good job with your money. In chapter eleven we will look at how you might construct just such a plan. You are going to use what you have learnt so far about investment, the world economy, financial accounts and funds to put an excellent structure in place for your money. You should see the logic behind the steps I am going to suggest you take and feel confident in them because of what you have learnt so far.

We will look at the detail below but for now it is perhaps worth summarising the approach briefly: The "keeping it simple" approach involves you setting up a monthly direct debit to pay money each month into good quality, low-cost funds which will benefit from the global growth and inflation themes we have discussed.

Even though you will not have to invest a great deal of time, taking this approach will still give you a high probability of making life-changing returns and protecting your downside. Again, your own common sense interpretation of the information that follows should give you confidence that this will be the case.

I would argue that the "keeping it simple" approach is also the one you should take if you are just starting out with investment or don't have a particularly large amount of money at the moment. For what it is worth, I would suggest that, for the sake of argument, if you have less than about £50,000 at the moment you should stick to the "keeping it simple" approach for the time being.

Once you have built a bigger pot, you might consider keeping 80% of your money (£40,000) in the keeping it simple strategy and using the remaining 20% (£10,000) to start trading more and think about buying individual shares – which is part of what we will look at in the "taking things further" chapter. This is simply because trading in and out of positions or doing the work on buying individual shares with much less than £10,000 is probably not really worth the effort.

I appreciate that many people might find the above paragraph exasperating as £50,000 may seem like a vast amount of money. I can understand this sentiment but I would argue that even if you are on the average UK salary, if you manage to invest 10% or so of your monthly income in your ISA account in the "keeping it simple" strategy, you have a good chance of getting to £50,000 in less than ten years.

If this seems like a horribly long and pointless amount of time and makes you feel like giving up, I would encourage you to stop for a moment and think about where you were and what you were doing ten years ago. If you are anything like me, it will seem like that the time has gone past in the blink of an eye. I would repeat that investment is a marathon, not a sprint. As I said right at the beginning of the book, this is not a get rich quick scheme but you will get rich. Wouldn't it be better to start on the road as soon as possible with the exciting prospect of building this sort of pot over the next few years? Remember that you make faster and faster progress in growing your money over time thanks to compound interest. Getting from zero to £50,000 takes quite a long time but, if you continue to invest successfully getting from £50,000 to much bigger numbers may only take the same again. It is crucial, however, that you start on the road.

The other good news if you have less than about £50,000 is that, for now, you won't have to spend too much more time thinking about finance or doing any more work on it. If, however, you are lucky enough to have a reasonably large amount of money already and feel willing to get more involved, you might consider "taking things further"...

CHAPTER TWELVE: "TAKING THINGS FURTHER..."
The "keeping it simple" approach outlined above should yield great results for your personal finances, will more than likely constitute a significant improvement over any arrangements you had in the past and is particularly appropriate if you are just starting out.

You may, however, decide that you place sufficient value on your financial future that you are willing to get more "hands on" with all things financial going forwards. You will want to "take things further", especially if you have a reasonable nest egg already.

I would hope that you have found many of the points we have made about finance in this book entirely logical and reasonably easy to grasp. Topics we have covered such as the importance of keeping costs down, the amazing possibilities that result from compound interest and the importance of diversification are not that complicated and, once you know about them, can help you significantly improve your financial situation.

Dare I suggest that some of you may even be excited about finance now that you have seen what a difference you can make with such relatively easy wins? Making money from your money is very liberating after all. As a result, I would hope that you might be interested in continuing to learn more about finance and investment.

To repeat the quote we met in chapter two:

"No one cares more about your money than you do. With a basic understanding of the investment process and a bit of discipline, you're perfectly capable of managing your own money... By managing your own money, you'll be able to earn higher returns and save many thousands ... in investment costs over your lifetime..." [1]

If you fall into this category and are eager to learn more, then chapter twelve, "taking things further" will provide you with a road map to really rev up your understanding of finance. The main difference between those of you who want to "keep things simple" and those who want to "take things further" is that the former method involves choosing some funds and automatically paying money into them each month. After that, there is very little additional work to do. You just have to "let it ride" and you will never be thinking about what the markets are doing or when the best time to invest is.

Those of you who choose to "take things further", however, will spend more time looking at your investments and making decisions about what to buy and sell and when to do so. You will begin a journey to learn more about financial markets generally and how to think about investing in shares, bonds, property, real estate, commodities and so on.

I hope as many of you as possible chose to "take things further" today, if you already have the means, or further down the road if you are just starting out. At the very least I would ask everyone to read both chapters eleven and twelve whichever category you think you fall into at this point. Doing so will mean you are best placed to decide which of these approaches is best for you personally and should get you excited about the opportunity that lies ahead...

1 From "The Gone Fishin' Portfolio", p. 4.

#10

MAKING A PLAN: YOU CAN'T GET TO YOUR DESTINATION UNLESS YOU KNOW WHERE IT IS...

"If you don't know where you're going, you might wind up someplace else..."

– Yogi Berra

"Without goals, and plans to reach them, you are like a ship that has set sail with no destination..."

– Fitzhugh Dodson

I would argue that working up a budget is one of the most important steps you will take on your road to financial success. It is probably fair to say that many people do this in some shape or form but it is also perhaps not controversial to suggest there are three things that relatively few people do:

1. Make a sufficiently detailed budget – throw in everything but the kitchen sink.
2. Budget for your dream life – the life that you actually want rather than the one you are limited to today. There is nothing like a reasonably detailed plan to keep you moving towards actually achieving it.
3. Stick to a budget once you've made it.

Human nature dictates that we are all pretty bad at point three (I am no exception). I am the first to suggest that trying to moderate your intake of overpriced coffees or spend less on having fun each weekend is often doomed to failure. Nevertheless if you go through steps one and two above at the very least, I genuinely believe you can start moving your mindset in the direction of doing a better job with sticking to a budget. Even if you miss by some margin, you will still do better than you would have done not having gone through the process.

As such, all I want to do in this chapter is suggest you work up a budget that is realistic for today based on your current income and then another one which is what you would need to live the life of your dreams. Once you have done this, you can set about doing some basic sums to work out how much you need to save to give you the best chance of achieving the latter.

Below you will find an example of how you might work out a reasonably detailed budget. Not everyone needs to cater for school fees or intends to pay for a gym membership or a massage each month but putting together this sort of document for your own particulars will give you a really good idea of where you stand.

It seems likely that the large majority of readers will have access to a spreadsheet programme. I would highly recommend taking the time to build a spreadsheet that looks something like the table below. You can then enter your expenses into the relevant column. Car insurance tends to be annual, for example, whereas utilities are monthly but you might think about your expenditure on nights out or grocery shopping weekly. It is entirely up to you how you work things out but I find that if you take the time to fill in all the columns so you get an idea of what everything costs daily, weekly, monthly and annually it gives you the very best visibility on all things financial.

I like to have things worked out daily quite simply because it gives me a daily trading target. If I can make enough each day just from trading / investing to cover all these costs calculated daily then I know I am living on my money alone which is incredibly liberating as you might imagine.

Many of you will know how to make the spreadsheet work so that something inputted annually is divided by twelve automatically to produce the monthly number and by fifty two for the weekly number, for example. This means you can easily produce a spreadsheet which gives you all the numbers you need. If you don't know how to do this yourself I suggest you find a nearby teenager since they almost certainly will.

As suggested above, it is worth taking the time to do this for your realistic expenditure at the moment given your current income. This must include an allocation to ISA investment. You can then work out what the numbers would be for your dream life. How much would the mortgage or rent be on your dream home, for example? Or, in an ideal world, how much would you like to be able to spend on amazing holidays each year?

Once you have worked out these numbers (twice), you will have a good idea of how to manage the income you have today (which must include an allocation to investment) and what you would ideally like to have in the future. These numbers can then serve as a target to aim for.

As you will have seen earlier in the book, annuity rates today are about 3%. At the most basic level, this means that when you retire, whatever lump sum you have in your pension can be exchanged for an annual income equivalent to about 3% of that lump sum. This is why I make the point on the website and earlier in this book that if you want an income of the average UK salary of about £26,000 a year at retirement, you will need a pot of about £867,000 (at 3%). If you have worked out that your dream life requires an annual income of, say, £80,000, then at an annuity rate of 3%, you will need about £2.67 million pounds.[1]

At first this probably seems rather depressing or daunting to say the least. You might be wondering how on earth you are going to build a pot of over £2.5 million. To respond to that concern I would make the following points:

First, as we saw in the section on compound interest earlier in the book, with a long term commitment to doing the best with your money, you really can aspire to turn relatively small amounts of money into large amounts. All you need is time (I would say at least ten years), a modicum of knowledge and a bit of effort in terms of taking care of the necessary administration.

---

1 As a reminder, the sum here is (target income/annuity rate so: £80,000/0.03 = £2,666,666 million).

PEF Budget Calculator				
	Daily	**Weekly**	**Monthly**	**Annual**
Books and music				
Car - Petrol, insurance, upkeep				
Cleaner				
Coffees out				
Council tax				
Credit card - annual fees, interest				
Dental				
Electricity (utility)				
Food, bathroom, kitchen etc...				
Gas (utility)				
Gym, personal trainer, other sports				
Household insurance				
Internet, phone, Skype				
Investment: ISA (and pension)				
Mobile phone				
Other - e.g. magazine subs.				
Rent or mortgage				
Restaurants and bars				
School fees				
Transport - i.e. for commute				
Travel & holiday (inc. Insurance)				
TV Licence / cable or satellite TV				
Vitamins & minerals / medicine				
Water (utility)				
Totals				

Secondly and linked to the first point, above we were looking only at passive income – that is to say that we are looking at the "perfect world" scenario of you being able to live your life entirely funded by the money you make from your money. In reality, we will all hopefully spend several decades of our life working in some shape or form. This is important, because your active income (the money you are paid for your work) can obviously make up a huge component of the costs of your dream lifestyle, for the decades you work. It can also, if you are sensible and take the right steps with a decent percentage of it for the duration of your working life, vastly increase your likelihood of building the "scary" seven figure retirement pot we are talking about.

Thirdly, whilst annuity rates may only be 3% today, by the time you have got through the material that follows and vastly improved your understanding of matters financial, you should aspire to return significantly more than 3% on your money. I feel that it is unlikely that I, personally, will ever buy an annuity product (unless it is a legal requirement when I retire). This is because, as you might imagine, I have great confidence that I can manage my financial affairs to return a good deal more than 3% per annum when I retire. My "pot" will be in a wide range of investments which, taken together, should provide me with a much higher income than 3% per annum and do so extremely safely.

It should be clear that if I can consistently make 6%, my pot need only be half the size or even one third of the size if I think I can make 9%. As we have seen earlier in the book, these sorts of returns are entirely possible: Simply buying a rental property at the right time in the cycle will give you reliable long term returns at these sorts of levels. Equally, buying shares in an extremely good quality business at the right price will more than likely give you these sorts of returns if you hold those shares for the long term and for their income in the way that investors like Warren Buffet do.

Finally, to go back to the notion of active income again: I, personally, hope to carry on making some kind of active income well past traditional retirement age. In common with all of the "old" people I respect, as long as I still have my critical faculties I aim to continue working in some shape or form well into my seventies, possibly even eighties. I am well aware that I am unlikely to be in any kind of high powered, full-time employment but on the basis that "every little helps" some kind of income in retirement will help to lower the amount of money I need to squirrel away and / or the returns I will have to achieve consistently on that money to live my own personal dream life.

Hopefully you can see that if, for example, I am able to pull in £10,000 a year as a DJ or cabaret singer in my seventies (!), I'm able to return about 6% on my savings and my dream income is £40,000 a year (given I would hope to be based somewhere cheap and hot where that kind of money goes a long way, like Croatia perhaps), my pension pot need only be £500,000 (£40,000 - £10,000 = £30,000 of income from my investments. At 6% - I therefore need £30,000/0.06 = £500,000 to live my dream life).

We all have different aspirations and plans. I would hope that what you take away from this chapter is the notion that having a real think about precisely where you want to get to financially and, by extension, what you will then need to do to get there will be hugely helpful in making your money really work for you.[2]

So... now we have dealt with where we are going, let's turn our attention finally to how we might get there.

2 There are a number of free online tools to help you with budgeting. I personally like using my own spreadsheet but I wouldn't hesitate to recommend using tools on the web if you find that easier.

#11

KEEPING IT SIMPLE: "OWNING THE WORLD"

"The most powerful tool an investor has working for him or her is diversification. True diversification allows you to build portfolios with higher returns for the same risk. Most investors... are far less diversified than they should be. They're way over-committed to (US) stocks..."

– Jack Meyer, manager of Harvard University's multi billion dollar investment funds. Mr. Meyer produced an average of 15.9% per year for fifteen years (a 910% compounded return).

I am aware that we've seen this quote before but I believe its message is important enough to bear repeating, especially given how impressive Mr. Meyer's track record as an investor is.

Think back to our two crucial investment themes from earlier in the book: The world economy keeps on growing and there is significant real inflation in the world. It should come as no surprise to you that if you are going to take our more "formulaic" approach to investing, you will want to ensure that you quite simply "own the world" and "own inflation".

This is the big picture starting point. We will now look in more detail at why we want to take this approach and at how we might achieve it as efficiently as possible given the financial accounts and products available today.

The other key feature of the "keeping it simple" investment approach we look at in this chapter is that you will be paying whatever money you have decided you can afford into your investments regularly every month with a direct debit.

Investing every month has two significant benefits: First, it is easy for you to set up and requires a minimum of effort going forwards. You will not have to worry about making complex decisions about when to put your money to work. This will maximise your chances of actually doing something with your finances sooner rather than later.

Secondly, investing regularly each month results in what is known as "averaging in" or "smoothing". To explain: Obviously the price of any financial asset or market goes up and down over time. By investing regularly each month you improve your chances of buying in at a good average price. For example, you ensure that you do not put a large amount of money in something just ahead of a crash. If anything you own does crash, by averaging in each month you will then pick it up when it is cheap in the months which follow that crash. Doing this removes a huge amount of stress and hassle and is key to keeping things manageable.

So let us look at the big picture first...

THE ADVANTAGE OF "OWNING THE WORLD": THIS IS VERY IMPORTANT

When I talk about "owning the world" I mean...

1. ...that you would like to own a wide variety of investment products or assets. In the long run you will want to have cash, shares, bonds, commodities and property, not just one or two of these like the vast majority of people...

2. ...that you will want to own assets from all over the world, not just one geographical area such as the UK or US...

You will recall from earlier in the book that the world economy as a whole continues to grow. You will also remember how important it is to be diversified. "Owning the world" means that you end up being diversified geographically and by asset class...

What does this mean?

GEOGRAPHICALLY DIVERSIFIED

"Geographically diversified" simply means that if one part of the world is having a difficult time, perhaps Europe or the USA for example, you still have a good chance of making money because you have exposure to another part of the world that is going up a great deal, perhaps certain emerging markets or Asia. Every year different parts of the world are stronger than others.

Rather than trying to work out where the best place for your money will be next year, which is difficult and time-consuming,[1] it is easiest just to be invested in every major part of the world. This means you benefit from the consistent growth of the world economy as a whole. Bear in mind that the world, in total, has only really ever had "down" years across the board in time of major wars.

One of the biggest mistakes people make with their investments is that they tend, in the main, to own assets from their own country. As we have highlighted already in the section on global growth in chapter three, if you had owned just the main UK and US stock markets (by which I mean the main indices, which many people have in their pension funds), over the last ten years you would have suffered a significant decline in your wealth, particularly after accounting for inflation at its true rate.

---

1 Although we will learn ways to think about this in the next chapter.

At the same time, many of the faster growing areas of the world have seen their stock markets double, triple or even better. With that sort of performance you didn't need to have a large share of your money exposed to these markets to enjoy a material impact on growing your wealth and achieve the sorts of numbers we saw at the beginning of the book.

There is no guarantee this will continue. The trend might even reverse and growth in the US and UK might be better than in China, India or Brazil for the next decade. My point is that you may not want to spend too much time trying to work out what is going to happen. A simpler approach is just to ensure that you have exposure to the world as a whole. As the world keeps growing and developing, which it will as a whole, this approach will give you the best chance of benefitting from that growth.

I would repeat that the only time the world as a whole has failed to grow has been in times of major wars. It is perhaps worth observing that if we are unlucky enough to live through "World War Three" in our lifetime, your investment performance might be the least of your concerns. Having said that, without wanting to sound horribly cynical, smart money has usually found even wartime reasonably lucrative. You may remember from right at the beginning of the book that the Chinese see "crisis" as the same as "opportunity". Even in the case of a World War, there will be opportunities for the informed and enlightened to keep their money safe and possibly even grow it.

Leaving aside that rather depressing possibility however, in the more normal run of things, "owning the world" will simply mean that you will want to end up with exposure to everywhere: The UK, Europe, the United States, Japan, the rest of Asia and various emerging markets all over the world. You want to own assets in as many places as possible so that you catch those doubles and triples over the years. In an ideal world you might also own a wide range of types of company, for example both small and large companies in all of these regions.

One of the reasons relatively few people pursued this sort of strategy in the past is that it used to be very hard for a private individual to invest like this. It is also the case that relatively few financial advisers have a grasp of how to do it or even why it is a good idea for all the reasons we looked at earlier in the book. Not that long ago this sort of strategy was realistically impossible. Today you can get closer than ever before to this sort of asset allocation without paying crazy fees and even if you only have a small amount of money to start with.

DIVERSIFIED BY ASSET CLASS

"Diversified by asset class" means that in a year when shares fall off a cliff as most of them did in 2008, for example, you do not lose a vast chunk of your money like everyone else. Instead you have a good chance of having a positive year or at least far less negative than most people because, even though some of your shares might have fallen in value, you will own other assets such as commercial property, bonds, gold, silver or oil and other commodities. Many of these will have held up very well in a bad year for shares. The reason this happens is due to a phenomenon called negative correlation.

It is often the case in investment that certain types of asset tend to go up when other types go down, that is to say they are "negatively correlated". The relationship in real life is never perfect but if you own a wide variety of types of asset, rather than, say, just shares or just property, you have a much better chance of seeing your money continue to grow if there is a stock market or property crash for example.

Gold has gone up every year for eleven years. What a shame that the vast majority of people in the world have not owned any and still don't. Before that, shares went up virtually every year for a decade or so and gold went sideways to down for a long time, just as shares have done in this last decade.

As such, in the long run, it is much easier to own a mixture of different assets so that you have a better chance of owning something that goes up when another type of asset crashes. Hopefully this makes sense to you.

To conclude on "owning the world" for the moment: Our holy grail here is that your money is put to work with the minimum of effort but so that you still gain exposure to the world as a whole. Ultimately you will want to end up the proud owner of a wide variety of assets: Shares from all over the world, commodities, bonds and property so that you will benefit from global growth, wherever it is in the future.

...AND THE ADVANTAGE OF "OWNING INFLATION"

You will also want to ensure that you invest a good percentage of your money each month to benefit from the inflation we have talked about earlier in the book. The best way to do this is to own the monetary metals (gold and silver) and a wide-range of other commodities. This will mean that, unlike nearly everyone else, you will actually benefit from inflation in the price of "stuff" rather than suffer a decrease in your living standards.

Monetary metals are in a very strong multi-year bull market primarily due to the money printing actions of the world's central banks we have already discussed. As long as central banks around the world keep printing (inventing) more money, precious metals and other "things" will continue to go up in price.[2] For this reason I feel strongly that exposure to monetary metals and commodities will enhance your overall performance without complicating matters or being prohibitively expensive. If central banks stop printing money and put interest rates up in the years ahead we will change our opinion[3] but whilst they continue to pursue the policies of the last several years we will need to invest accordingly.

VERY SMART INVESTORS DO THIS – INCLUDING HARVARD AND YALE
Before I continue, I would like to point out that I am most certainly not the first person to advocate this method of investing. This broad approach has been used with stunning results by some of the very smartest investors in the world for several decades. Award winning British wealth manager Tim Price has called diversification the "only free lunch" in investing, for example. As I said in the first section of the book, I think the best thing to do is to invest with the smartest investors in the world or, failing that, like them.

There are two particularly good books that highlight the strength of this strategy. The first is called: "The Ivy Portfolio" by Mebane Faber and Eric Richardson (see bibliography). Faber and Richardson focus on Harvard and Yale Universities' investment funds.

Harvard and Yale Universities in the United States both have very large (multi billion pound) investment funds called endowments. The Yale fund returned 16.62% per annum from 1985 until 2008 (the last year for which numbers were available before the book was written). The Harvard fund returned over 15% every year over the same time period. "The Ivy Portfolio" studies how these funds achieved such fantastic and consistent returns.

It is worth noting that in the crisis year of 2008, when many funds fell by as much as 50% Harvard, was up 8.6% and Yale by 4.5%.[4] The shares both funds were invested in fell in value by 10-15% but they were able to make a positive return overall as their commodity holdings were up over 75%.

This perfectly illustrates the point I am making in this chapter...

DON'T FORGET WHAT THESE SORTS OF NUMBERS MEAN FOR YOUR WEALTH
It is worth flagging that, thanks to the power of compound interest, if you had

---

2 At the time of writing the central banks are as committed as ever to printing money. Europe is following the UK and the US adding billions worth of new money conjured from thin air. They call it the LTRO rather than QE but it is the same thing.

3 If you subscribe to the free Plain English Finance email list I will be sure to let you know if things ever do change and suggest what you might do about it at that point.

4 Source: http://seekingalpha.com/article/96448-performance-for-harvard-yale-endowments-in-2008

been able to invest in either fund in 1985 you would have made around forty times your money by 2008. This is based on making just one lump-sum investment. If you had been paying money into funds with this sort of performance every month as we are suggesting in this chapter, the number would most likely be higher.

This should remind us of the point I have made previously about compound interest. As we have already seen, paying just a few hundred pounds each month into a fund returning 15% or more really will result in your having at least a million pounds at retirement, probably far more.

I repeat: Hundreds of pounds regularly invested at these rates of return become millions of pounds…

Jack Meyer ran the Harvard Fund from 1990 to 2005. During the last decade of his tenure, the endowment earned an annualized return of 15.9%. We have already seen what he has to say about investment but why not hammer the point home (!):

"The most powerful tool an investor has working for him or her is diversification. True diversification allows you to build portfolios with higher returns for the same risk. Most investors… are far less diversified than they should be. They're way over-committed to (US) stocks…"[5]

Being American, Mr. Meyer refers to US stocks but the same holds true to people in the UK having too many British assets or in Germany owning only German stocks and so on. Sadly, it is not possible for private individuals to invest in the Harvard or Yale funds but more than ever we are able to invest like them.

THE PERMANENT PORTFOLIO

A similar approach to that taken by Harvard and Yale is called "The Permanent Portfolio". It was invented in 1981 by top-selling investment author, Harry Browne. Just like Harvard and Yale, his idea was that if you own well distributed assets you should always have something which performs well. Mr. Browne's portfolio consisted of gold, a basket of international shares, cash and bonds. Here is how this structure has performed since 1972 and an illustration of the returns you would have made investing £10,000:

5 Jack Meyer quoted in "The Ivy Portfolio" p. 50.

The Permanent Portfolio's returns since 1972					
Year	Return	Cash	Year	Return	Cash
		£10,000			
1972	18.8%	£11,880	1992	4.4%	£100,258
1973	15.6%	£13,733	1993	12.9%	£113,191
1974	14.2%	£15,683	1994	-2.5%	*£110,361*
1975	8.3%	£16,985	1995	18.0%	£130,226
1976	12.2%	£19,057	1996	4.9%	£136,607
1977	5.6%	£20,125	1997	7.5%	£144,853
1978	12.1%	£22,560	1998	10.8%	£162,713
1979	42.1%	£32,057	1999	4.2%	£169,547
1980	13.4%	£36,353	2000	3.2%	£174,972
1981	-3.9%	*£34,935*	2001	0.9%	£176,547
1982	23.2%	£43,075	2002	7.0%	£188,905
1983	4.2%	£44,884	2003	14.0%	£215,352
1984	3.2%	£46,320	2004	6.6%	£229,565
1985	20.8%	£55,055	2005	8.1%	£248,160
1986	18.8%	£66,475	2006	11.0%	£275,475
1987	6.2%	£75,596	2007	12.9%	£310,991
1988	4.3%	£73,632	2008	1.9%	£316,900
1989	13.5%	£83,572	2009	7.8%	£341,618
1990	1.6%	£84,909	2010	14.5%	**£391,153**
1991	13.1%	£96,032			
Source: www.agorafinancial.com					

Just like Harvard and Yale, this strategy even had a positive year in 2008, when nearly everyone else was losing vast sums of money. For investors based in America, it is possible to buy a fund which replicates this strategy very closely. It is called the Permanent Portfolio mutual fund. Over the last fifteen years it has produced twice the return of the S&P 500 and beaten the famous investor, Warren Buffet, by some margin.[6] As UK based investors, however, we are perfectly

6 Source: http://dailyreckoning.com/the-permanent-portfolio-revisited/

capable of investing in a similar way. We shall see how shortly.

THE GONE FISHIN' PORTFOLIO
Another similar strategy to the two outlined above and aimed at the private investor, is called "The Gone Fishin' Portfolio", the detail of which is found in the second of the two books I referred above: "The Gone Fishin' Portfolio: Get wise, get wealthy and get on with your life" by Alex Green.[7] Mr. Green is the Investment Director of one of the best investment clubs in the world, the Oxford Club.

His "Gone Fishin' " portfolio is basically a slightly more complicated and American-centric version of the method we are looking at in this chapter. He shows his readers how to set their money up to own a wide range of assets with the minimum of effort, just as we are going to be doing.

For those of you who wish to pursue the "keeping things simple" approach in this chapter but who are prepared to invest the time to read only one book, I would highly recommend this one as it will give you a deep understanding of the value of the approach. You can find it in the resources section of the website.

For what it is worth, the Gone Fishin' portfolio achieved the following performance numbers from 2003 until 2007 (when the book was written):

- 2003: +32.72%
- 2004: +15.28%
- 2005: +11.93%
- 2006: +16.99%
- 2007: +10.75%

Yet again we see the kind of consistent returns which will literally turn hundreds of pounds into millions if you keep plugging away year after year. If you are saving every month, your annual returns will very possibly be higher than the numbers above.

So we are going to own the world and own inflation. We will now look in more detail at how we might do this. Before we do however, let us answer an important question:

IF THIS IS SUCH A GREAT APPROACH TO INVESTMENT THEN WHY ISN'T EVERYONE DOING IT?
The first and most obvious answer, which you have already seen me write about,

---

7 See the resources section of the website.

is because no one ever spends enough time learning about finance. Most people have no idea how to invest in Brazilian equities or Asian bonds for example. It is also fair to say that relatively few financial advisers are up to speed on this knowledge or would have a good idea how to put this together for their clients in a cost-effective way if they were. We have already seen why this is in chapter two.

Perhaps more importantly, it used to be nearly impossible to "own the world". Until relatively recently, you would have needed to be a multi-millionaire to get such a wide investment exposure (yet another reason why many of the rich have remained rich through history).

To end up owning a wide range of financial assets from all over the world, which is what you want to do here, meant you had to own a large number of funds. This had two problems:

1. Unless you had a very large amount of money, the costs were prohibitive. Too much of the money you were trying to invest would be eaten up in fees, resulting in poor performance. In fact, to a great extent, this is actually still true for many people given how expensive financial advice and the wrong financial accounts and products can be (costs we are learning to avoid).

2. In addition, you can no doubt imagine that owning a large number of funds was a real pain administratively. We are trying to make things easy enough so that this doesn't take very much of your time. We do not want to spend hours and hours keeping on top of the administration involved in owning dozens of different funds.

Importantly, in the recent past it has finally become possible to get the exposure we want easily and cheaply.

EXACTLY WHAT TO DO...

In order to implement the Plain English Finance "keeping it simple" methodology, then, you will need to take the following steps:

STEP ONE: OPEN A STOCKS AND SHARES ISA ACCOUNT WITH A TOP QUALITY, LOW COST COMPANY

As we have said before, you can see suggestions for who you might use on the website. Using the correct ISA provider will ensure you pay lower costs than you might using a high street bank or lower quality firm. It will also mean you are able to invest in a much wider range of investments. You will remember how important both of these points are for you to succeed financially.

I have not named my favourite UK ISA providers here since this book is, by its very nature, a static information source. I am well aware of who my favourite ISA providers are at the time of writing but financial services companies are constantly launching new accounts and improved products.

As such, please use the Plain English Finance website for suggestions as to the best ISA companies. This will ensure you know who is currently offering the best value, best quality ISA accounts.

STEP TWO: SET UP A DIRECT DEBIT TO YOUR STOCKS AND SHARES ISA ACCOUNT

We have already looked at how you might find a certain amount of money to invest each month. Once you have worked out what you can afford, you can set up a direct debit instruction with your ISA provider. They will usually give you a choice of which day of the month funds will automatically be transferred from your current account to your ISA account.

STEP THREE: SPLIT YOUR MONEY BETWEEN "OWNING THE WORLD", "OWNING INFLATION" AND CASH

We will look in more detail at how to "own the world" and "own inflation" below. An important consideration is what percentage of your monthly investment you allocate to each. In general, I would suggest you allocate 60% to 70% of whatever you are able to invest monthly into "owning the world", 20% to 30% into "owning inflation" and keep 10% in cash.

Keeping a certain amount of your savings in cash is a good idea for three reasons: First, as we have already seen, cash cannot fall in (notional) value. The only risk to cash is inflation eating it up. Second, it is always good to keep some cash on hand in your savings to take advantage of investment opportunities that might arise in future. Third, you also need to hold cash to be properly diversified.

Although what we are looking at in this chapter is a method of investing which does not require you to learn much more about finance, I think it is very likely that you will have some excellent thoughts of your own about where you might invest that money at some stage in the future. If you subscribe to the free email from Plain English Finance, for example, you will no doubt be inspired by certain investment thoughts in the months and years ahead. You will want to have some cash on hand to take advantage of those thoughts.

Either that or some time in the future you might use the cash for any number of exciting purchases without having to sell any of your investments. Whatever happens, it is likely you will be glad that you have kept some of the money you are saving every month as cash.

It is also worth noting that many experts in personal finance suggest that when you start saving, you should keep 100% of those savings in cash until you have built up a "rainy day" pot which can cover you for a certain amount of time if you were to lose your job. Different commentators advocate different sums of money but the convention seems to be anywhere from one month to six months of salary. What you decide to do in this respect is entirely up to you. I would suggest that if you feel safe in your job you might consider one month sufficient.

To be clear, I am suggesting that you do not begin to invest money into the financial assets we are looking at in this chapter such as investment funds or stock exchange listed precious metals until you have first saved at least a month's salary as cash, possibly more. Once you have done this, however, you can start allocating some of your monthly savings to investment.

Given the percentages I suggested above, below are two tables detailing how you might split your money between the three categories of the "keeping it simple" approach, depending on how much you are able to save.

SOME POINTS TO MAKE ABOUT THESE TABLES:

1. The table goes up to £940, purely because that is the most you are able to save in a stocks and shares ISA account each month given this year's ISA allowance of £11,280.
2. Our method for "owning inflation" is to invest in precious metals. We will look at why this is in more detail shortly. As you shall see, I am a strong advocate of investing in both gold and silver where possible. In a bid to keep dealing costs low, however, I don't think you should invest in silver as well as gold unless you are saving quite a substantial amount of money each month. This is why the table above suggests a 0% allocation to silver until you have about £500 a month to invest. Owning gold alone will ensure that you "own inflation" for the time being.
3. You will note that I include dealing costs at £1.50 to buy gold and £3 to buy gold and silver. This assumes you use an ISA provider that offers an account with the option to buy shares monthly for only £1.50. You will not be able to achieve these low dealing fees with most ISA providers in the UK market. You can see who does offer this sort of value account on the website.
4. I do not include an assessment of the cost of whichever product you use to own the world. This is because it is likely that this product will be a fund which does not trade on a stock exchange. The costs of this sort of product will be a small percentage of the funds invested rather than the dealing commission you will pay to buy gold or silver each month. We covered these points about how you pay for funds in chapter eight. Please re-read that section if you need to refresh your memory about the costs associated with buying funds.

PEF Keeping It Simple - Split (£100 – £450 invested each month)						
Total to invest each month	% in Owning The World	% in Owning Inflation		% kept in cash	Costs with £1.50 rate e.g.@ TD	COSTS as % of investment
		% in gold (e.g. PHAU.L)	% in silver (e.g. PHAG.L)			
£100.00	£60.00	£30.00	£0.00	£10.00	£1.50	1.50%
£150.00	£90.00	£45.00	£0.00	£15.00	£1.50	1.00%
£200.00	£120.00	£60.00	£0.00	£20.00	£1.50	0.75%
£250.00	£150.00	£75.00	£0.00	£25.00	£1.50	0.60%
£300.00	£180.00	£90.00	£0.00	£30.00	£1.50	0.50%
£350.00	£210.00	£105.00	£0.00	£35.00	£1.50	0.43%
£400.00	£240.00	£120.00	£0.00	£40.00	£1.50	0.38%
£450.00	£270.00	£135.00	£0.00	£45.00	£1.50	0.33%

		PEF Keeping It Simple - Split (£500 – £940 invested each month)				
Total to invest each month	% in Owning The World	% in Owning Inflation		% kept in cash	Costs with £1.50 rate e.g.@ TD	COSTS as % of investment
		% in gold (e.g. PHAU.L)	% in silver (e.g. PHAG.L)			
£500.00	£300.00	£100.00	£50.00	£50.00	£3.00	0.60%
£550.00	£330.00	£110.00	£55.00	£55.00	£3.00	0.55%
£600.00	£360.00	£120.00	£60.00	£60.00	£3.00	0.50%
£650.00	£390.00	£130.00	£65.00	£65.00	£3.00	0.46%
£700.00	£420.00	£140.00	£70.00	£70.00	£3.00	0.43%
£750.00	£450.00	£150.00	£75.00	£75.00	£3.00	0.40%
£800.00	£480.00	£160.00	£80.00	£80.00	£3.00	0.38%
£850.00	£510.00	£170.00	£85.00	£85.00	£3.00	0.35%
£900.00	£540.00	£180.00	£90.00	£90.00	£3.00	0.33%
£940.00	£564.00	£188.00	£94.00	£94.00	£3.00	0.32%

So let us now look at how we might own the world and own inflation:

OWNING THE WORLD

As we've already said, when we talk about "owning the world", we mean that you would ideally own a good range of assets with truly global exposure. Having come this far and read the section on funds in chapter eight, you might already have an idea of how it might be possible to "own the world" in this way: You will hopefully remember that you can buy a tracker or index fund for a vast range of different types of asset (assuming, of course, that you have an ISA provider that offers such a range).

One method you might use, therefore, would be to buy one fund for each geographical area and one or two for each asset class. You could buy a FTSE 100 tracker to own UK shares and an S&P 500 tracker to own the US for example. You might then do the same for Europe, Asia and Latin America et al. and in order to get exposure to real estate and the bond market.

Again, having read this far, you may realise that this approach can only work if you have a significant amount of money to invest. This is because every time you buy a financial product, you pay a fee. To get a truly global and diversified asset exposure this way will obviously require you to buy a large number of funds. An example might be instructive.

Below is a table which lists the funds we might consider buying in order to end up "owning the world" in a reasonably comprehensive way:

One Way to "Own The World"			
Shares	**Large Cap**	**Mid & Small Cap**	**Dividend**
UK funds	1	18	23
US funds	2	19	24
Europe including Switzerland	3	20	25
Japan	4	21	26
China	5	22	n/a
Rest of Asia	6	n/a	n/a
Latin America including Brazil	7	n/a	n/a
Russia & Eastern Europe	8	n/a	n/a
India	9	n/a	n/a
Africa or frontier fund	10	n/a	n/a
Middle East	11	n/a	n/a
Bonds			
Global bond fund to include government and corporate bonds	12		
Real Estate (Property)			
Global real estate fund	13		
Commodities			
Agricultural commodities fund	14		
Energy commodities fund (oil, gas,...)	15		
Industrial metals (copper, zinc, platinum,...)	16		
Precious metals (gold and silver)	17		

The above is just an example and some might argue is actually a conservative number of funds to get a truly global and diversified exposure. A purist might argue, for example, that we don't own any "hot" sector or thematic funds within this structure (such as biotechnology, pharmaceuticals or oil for example). Even with the twenty six funds above, however, the point I am trying to make still stands: As you will recall from the section on funds in chapter eight, each time we buy a fund we have to pay commission or other fees. The above approach would, therefore, only be suitable for someone with a large amount of money to invest.

That lucky individual could quite simply split their money up between a large number of funds, sit back and watch their money grow, very possibly every year as per Harvard and Yale's endowment funds. In the future, when you have built a seven figure pot of money and are confident in your financial knowledge, you might aspire to invest in this way. For now, however, owning twenty six or even more funds in order to "own the world" simply isn't practicable. We need to think of a more suitable method.

ONE FUND TO "OWN THE WORLD"

The more suitable method, for the time being, then is to look for one fund which gives you as much of the above exposure as possible. One fund implies keeping things simple administratively and keeping your costs as low as possible. Thankfully, in the relatively recent past it has become possible to find just this sort of product at the right price.

Earlier in the chapter I explained how I would not name my favourite ISA providers in this book given the dynamic nature of that advice. As you might imagine the same holds even truer for fund products. At the time of writing there are a number of funds in the UK market that you might use to "own the world". No doubt more will be offered by the best financial services companies in the months and years ahead.

As such, please use the website for suggestions as to the best fund products you might consider putting in your ISA in order to "own the world".

SO HOW DO WE OWN INFLATION?

You will no doubt remember from earlier in the book that "stuff" goes up in price when there is inflation. In fact, inflation is an increase of the price of stuff if you think about it. These are two sides of the same coin. In the vernacular of investing, "stuff" is better known as "commodities". If we want to own inflation, we just need to own some commodities. We have already looked in some detail at the case for commodities in chapter eight.

Before we go on, it is worth noting that once you have invested money in "owning the world" as per the section above and as recommended on the website, you will already have a reasonable degree of natural exposure to commodities (and global currencies for that matter) by virtue of owning companies that are involved with commodities in one way or another.

This is good news but, in my opinion, the exposure you get through these two factors is not as much as you will want to have for the next several years for all the reasons we have already considered: Governments inventing money and resource scarcity in the face of population growth and increased demand for raw materials. You will want to have a bigger exposure to commodities whilst western governments continue to create vast amounts of money out of thin air and whilst the developing world continues to grow and urbanise.

The simplest way to do this is to own gold and silver. Gold and silver benefit from all the positive metrics we looked at in the commodity section above but have an important additional benefit: They have historically been seen as money. This is particularly important.

WHY GOLD AND SILVER ARE THE BEST COMMODITIES TO OWN: THEY ARE MONEY...

"Gold is money. Everything else is just credit..."

– John Pierpoint (JP) Morgan.

Whilst I completely believe in our general view of commodities as outlined above, industrial and agricultural commodities are famously volatile and when the global economy slows down they can suffer severe falls in price. A good example is copper. Copper is a metal just as gold and silver are, but its use globally is basically 100% industrial. As such, if the world is manufacturing fewer cars or building fewer skyscrapers, the copper price can fall drastically. We have seen this recently as commodity investors around the world have taken to worrying about the Chinese economy slowing down (China is a huge consumer of copper for obvious reasons).

Gold and silver are not immune to the same phenomenon and they will periodically fall by a meaningful percentage. The crucial difference between gold and silver and all other commodities, as we have already seen, is that they have been used as money for several thousand years. Both metals have industrial and retail applications (for example in jewellery) but an increasingly large part of the demand for both of them from all over the world derives from their use as a financial asset, as money. This is something they have both been used for to a greater or lesser degree for several thousand years.

Given the general commodity exposure you will have by virtue of "owning the world", I firmly believe that the best assets for you to buy to gain additional exposure to "commodities" and to "own inflation" as a result are the precious metals. Unlike all other commodities, they benefit from industrial demand *and* monetary inflation. They are very easy to buy and have a very strong individual investment story which we will look at now.

Please note in the discussion that follows that all the points I make about gold hold doubly true for silver. Silver tends to amplify what gold does. If the price of gold goes up by 10%, silver will tend to go up by two or three times that amount. This is also true when the price goes down, which is why the prudent investor will usually own more gold than silver.

In order to understand why gold and silver are particularly important to own beyond the general upward trend in commodities we have already outlined, we must look quickly at exactly what "money" is.

WHAT IS MONEY?

It might seem ridiculous to have a section explaining what "money" is but I would contend that most people actually don't understand enough about what money really is. Failing to understand what money is will have a big negative impact on your ability to make it. I hope, therefore, that you will persevere with what follows and trust that it is important in helping you grow your real wealth.

To really get to grips with what money is, we need to go back a little bit in history to understand why it was invented: In early human societies the "economy" such as it existed, worked with a barter system. An individual with food would exchange some of that food for clothing or for a weapon, for example. This system enabled early human societies to significantly improve their productivity through specialisation: One group could focus on food production (farmers, fishermen) and another on the production of other relatively vital goods such as clothing (tanners, weavers) or tools and weapons (blacksmiths).

As you can imagine, a barter system had severe limitations: A farmer who wanted some new clothes or shoes for his family would have to find someone with those products available who, at that precise moment in time, wanted what the farmer had just produced. This was particularly problematic when you consider how perishable and seasonal most of the farmer's products were and how difficult they were to store and transport.

As a result, several thousand years ago, some bright spark came up with the idea of using something as a medium of exchange and store of value, what we now describe as "money". It is important that we think for a moment about what qualities were required to perform the function early societies required money to perform. When you think about it, these qualities are reasonably self-evident and, at a fundamental level, have not changed over time. Whatever they chose to use needed to be:

PORTABLE

A key feature of anything which would serve the purposes required here would be the ability to carry enough of it with you. Portability was one of the key problems with a barter system: A farmer needed to herd animals into town, or bring a wagon full of crops just to have enough to exchange for something reasonably "expensive" such as a plough or some good boots. Portable money also enabled people to travel further than ever before, secure in the knowledge that they would be able to buy vital supplies far from their homes rather than having to face the uncertainty of hunting or foraging for food and fresh water.

REASONABLY READILY AVAILABLE, YET RELATIVELY SCARCE

There would have been no point in choosing to use something which was virtually impossible to find or that would require a large percentage of the population to work to produce. It is probably for this reason that precious gemstones, despite coming to be highly valued, were never used as a common currency for day-to-day transactions such as buying food. On the other hand, choosing something which was extremely common (timber, for example) would have resulted in the use of something insufficiently portable: Using the example of timber, people would have simply chopped trees down to the point of then having to carry a pointlessly large amount around with them, no better than a barter system.

DURABLE

For something to act as a "store of value" it was crucial that it would last for long periods of time and not be too fragile and easily damaged. There would be no point in using something that would rot away or easily be broken in two for example. Gold and silver perform this function particularly well.

FUNGIBLE AND DIVISIBLE

To really work, money also needed to be reliably the same within the society that was using it and divisible into reliable units. Some early societies in the Pacific islands and elsewhere used seashells and feathers as "money". Problems clearly arose when one islander had a particularly large seashell or unusually beautiful feather: How much more was a big seashell worth than a small one when exchanging it for a quantity of fish for example? More advanced societies ensured that the size and weight of their "money" was standardised to avoid such issues. That is to say that their money was fungible.

When you consider the above requirements it is unsurprising that in almost every human society in the world:

> *"…metals such as gold, silver and bronze were … regarded as the ideal monetary raw material…"*[8]

Precious metals were made into coins as early as 600 BC, possibly earlier. Metal coins were then used pretty much universally for several centuries before the next major development: The arrival of paper money.

PAPER MONEY

For the first few hundred years of its existence, paper money was very simply an "IOU": It came about because another bright spark realised several centuries ago that rather than taking the high risk and paying the significant costs (soldiers, ships, sailors) of transporting large amounts of precious metals over long distances, it would be easier to leave the physical metal in a vault somewhere safe and use a piece of paper representing that metal to perform transactions. These pieces of paper became the original bank notes.

This is why it says on a British bank note: "I promise to pay the bearer on demand the sum of…" What this originally meant was that someone holding a one "pound sterling" note could go to the Bank of England and demand one pound (weight) of "sterling" silver (92.5% pure silver) in physical form. [9]

The point here is that gold and silver have been used as money by countless human societies over thousands of years for all the above reasons. Precious metals came to be used almost universally across human civilization because they possessed these key characteristics of portability, relative availability, durability, divisibility and fungibility. It is precisely because they possess these characteristics that precious metals constitute a superior "money" to paper or, for that matter, zeros invented by a government in a computer.

MORE ON GOLD AND SILVER SPECIFICALLY AND WHY THEY ARE NOT "IN A BUBBLE"

As we have just seen, for the first few hundred years of its existence; paper money was only ever an IOU backed by a precious metal somewhere. In 1971, faced with the enormous cost of the Vietnam war and unable to pay America's creditors in gold bullion (real money), President Nixon suspended the convertibility of the US dollar into gold and America's creditors had to accept being paid back in paper dollars.

---

8 This quote is taken from Professor Niall Ferguson's superb book: "The Ascent of Money", an extremely good history of the development of money for anyone interested. See the resources section of the website.

9 As I write, you would be able to exchange £1 for 1/310th of a pound of silver. That is to say that the £ is 310 times less valuable in real terms. That is what inflation does to your money.

The result was that the gold price (in paper dollars) went up by a factor of TWENTY FOUR times in the following nine years – from $35 to $850.

Today, people are saying gold is "in a bubble" because it has gone up approximately five times in eight years. This is very simplistic analysis. History teaches us that big structural bull markets can go up far further and longer than this. Saying that something has gone up a lot is not a real analysis of whether it is in a bubble.

In considering the gold market today, it is perhaps more instructive to look at the following points:

POINT ONE: THIS BULL MARKET IS A FRACTION OF WHAT HAPPENED IN THE 1970S

As I have mentioned above, the 1970s bull market in gold was a vastly higher percentage increase than we have seen this time around. We are nowhere near it today.

To repeat: Between 1971 and 1980, the gold price increased from around $35 to $850. That is to say it went up by a factor of approximately twenty four times. If the gold market achieved the same growth in this bull market as it did in the 1970s this would imply around $250 x 24 or $6,000 compared to the price at the time of writing of about $1,600.

The current bull market started at about $250 in 1999. It is perhaps worth noting that this is around the level that Britain's ex Prime Minister, Gordon Brown, sold most of the UK's national reserves when he was Chancellor of the Exchequer.

It might be tempting for anyone reading this argument to say that "hindsight is 20:20" and suggest Gordon Brown can't be blamed for failing to see what might happen in the gold market. This might seem like a fair comment but I would argue differently: There were plenty of commentators at the time highlighting the likely long term value in gold and there are ways of looking at gold's value which positively screamed that it was cheap at the time.

One such commentator was Jim Rogers who's track record of correctly calling every major market theme since the 1970s and delivery 4,200% growth as a result at George Soros's Quantum Fund should have suggested he was well worth listening to. As we shall see, just as with all asset classes, there are ways of working out whether gold is inherently expensive or cheap over the long run.

There are strong arguments to suggest that this time the rise in the price of gold should be even more dramatic than in the 1970s. Let's look at why:

POINT TWO: THE DEMAND FOR GOLD AND SILVER

In the 1970s bull market there were a tiny fraction of the possible buyers there are today. Buying came almost entirely from "sophisticated", "professional" investors and basically only from Europe and the USA. There were no Exchange Traded Funds in gold and essentially no other gold funds. In terms of private individuals, only the very richest people in the developed world could be involved in the market through their private bankers. The market was a physical market and you owned ingots or coins in a vault.

In fact, for much of the twentieth century it was actually illegal for private individuals to own gold, even in the west. With China and the USSR under communist rule, effectively no one in either of those enormous countries could invest in gold. The only people permitted to do so were a tiny elite in the ruling parties who were able to travel and keep wealth outside of their country, in Swiss banks for example. The situation now is 180 degrees different with today's authorities in China proactively encouraging their vast population to own gold through a national advertising campaign.

In addition, in the 1970s, developing countries with massive populations such as India, Brazil, Indonesia et al. were all immeasurably poorer than they are today, putting gold as an investment out of the reach of all but the tiniest minority. Today these countries have affluent middle classes totalling around 400 million individuals – a number which is growing all the time.

There was some government or central bank buying from many of these countries but remember how incredibly poor they were compared to the US and Europe in that era. They were tiny economies. Even a concerted effort on any of their parts to buy gold was fundamentally irrelevant to the global market and to the price of gold as a result.

Even in the developed world it was very hard for the private individual to own gold compared to today. Today, people all over the world can buy gold with the click of a mouse button. As a result, the potential market is a significant multiple of what it was in the 1970s.

Despite this reality, actual allocation of overall investment assets to gold even now is historically small. Even after the incredible price move of the last ten years, gold as a proportion of total invested assets is actually at historical lows. It currently stands at less then 1% compared to more like 3-5% historically. If, as I suspect will be the case, gold takes back its long run share or more of invested assets globally, this will constitute nothing short of a tidal wave of money chasing an ever shrinking supply of the yellow metal. The implications of this for the price are extremely positive. Here is a chart to illustrate this point:

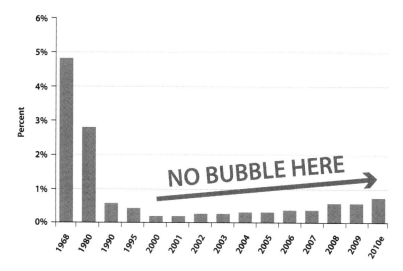

Gold as a Percent of Global Financial Assets

Source: CPM Gold YearBook 2011

This fall in the percentage allocation to gold has happened because of how much paper money has been printed all over the world and ended up in shares, property and bonds.

NET CENTRAL BANK BUYING

Another very important argument when looking at the demand side of the gold equation is the resurgence of gold buying by central banks (those outside of Europe and the US that actually have any money left). An article published in June of 2011 highlighted that China had sold out of 97% of its US Treasury (government) bills.[10]

China has been selling dollar assets and buying gold more or less quietly for several years and has bought at least $700 billion worth of it in the process. It is perhaps also worth mentioning that China has been extremely active in other commodities, acquiring vast amounts of agricultural and resource assets in Africa and Latin America. The Chinese would seem to have the same view on "stuff" as we are outlining in this chapter.[11]

10 http://cnsnews.com/news/article/china-has-divested-97-percent-its-holdings-us-treasury-bills

11 This is discussed in the book: "Winner Takes All: China's Race for Resources and What it Means for the World" by Dambisa Moyo. See bibliography.

The Chinese are not the only country to have been substantial net buyers of gold. Central banks all over the world have been buying gold where possible. As a whole they became net buyers of gold in the second quarter of 2009 and have been buying increasing quantities ever since.[12] Net central bank buying of gold from all over the world is obviously very positive for the gold price.

POINT THREE: A COMPARATIVE ANALYSIS OF PRECIOUS METALS VALUATION:

Another consideration here is that looking at the US dollar ($) price of gold is a terribly simplistic approach to trying to work out its value. A better way of looking at many assets to establish value is to compare them to other key assets over time.

WAYS OF LOOKING AT THE REAL VALUE OF GOLD AND SILVER:

1. GOLD VS. OIL

A great way of measuring the value of something like gold is to look at its ratio to things like oil, property or stock markets. The average ratio of the gold price to a barrel of Brent crude (oil) since 1970 has been about 16x. At the time of writing this is almost exactly where gold is trading. This would indicate that gold is in no way "expensive". For gold to be "expensive" using oil as a valuation tool, that ratio could double, as has been the case in the past on several occasions. This implies that oil will halve in price or gold will double in price from here, or a mixture of the two.

2. GOLD VS. HOUSE PRICES

Another useful ratio, when considering both property and gold prices is the ratio of gold prices to house prices. Here is a chart of UK house prices for the last few years priced in pounds (£s):

12 Have a look at the link below for an interesting November 2011 article on central bank gold buying. Perhaps most instructive is the UBS analyst's estimate for the last quarter was 1/3rd of the real number. Is it any surprise that mainstream analysts keep underestimating the gold bull market with assumptions like these? http://online.wsj.com/article/SB10001424052970203611404577043652396383484.html

Average UK House Price (GBP)

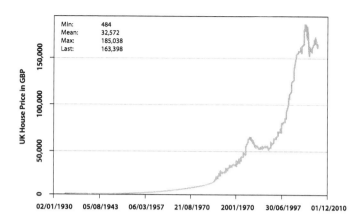

Min:	484
Mean:	32,572
Max:	185,038
Last:	163,398

You will remember from earlier in the book that the purchasing power of a pound has fallen by about 90% since 1971 and that this, more than anything, accounts of the increase in the price (if not value) of UK property.

Gold is a much better long term store of value. If we look at the price of UK houses in terms of oz. of gold we can draw some very interesting conclusions:

Average UK House Price Ounces of Gold

Min:	55.69
Mean:	215.68
Max:	725.25
Last:	183.56

Min - Max Value in this Chart might sligthly vary over time due to data interpolation

First, we can see, that going back no less than eighty years, 2002 was a terrible time to sell gold given it was as cheap as it had ever been historically compared to house prices. Without wishing to sound like a broken record, I really would love to know if Gordon Brown and his advisers were looking at charts like these when they took their decision to sell the UK's gold.

The point here is that the smart money will always be looking at long run relative value. Folks like the aforementioned Jim Rogers could never guarantee that a British house costing 700 oz. of gold was inherently totally the wrong price but there was most certainly a very good chance that it was. You simply can't escape mean reversion in any market.

People are forever suggesting that you "can't time the market". I would argue that if you are prepared to spend a little bit of time looking at the relative value of a wide variety of assets you have a good chance of making better long term decisions about your finances. This chart tells you that the smart money sold property in about 2006 / 2007 and purchased gold. If UK house prices get back down to less than 100 oz. of gold as they have done in the past, this implies either that gold will double from here or UK house prices will halve. My best guess is that it will be a combination of the two and they will meet somewhere in the middle, at which point a UK house will be good value again and a bar of gold will be inherently expensive.[13]

Whatever happens, people who sold out of property to buy precious metals in 2006 / 2007 are very likely to be able to sell their precious metals and buy a much nicer house than the one they sold a few years ago.[14]

3. GOLD VS. STOCK MARKETS

Another metric used by the smart money is to compare gold to a stock market index such as the Dow Jones Industrial Average. At the time of writing the DJIA is trading at 12,000. With the gold price at $1600, the current ratio of gold to the Dow Jones is therefore about 7.5:1. This ratio has been as low as 2:1 on more than one occasion in the last century and was nearly 1:1 in the early 1980s. If we were to see a 2:1 ratio again, this would imply the possibility of gold increasing to $6,000 p. oz. with the Dow at current levels or, perhaps more likely given current circumstances, a crash in the Dow and a slightly less extreme rise in the price of gold.

13 These excellent charts come from a superb article by MoneyWeek magazine's resident precious metals expert, Dominic Frisby: http://www.moneyweek.com/investments/property/gold-price-and-uk-house-prices-04909

14 It is worth noting that this analysis does not hold for central London property for all the reasons discussed in chapter six. Central London property is still very expensive in terms of gold. This suggests to me that London house prices have some way to fall or gold some way to rise. The likelihood is that it will probably be a combination of both over the next decade or so.

I am not alone in believing we could see a 2:1 ratio again. Many of the financial commentators who best predicted the gold bull market and the financial crisis of the last few years see the end game as a likely return of the gold to Dow ratio to 2:1 or worse (read "better" for gold investors).

Their views are controversial but I would highlight that the mainstream financial commentators who argue they are crazy to believe the Dow and gold could ever trade in line are the very same people who have argued against their bullish call on gold for the last ten years or so, have been wrong the entire time and have missed out on about 600% so far as a result.

In my experience precisely none of them do the comparative analysis against other assets we are looking at here. Many of the conditions that we are discussing in this chapter which exist today are those that caused this ratio to be reached in the past. If anything, many of the arguments for us seeing a 2:1 ratio again which we are outlining here are materially stronger today than on the previous occasions it has occurred.

I think there is a very strong likelihood that people who see the 2:1 ratio as beyond the realms of possibility will prove in the long run to have been suffering from a nasty dose of the phenomenon of anchoring we met in the section on property in chapter six. As you should be able to see, considering these ratios suggests we are not yet near "bubble" territory for gold. There is still vastly more money in other assets and compelling reasons why much of that money could be chasing gold in the months and years ahead.

4. INTEREST RATES

The final demand side argument for continued strength in the gold price concerns global interest rates. Although you will by now be well aware that I expect the global bond market to drive interest rates up in the years ahead, real interest rates today are basically at a three hundred year low. In nearly every corner of the world real interest rates are negative as inflation, even on the science fiction government numbers, is higher than the interest rate.

Bear in mind that one of the biggest negatives about holding gold in the normal run of history is that you do not earn any interest. When interest rates are high, owners of gold miss out on this return. Economists call this the "opportunity cost" of holding gold. This is the main reason gold performed so weakly in the early 1980s. At that time, Paul Volcker became Chairman of the Federal Reserve and instituted high interest rates in a bid to control inflation. Inevitably a great deal of money left gold, chasing what were historically high interest rates it could now earn elsewhere and the gold price fell.

With the negative real interest rates we have today there is no such downside to owning gold and, given where real inflation is, nominal interest rates could increase by several percent before this was no longer a bullish argument for gold.

5. THE SUPPLY OF GOLD AND SILVER

We have, hopefully, established quite a strong case for the growth in demand for gold above. Let us now turn our attention to supply: Simply put, it is falling significantly. It is getting harder and harder to find and extract gold. Earlier in the book I highlighted the fact that finding one wedding ring's worth of gold involves mining no less than twenty tonnes of rock today.

The world's biggest mines in the world are seeing supply fall. The largest mines in the world in South Africa are finding it harder and harder to extract gold and their production is going backwards. To give you an idea of just how scarce gold is, a little known but interesting fact is that all the gold in the world ever mined could fit into two Olympic swimming pools.

There are strong arguments to suggest that there is likely to be much more demand for gold in the future. At the same time the supply picture for gold is far from rosy. As I have mentioned before, one of the fundamental truths of economics is that when demand of something is rising yet the supply of that something is fixed or falling, price has to rise.

6. THE SUPPLY OF PAPER MONEY

Finally, as mentioned already, there is one further factor to consider: The supply of paper money.

I hope you will forgive my repetition but we should by now be familiar with the fact that the supply of paper money all over the world is increasing at quite a clip. If there are three times the number of dollars in the world and the same amount of gold, then all other things being equal, the price of gold in dollars should be three times higher before you even begin to consider the demand and supply figures I outlined about gold itself above.

In actual fact, the dollar money supply has grown so much since it was last linked to gold in 1971 that the implied price of gold today should be many thousand dollars. I'm not saying the price will get there any time soon but it is an interesting ratio underscoring the potential in the long term. For those of you who would like more detail please check out the article in the footnote below[15] or this excellent

---

15 This is one of the best articles I have found on line summarizing this argument:
http://www.caseyresearch.com/editorial.php?page=articles/gold-still-answer-investors&ppref=DLC231ED1111A

video.[16]

Before we move on to the next section of this chapter I want to repeat the important point that pretty much everything we have said about gold is relevant to silver. Silver has traditionally played the same monetary role as gold and I see no reason why it will not continue to do so.

In fact the outlook for silver is arguably significantly more positive than for gold. There are a number of reasons for this: First, silver has significantly more industrial uses than gold and so there is more non-monetary demand for it. It is also worth noting that there is roughly sixteen times more silver in the world than gold. This implies, all other things being equal, that the long run price of silver should be roughly 1/16th of the price of gold. As such, with the gold price at $1600 at the time of writing, silver "should" be trading at about $100. The actual price today is about $30.[17]

TO CONCLUDE ON "OWNING INFLATION": WHAT YOU MIGHT BUY

We have outlined in some detail why we need to own inflation and I have explained how the best way to do this is to own precious metals. This is very easy and inexpensive to do. With the 20-30% of your monthly investment funds left after investing in the world as per the previous section, you simply need to buy some gold and silver.

For a UK investor, this is done very easily by buying the fund ETF Securities Physical Gold. The code on the London Stock Exchange is PHAU.L. If you wish to own silver as well, you can buy the fund ETF Securities Physical Silver, code: PHAG.L. Both of these will be available to buy in your ISA account, assuming you have the right one.

I provide more detailed information about these funds and funds that will help you to "own the world" on the website. It is worth noting that the fees you will pay to own all of these assets if you have an account with a good quality, low cost stockbroking firm will be tiny compared to the fees you would usually pay using financial advice from high street banks or the vast majority of IFAs.

A NOTE ON LUMP SUMS

One final thing to say is that if you already have a lump sum you would like to invest (a very good idea) and if you want to keep things very simple, then I suggest

---

16 http://theelevationgroup.net/gold-and-silver/click-here-to-see-whats-going-to-happen-to-the-price-of-gold-and-silver/

17 I would also repeat that many veteran commentators on the silver market are genuinely concerned it could entirely run out at the current rate of industrial consumption (by 2020). If this is even a vague possibly the price of silver will skyrocket very soon.

you simply divide that sum into twelve and pay 1/12th of it in to the above investments each month for the next year along with what you intend to save monthly. We already saw how investing every month like this achieves "averaging in" or "smoothing" hence why taking this approach is a good idea. This will reduce the risk that you invest a big lump of cash days before a market crash. Don't forget, however, that you should suffer far less from any kind of market crash than most given your geographical and asset diversification.

REBALANCING

A final consideration of the "keeping it simple" approach is an idea called "rebalancing". Imagine if you invested £3,000 in gold and silver at the beginning of a year and £6,000 in your chosen "own the world" fund (and kept another £1,000 in cash). This would imply that you had allocated 30% of your money to gold and silver, 60% to "owning the world" and 10% to cash.

Now imagine that, over the year, gold and silver go up by 20%, your world fund by 10% and cash by 0% (as interest rates are basically 0%). This would mean that one year later you would have £3,600 in gold and silver, £6,600 in your world fund and still £1,000 in cash. The crucial thing to understand here is that your percentage allocation to each asset will have changed slightly. You will now have £11,200 in total and it will be split: 32.1% gold and silver, 58.9% in your world fund and 9% in cash[18] compared to your target split of 30%, 60% and 10%.

Obviously the percentages have not changed by a huge amount but over time if you did nothing to deal with this situation you could end up with a split which is some way away from the 30/60/10 that you are looking for. The solution to this is what we call "rebalancing". Once a year or so, you would look at the proportion of assets you hold and sell the ones which have gone up most to buy the ones that have gone up less (or fallen). In the example above, if your target is 30/60/10 then this would imply you would like to own: £3,360 of gold and silver, £6,720 in your world fund and have £1,120 in cash. All you would need to do would be to sell £240 worth of gold and silver and put half of it into your world fund and keep half in cash.

This approach ensures that you stick to your target asset allocation but it also has the benefit that you automatically take some profit from your best performing assets and use that profit to buy other assets at a relatively cheaper level.

The more mathematically minded of you will have noticed that, if you are buying assets every month in the right proportions, the differences in percentage change at the end of the year are likely to be very small indeed, unless there have been

---

18 Gold and silver %age = 3,600/11,200 x 100. World fund %age = 6,600/11,200 x100 and cash = 1,000/11,200 x 100.

some very big moves in a short space of time.

You will not need to worry too much about rebalancing if you are following the methodology of monthly investment. Nevertheless, I would argue that you should just check your percentage allocation at least once a year to make sure things haven't moved too far away from your target. I tend to do my rebalancing on new year's day each year to punish myself for having a hangover. That is the only work you will need to do after you have set things up with this approach.

"PAST PERFORMANCE IS NOT INDICATIVE OF FUTURE RESULTS..."

Many of you will have seen this phrase in the literature of financial services companies. Depending on the type of firm you are dealing with or product you are considering, it is usually compulsory for it to appear.

I have serious misgivings about the usefulness of the statement. If past performance was no guide to future results how would we pick football teams, why would we choose a certain brand of car over another and why might we decide to vote a government out of office at election time?

The reality is that past performance can be indicative of future results. We do, however, need to be careful how heavily we rely on it and ensure that we use it as only one possible indicator of future performance amongst many. In my opinion, sound analysis of what is going on around us is generally more useful for predicting what might happen in the future than focussing overly on performance numbers. You will quite possibly be bored of me repeating the example of gold's fantastic performance over the last decade but let us use it once more to illustrate this point. It is certainly very interesting that gold has risen by a double digit amount every year over this period.

However, were central banks around the world to reverse their policy of inventing vast amounts of money every year, or if we developed a technology to easily extract gold from sea water, something certain scientists believe is a possibility, we would be sensible to revise our thoughts about where gold prices might go in future. If we had a fiscally prudent Federal Reserve Chairman along the lines of Paul Volcker who held that position in the early eighties and we saw US interest rates back at levels last seen back then, it would be very damaging to the gold price.

Given this backdrop, gold's performance over the last decade would become fundamentally irrelevant to its likely future performance. This is a very key point. Past performance is no doubt something we should be aware of and keep an eye on but I would contend that solid analysis and logic will trump it every time.

I would hope that after reading this far you would agree that the strategy we have outlined in this chapter is based on just such solid analysis and logic: We have seen a great deal of evidence to support the ideas of owning the world and owning inflation and we have seen how important it is to do this as effectively and cheaply as possible.

TO SUMMARISE...

If you remember the magic of compounding, you will hopefully see that if you pay as much money into these accounts as possible and leave that money there for as long as possible you will achieve the biggest result in terms of building your money. The more money you invest and the more you leave invested, the more "free" money you can generate from compounding (interest on your interest or return on your return).

You will have to make your own decisions about when and for what reason you withdraw money from your ISA account but the longer you can leave it before upgrading your car or taking that exotic holiday, the more cars and amazing holidays you will be able to buy in the not too distant future and the more comfortable your retirement will be in the long run. As Economists say: "Jam today or more jam tomorrow...".

As you might imagine, it is my firmly held opinion that if you use the logic outlined in this chapter you will have done an extremely good job of setting up your financial affairs, particularly for someone who doesn't want to invest any real time or effort.

As we have seen, this methodology means that:

- You are well diversified geographically and in terms of assets: You are invested in the world...
- You stand to benefit from the inflationary policies of central banks all over the world whilst everyone else sees their purchasing power gradually destroyed...
- You achieve this as cheaply and effectively as possible by leaving out expensive financial advisers, high cost products and poor quality investment accounts.

For those of you who you who want to get your house in order with as little effort as possible, to the best of my knowledge and ability, this is a superb approach to take. It will give you an excellent chance of making more money from your money than the very large majority of people. As we have seen it has worked for the likes of Harvard and Yale for decades.

In reasonably short order you should see a significant impact on your finances. Your money will start making you money. If you stick with the above plan over several years, your money will very possibly end up making you more than you can earn by working – our ultimate goal. By getting your financial affairs in order you give yourself the best chance of building a pot that could quite possibly make having a mortgage or any other kind of debt a thing of the past.

I can't say that this approach will always make money. You may well experience the odd down year as there is no certainty in investment. What I can say with a high degree of confidence is that it is highly likely that following this approach will grow your real wealth over time as demonstrated by the permanent portfolio table above. If the material you have read so far has succeeded in its job you will hopefully find the ideas sufficiently compelling to agree with this assessment.

A VERY IMPORTANT FINAL POINT

The above notwithstanding, I want to make a very important final point: Which is to say that although I am confident the approach outlined in this chapter is a very good one, there really is no substitute for taking a more proactive approach to looking after your money. Arguably this has never been truer than today.

There are some very serious and frankly rather frightening structural changes going on in the world today, not least the possibility of rampant real inflation. If you really don't have the inclination to spend a bit more time in your life learning about finance then please do implement the ideas in this chapter.

In order to give yourself the very best chance of surviving and thriving, however, I would strongly recommend that you take further steps to improve your understanding of finance. Once you open the Pandora's box of learning about money there is a good chance you might even find it fun or interesting at the very least.

Whatever happens you will certainly give yourself the best chance of spotting a big trend or change in the way the world economy is working and this will maximise your chances of avoiding being caught out in a crash on the one hand and in investing in the right places on the other. Taking responsibility for your own financial affairs will also save you a great deal of money in fees and costs, which can have a very significant impact on your finances as a whole, as we have seen.

The simplest way to start on this path is to ensure you subscribe to the Plain English Finance free email and to read the final chapter of this book. The email will ensure that you will be aware of any big change in the global financial picture that might alter the strategy outlined in this chapter and will serve as a regular reminder to keep on top of your investment situation. The final chapter of this book aims to point you in the right direction in terms of how you might most effectively go about improving your financial literacy and to give you some examples of what can be achieved and how to proceed.

So that is the Plain English Finance "keeping it simple" approach. Create some financial surplus as per chapter six, get your accounts set up as per chapter seven, invest as per the last two chapters and get going. For those of you who wanted to "keep things simple". That is it. I hope you have found what you have read so far to be compelling and I hope that you will take action to revolutionise your financial affairs. If you have any concerns or questions, please do not hesitate to get hold of me via the website: www.plainenglishfinance.com

If, as I hope, you are interested in "taking things further" and maximizing your chances of doing an even better job with your money longer term then please continue to the next chapter. It is well worth at least looking at the next chapter even if you see yourself as one of the "keeping it simple" crowd...

#12

TAKING THINGS FURTHER...

"...how you go about investing is vastly more important than which stocks you buy..."

– Porter Stansberry, founder of one of America's best investment advisory companies, Stansberry & Associates.

In the previous chapter we looked at how you might invest successfully, using what we've looked at so far but without having to do any more learning about finance or ongoing work.

It is my belief that the investment method outlined in that chapter is a great approach if you fall into this category and would rather not spend a significant amount more time learning about money and finance. It will ensure you pay low fees, end up with an excellent spread of assets and have a high chance of making consistent returns. This can yield wonderful results in the long run thanks to the power of compounding. I would hope that those of you who have read this far have found the arguments logical, backed by evidence and compelling as a result.

Given how dynamic the financial world is today and given how big a subject investment is, however, I believe it is worth taking a more proactive approach to looking after your money, particularly if you have a reasonable sum to invest. Learning more about finance and investment will mean that you raise your chances of growing your money more quickly whilst simultaneously increasing your confidence that you can do so as safely as possible.

Given what a huge subject finance is and how it is constantly changing, this chapter is absolutely not intended to be a comprehensive guide to everything you need to know in order to become a successful investor. Such a chapter would have to run to thousands of pages and would need updating weekly, possibly even daily.

What I do hope to achieve in this chapter, is:

1. ...highlight some of the key concepts you will want to understand to get up to speed on finance...
2. ...point you in the direction of some top quality resources which will help you get to grips with these concepts...
3. ...give you some examples of what can be achieved if you do...

Once you have finished this chapter you should be able to start on the road to knowing how to do three important things:

1. MAKE DECISIONS ABOUT ASSET ALLOCATION

Throughout the book and particularly in the last chapter we have established how important it is to invest in a wide variety of assets. We then looked at a largely formulaic way of achieving this. If you are prepared to get to grips with various aspects of finance, some of which we will look at in this chapter, you will get to the stage where you can finesse your asset allocation to take advantage of phases where one asset is performing more strongly than the others.

Armed with a reasonable knowledge of basic financial analysis, economics and economic history, you are capable of making big picture decisions about when certain assets are more likely to perform better than others. As an example, anyone with a good grasp of relative value between the various asset classes might have decided to be heavily weighted towards the precious metals from 1971 until about 1980, towards equities from the early 1980s until about 2000 and then back to precious metals at that point until today. This approach would have resulted in very high returns indeed for no less than forty years.

Many people will read the above and argue that making these calls successfully is impossible. This is certainly a fashionable view in the finance industry. That is to say that "hindsight is 20:20" but it is unrealistic to think that anyone can time markets as successfully as in my example above.

I politely disagree. As I have said several times before, you will never be able to make these sorts of calls with perfect timing but without question there are ways of comparing the main asset classes to each other which highlight times when one or other of them is more likely to be good value. We have already seen some of these methods, for example in the section on gold from the last chapter when we compared the gold price to the price of oil and the level of the stock market. I would repeat that one of the reasons relatively few people succeed in making these big picture asset allocation decisions is quite simply that relatively few people take the time to understand and look at all asset classes or even work out how to invest in them. I would argue that this is true for most private individuals and many professional investors.

That said, there are plenty of examples of professional investors who have made these calls over the years. Increasingly you are able to learn who these people are and follow their advice, often entirely free of charge.

OPTIMAL ASSET ALLOCATION ALSO CHANGES WITH YOUR AGE

The other thing to bear in mind here is that one of the universal rules of sensible investment is that you should become more conservative with your investments the closer you get to retirement. When you are young, you can afford to be a bit racier in a bid to grow your money as much as possible. At the most basic level, this implies owning more shares and less bonds, all other things being equal. As you get older, however, you should be thinking more about the return *of* your money than the return *on* your money.

There would be nothing more tragic than having a nasty negative year in your late fifties, for example and giving up a large amount of the pot you have worked so hard to build. Having a down year in your twenties or thirties will mean you lose less money in total (given your pot is smaller at that point) and have more time to make it back. Generally this means that as you approach retirement you ensure that you keep more of your money in bonds and cash and less in shares.

As you gain a deeper understanding of these things, you will be able to make your own decisions about how to allocate your money to shares, bonds, commodities, cash and real estate as you get older. This is not easy by any means but the more you learn, the better chance you will have of getting it broadly right over the years and this will have a very positive impact on your ability to make great returns whilst minimising your risk.

2. START THINKING ABOUT INVESTING IN INDIVIDUAL ASSETS

Once you have learned a bit more about finance you might also consider investing in individual assets yourself (rather than just funds as discussed in the last chapter). For example, armed with the knowledge that follows, you might soon feel confident enough to choose an individual share or commodity that you think has a particularly bright future.

I have owned a fair few things over the years which have gone up 100% or more. As I have already written, last year I made over 160% profit in just over eight months in silver and sold a share that was up 350% in about 18 months. (Sadly this share is now up 675% from my purchase price. I sold it early because I wanted the funds at the time. No point in crying over spilt milk).

Obviously, these sorts of gains don't happen all the time and there are always losers to contend with but, as you can imagine, you don't need too many successes like these over the years to have a significant positive impact on growing your pot to the target lifestyle we discussed in chapter ten.

You are unlikely to experience these sorts of returns owning a basket of funds as suggested in the "keeping things simple" section. Finding and investing in big winners and avoiding losers requires more knowledge than you learnt in the last chapter but it is still not that difficult to get a point where you can start to have a go at this if you are prepared to learn a little and ensure you are using the right resources.

3. START THINKING ABOUT LEARNING HOW TO "TRADE"

Once you have had a look at the material that follows, you will be more likely to start "trading". That is to say, you will consider making more regular purchases and sales of financial assets and holding them for a shorter period of time than if you were following the method I suggest in the previous chapter. If you manage to do this successfully it can have a significant positive impact on your returns as we shall see.

If you can use certain techniques to improve your chances of buying the right assets at the right time and to buy low and sell high, you stand to make significant returns. This isn't easy but, as we have already seen earlier in the book there are methods of investing which achieve consistent returns, particularly if you understand certain valuation metrics and are willing to think globally and about a diverse range of assets.

One thing worth bearing in mind when thinking about becoming more of a "trader" rather than an "investor" is that, in my opinion, you should only use part of your capital to do so. This is related to the point about asset allocation above. Even if you have a reasonable amount of money to look after and feel confident that you have learnt a good deal about exciting trading strategies, I would suggest you continue to keep a large portion of it in more conservative, longer term investments. Another tragic scenario in investment, which too many people fall foul of, is to decide to use more aggressive short term trading strategies that you are excited about with all of your investment capital.

It is perhaps helpful to think of "trading capital" as another one of the fundamental components of your asset allocation strategy. That is to say that even if you think you've become quite good at short term trading you might allocate your money something like:

- 40% longer term investments in shares and share funds.
- 25% in precious metals and other commodities.
- 10% in bonds.
- 10% in real estate.
- 15% to "wing around" trading more risky assets (perhaps foreign exchange or very small, higher risk shares or in a spread betting account).

To continue the example: As a UK resident you can use a spread betting account to have lots of fun with trading. You might, therefore, allocate the "wing around" 15% of your capital to a spread betting account. A small minority of people who become good at this after putting in the work can make extraordinary returns with spread betting. My point is that, arguably, even those people should still only use about 15% of their overall pot for that purpose. Any profits they make might then be used to buy more of the other four asset classes listed above. This is far safer than using 100% of your capital to spread bet.

A FINAL POINT ON "TAKING THINGS FURTHER"

Before we move on, I want to make a key point about what follows in this chapter: There is a chance that as you read it for the first time, much of the information and terminology will seem alien and quite possibly rather daunting and complicated as a result. To a certain extent the ideas in this chapter are rather complicated. Getting up to speed on finance in any detail is no walk in the park. I stand by the statement I made at the beginning of the book, that you would be able to make a great positive difference to your finances in less than the time it took you to learn how to drive because I believe reading chapters one to eleven and setting your affairs up as recommend qualifies as taking less time than learning to drive.

The journey to true financial literacy advocated by this chapter, however, is a longer road to travel but one I hope you are prepared to at least consider. You may find some of the sections to be rather complicated to begin with but I would hope that if you are willing to persevere and, most particularly, to start to immerse yourself in the resources suggested, you will find you start to get these concepts reasonably soon. I repeat that the benefits of doing so are truly life changing. It is also worth mentioning that the website www.plainenglishfinance.com will help you on this journey in the months and years ahead.

So now let us turn our attention to the basic ideas and resources which will help you to achieve the three goals above...

FOUR KEY CONCEPTS FOR INVESTMENT SUCCESS

It is my belief that there are four key concepts which you need to think about for consistent investment success:

1. You will want to understand a little about human psychology as it relates to investment decisions…
2. You must be able to perform basic "top down" analysis: That is to say, work out big themes which help you to asset allocate most effectively. (To to this requires a basic grasp of current affairs, economics and economic history)...
3. You will want to be able to perform basic "bottom up" analysis to chose specific assets and make sure you buy them at the right price. (To do this you will need to gain a basic understanding of both fundamental and technical analysis)...

4. You will want to arrange your financial affairs with various third parties so that:
- ...you are able to invest cheaply in all the main asset classes...
- ...you receive a constant stream of possible investment ideas...

If you can get moderately up to speed on these four things you have a very good chance of making returns in advance of many professional investors and of what many people think is possible.

I would argue that relatively few people are up to speed on all four of these, including many finance professionals for the sorts of reasons we discussed in chapter two. Largely as a function of human nature, many professional and private investors fall down on one or more of these ways of thinking about investment.

It is a relatively rare person who thinks explicitly about human psychology, has a basic grasp of economics and economic history, follows current affairs, respects and has at least a basic understanding of both fundamental and technical analysis and, in addition, knows how to arrange their affairs to be able to invest in all major asset classes in a cost effective fashion. If you really want to "take things further" you should aim to become one of them.

Getting up to speed on these key concepts may seem like a tall order. You might have read the above and thought that you are not even familiar with what some of it means. Nevertheless, it is not as out of reach as you might think. If you are willing to make the effort to focus your attention on the most important information you can give yourself a good chance of being in a small minority of investors in the world who have taken account of all four of the above key concepts and given themselves the best chance of making money on their money as a result.

So let us deal with each of these concepts and the resources you might consider to get you up to speed on them...

KEY CONCEPT ONE: THE IMPORTANCE OF HUMAN PSYCHOLOGY

It is probably quite obvious that human psychology has a significant role to play in investment success. It is therefore quite surprising how few investors think about it explicitly or spend much time learning about it.

"Behavioural finance" is an area of study within economics and finance which attempts to factor fundamental traits of human psychology into assumptions about how we make investment decisions. Many of these traits are not immediately obvious, in fact quite a few of them are counter intuitive. This is why many people are often entirely unaware that they are falling foul of one or other of them when they make poor investment decisions.

The Chartered Institute for Securities and Investment (CISI) work book for the "Principles of Investment Risk and Return" examination has a section on behavioural finance in which it describes no less than forty six psychological biases or theories that can negatively affect our ability to make sensible investment decisions.

We have already talked about three of these before, for example in the section on property in chapter six: Money illusion, anchoring and the endowment effect. As a quick reminder: Money illusion refers to our tendency to ignore inflation when assessing the value of something. Anchoring concerns how people are inclined to give too much weight to their recent experience and ignore what happens in the long term and the endowment effect is where individuals demand more to sell something than they would be willing to pay for it themselves and are unwilling to acknowledge their asset is worth less than it was previously. Just being aware of these three biases is a good start.

You will no doubt be relieved that it is not my intention to list and explain all forty six psychological biases here. This would take up a great deal of space and I don't believe you need to know about them all in detail. Two things are important, however:

1. That you understand and acknowledge that psychology has an impact on your ability to invest successfully.
2. That, as a result, you do take the time to read at least one of the three books I highlight at the end of this section: "Trade Your Way to Financial Freedom" by Dr. Van K. Tharp.

"Trade Your Way to Financial Freedom" should appear in any list of the best investment books of all time. One of the key reasons for this is the excellent job Dr. Tharp does explaining how crucial your psychology and beliefs about money are for financial success.

If you have the wrong attitude and beliefs about money you are unlikely to get ahead financially. This isn't new age psycho babble nonsense, it is just that if you believe "the stock market is a casino" or that "investment is very risky", you will never bother to take the time to learn what you need to learn. You will not equip yourself with the knowledge or a plan to get ahead and you will not save or invest any money. On the other hand, if you see the incredible things that are possible through investment you might take a different view and start learning, saving and investing.

"THE MAGIC OF BELIEVING"

Perhaps most important with respect to investing psychology is believing that it is possible to make significant returns on your money. Hopefully you remember my "sprinter" analogy from earlier in the book: When looking at stock market returns, too many people fixate on the returns made by the "average" fund or share or on the fact that a particular country index has gone sideways or down. The more you read about the world of investment, the more you realise that there are plenty of investors who consistently make high returns from whom you can learn, or with whom you can invest. As Dr. Tharp says:

"Financial freedom is really a new way to think about money... Financial freedom means that your money working for you makes more money than you need to meet your monthly expenses..."

If this sounds unrealistic to you then the first thing I would say is that there are thousands, if not hundreds of thousands of people in the world today for whom this is a reality. The only thing standing between you and joining that group of people are knowledge, belief, time and a little effort.

The title of the first section of "Trade Your Way to Financial Freedom..." is: "The Most Important Factor in Your Success: You!". We all have different personalities, different attitudes to risk, different work ethics, different commitments. It is important as you get to know more about investing that you choose strategies which fit you personally. This is another key reason why we must think about human psychology in order to achieve investment success.

A key consideration, for example, is how much time you have to devote to running your money. For most people, when you start on this journey you will have a full time job. It would be foolish for you to choose an approach to investment that required you to monitor share prices for most of the day. You would need to use an approach to growing your money which could yield decent results in a few minutes a day or an hour a week at the weekend perhaps.

A full discussion of how you might do this is beyond the scope of this book but you will start learning about these things when you immerse yourself in the resources I am about to recommend. For now, please just be aware of the fundamental point that we are making here: That psychology and attitude are key. If you believe that you can make good money from your money this is an important step on the way to true wealth (and / or an early retirement).

AN EXAMPLE OF WHAT IS POSSIBLE: CURTIS FAITH AND "THE TURTLES". LEARNING HOW TO BE AN AMAZING TRADER IN ONE WEEK...

In chapter four, we saw examples of some fantastic returns made by conventional professional investors with a reasonably conventional, long term approach to investing money. I thought it might be worth giving another example of what can be achieved by people with no previous knowledge of how to run money learning how to trade in a very short space of time.

Relatively few people are aware of some of the spectacular results achieved by completely inexperienced traders who are taught how to use a systematic approach to running their money. Many people have made huge amounts of money impressively quickly doing this. A great example I am aware of concerns a group of novice traders called "the turtles".

In 1983 two of Chicago's most famous traders made a bet with each other: Richard Dennis bet his friend William Eckhardt that he could show anyone how to be a successful trader in only two weeks. They were on holiday and, rather randomly, happened to be visiting a turtle farm in Singapore. Dennis was convinced he could "raise traders like the farm raised turtles", hence the rather strange name they gave the group. For what it is worth, this bet is rumoured to have been part of the inspiration behind the Eddie Murphy and Dan Ackroyd film "Trading Places".

On returning from their holiday, Dennis and Eckhardt put an advert in the paper inviting people to apply to be taught about trading. Within a few weeks they had chosen a small group of individuals with no previous trading experience. They taught the first group about basic technical analysis and human psychology for two weeks and taught a second group the same lessons in one week after honing their message.

What then happened is legendary in trading circles: "Over the next five years the Turtles each earned an average return of over 80% per year..." The best performing member of the group, Curtis Faith, who was 19 years old when he started as a "turtle", made over 100% per year...

As a result, Mr. Faith turned $2 million into $31 million in just over four years... (remember at 100%, $2m becomes $4m, then $8m, then $16m, then $32m)... How they did it is detailed in his excellent book: "The Way of the Turtle".

We are already aware that there are plenty of investment professionals who have made consistently good returns over a large number of years. The point I am making here is that there are also people making spectacular returns after a relatively short period of learning about money. One of the most important things these people have in common is their attitude and belief.

As I have already said, rather than obsessing over the statistical "fact" that it is very difficult to make high returns on your money it would seem to me that a more enlightened and fruitful approach would be to seek out individuals that have made high returns and study them and the techniques that made them successful. The following resources will put you squarely on that path:

ACTION POINTS AND RESOURCES YOU MIGHT CONSIDER FOR KEY CONCEPT ONE:[1]

Here are some of the resources you might consider looking at to help you really understand the first of our key concepts:

If you take only one action…

> …*take the time to read "Trade Your Way to Financial Freedom".*

Even better, find a little more time and read the other three fantastic books listed below. I would highly recommend that you do take the time to read them. Remember, there is no hurry, everything you read will add to your financial skills.

"RICH DAD, POOR DAD: WHAT THE RICH TEACH THEIR KIDS ABOUT MONEY THAT THE POOR AND THE MIDDLE CLASS DO NOT" BY ROBERT KYOSAKI.

This book is not specifically about investment or trading. It is a more general book about personal finance. A key message in the book is that "…the poor and the middle class work for money… the rich have money work for them." This is clearly one of the fundamental ideas behind Plain English Finance. Another point the book makes is how poorly education systems around the world prepare people to look after their personal financial situation. You will know by now that this is a view I share very strongly. This book has changed the lives of a vast number of people since it was first published and is one of the best selling books on general finance ever written.

"THINK AND GROW RICH" BY NAPOLEON HILL.

In this section we have seen how important your attitude to money is. People who believe that money is scarce and hard to come by are the least likely to succeed in getting hold of any. Those who believe that it is within their power to become wealthy vastly increase their chances of this coming true. Napoleon Hill's classic book on this very subject was originally published in the 1930s and has changed the lives of millions of people ever since. A quick glance at the Amazon reviews will show you that this book has the power to improve more than just your financial

1 Remember you can find details of the resources suggested in this chapter and links to them at: www.plainenglishfinance.com/resources

situation. This book is absolutely first class and required reading in my opinion.

"WAY OF THE TURTLE: THE SECRET METHODS THAT TURNED ORDINARY PEOPLE INTO LEGENDARY TRADERS" BY CURTIS FAITH.

I have already outlined what this book is about. It is a fascinating study in what is possible. I confess there are some slightly dry sections on specific trading methodology which some people might find a bit off-putting, hence why I have listed it at the bottom of the books you might consider from this section.

So that is human psychology and your attitude to money taken care of, now let's carry on to the next section and have a look at how to get up to speed on top down analysis by looking at how you might improve your understanding of current affairs, economics and economic history...

KEY CONCEPT TWO: USING "TOP DOWN" ANALYSIS TO FIND THEMES...

As I suggested in the introduction to this section of the book, once you have a reasonable sum saved, you might think about using a proportion of it more proactively. To do this, you will need to come up with ideas about what to do with that proportion of your money.

The first "filter" for finding these ideas, might be described as "top down" analysis. This is where you use your knowledge of current affairs, economics and things financial to come up with fundamental themes that, for logical reasons, are likely to be a good place to put your money to work.

We have already looked at two such investment themes in this book: That the world as a whole continues to grow and that inflation is higher than many people realise. Once you start to look at the world with your "investor's" hat on, you will, I hope, start to recognise other similar themes. Here are a couple of quick examples:

EXAMPLE ONE: GROWTH IN THE DEVELOPING WORLD

We have already established that the world's population is growing significantly. At the moment, there are about 200,000 people being added per day to the global population. At the same time, the standard of living in many countries in the world is improving such that hundreds of millions of people in countries like India, China, Brazil or Turkey can now aspire to a "middle class" lifestyle in a way their parents' generation never could.

This has given us our "big picture" idea to "own the world" but if we think in more detail about the implications of this reality we should be able to identify more specific investment themes. For example, the fact there are millions of new mouths to feed in the developing world should be very positive for agriculture as a whole. It will also no doubt be positive for the energy sector and for any company involved in construction in these high growth economies. Another correlated theme would be the improvement in water or telecom infrastructure required. In fact, if you stop to think about it, you would most likely be able to brainstorm any number of investment themes which stand to benefit from global growth.

EXAMPLE TWO: AN AGING DEMOGRAPHIC IN THE OLD WORLD

At the same time that populations are growing and becoming wealthier in most of the developing world, they are doing something rather different in most of the developed world: Specifically much of the population in the developed world is aging. In Japan and Europe in particular, an increasing proportion of the population is approaching and passing retirement age. Again, a moment's reflection on this reality should yield some logical conclusions about the sort of investments which will benefit: We might conclude that any companies making products for or providing services to the elderly are likely to see the demand for those products and services increase.

As a result, they are likely to enjoy less of an uphill battle to grow their sales and profits than companies in other sectors. You probably don't need me to tell you that these might include companies in the healthcare space: Companies that make drugs or medical devices such as pharmaceutical and biotech firms or who build or service nursing homes for example.

These are only two themes. I would hope that both of them seem entirely logical to you and, moreover, that you can see how starting to think like this can yield quite obvious places to go looking for superior investment returns. Once you start to think like an investor you will get an intuitive feel for things you believe might give you the best chance of making superior returns on your money.

YOUR VERY OWN THEME DRIVEN INVESTMENT SHOPPING LIST

Each time you think of something which seems like a good idea, I suggest you write it down and start to build a shopping list of things that you would like to invest in, all other things being equal. This is a great place to start. Given my own "top down" analysis of what is going on in the world at the moment, my personal top ten at the time of writing might look something like this:

1. Precious metals and precious metal mining funds / companies.

2. Oil / energy / oil services funds / companies.
3. Healthcare, pharmaceutical and biotechnology funds / companies.
4. Emerging market infrastructure: Water, railways, automotive, agriculture.
5. Potentially explosive frontier markets: Zimbabwe, Mongolia, Burma, others?
6. Rich country funds (bonds and shares): Singapore, Qatar, Norway, Canada, Australia.
7. The world's best technology companies: Microsoft, Oracle, Intel, Apple.
8. The world's best consumer goods companies: P&G, Unilever etc.
9. The world's best tobacco, gambling and brewing companies ("sin" investing).
10. Clean energy / new energy technologies that don't require government subsidy. Uranium, thorium, rare earths etc.

To be honest, the list of themes that I am keeping an eye on is substantially longer than this as I am constantly getting excited about all sorts of things but hopefully you can see how helpful it is to start drilling down from the hundreds of thousands of things you might invest in to ones which are likely to enjoy a fair wind for structural reasons. Dare I confess that I think it is also actually very good fun working out how to make money from the news?

THE "TOO HARD BUCKET"
For what it is worth, in the process of thinking about investable themes I will often save myself a great deal of time and effort by completely discarding themes which I would describe as being in what I call the "too hard bucket". There are many areas of investment where I believe the individual investment vehicles are just too complicated to analyse with consistent success.

Two examples of this, as far as I am concerned personally, are financial services companies, particularly big banking groups and any company that relies to a great extent on big, lumpy government contracts, a good example of which would be defence companies.

It is entirely possible to make a great deal of money investing in banks if you are very clever and have a deep knowledge of a large number of complex investment ratios but for the average investor, banks are just too complicated. An important thing to bear in mind about investment generally is that you should limit the number of things you invest in, I would argue to less than about twenty to thirty assets in total. This sort of number gives you the advantages of diversification and the ability to keep on top of them all. If you own much more than this, things become rather too complicated.

Given there are so many things you are able to invest in (if you have your accounts with the right provider), there really is no great loss in deciding to ignore anything that you feel is too complicated. There will always be plenty of options left for you to succeed with.

For this reason, I am very quick to put any area of investment that I consider too much work to keep on top of in the "too hard bucket". The downside is that you might miss out on spectacular growth in a sector from time to time but I think this is a small price to pay to avoid the enormous headache of trying to follow a fundamentally complicated and opaque industry sector like banks or defence companies. Never be afraid to put things in the "too hard bucket" and move on to something that is simpler to understand.

TO CONCLUDE

Building your list of investable themes is your crucial first step. The next and more important step is to work out the specific investment vehicles (funds, shares etc.) to own within those themes to give you exposure to them. You will also want to do your best to buy those specific vehicles at the right price – i.e. a price which gives you the best chance of investment success in the years ahead.

This is where our third key concept comes in: "Bottom Up Analysis" of which the two main types are fundamental and technical analysis. We will look at the basics of these in the next section. Before we move on, however, let us look at some resources that will help you get a handle on our second key concept as quickly as possible: I recommend the following three action points and resources in order of importance...

RESOURCES YOU MIGHT CONSIDER FOR KEY CONCEPT TWO:[2]

1. SUBSCRIBE TO MONEYWEEK MAGAZINE AND READ IT AS OFTEN AS POSSIBLE.
...If you take only ONE action after reading this book I would recommend subscribing to this magazine and getting into the habit of reading it...

It is my heartfelt belief that if you live in the UK, the single best financial publication you should ensure you subscribe to and read as often as possible is MoneyWeek Magazine. This is most likely the best investment in your financial future you can make. By doing so you will ensure that you enjoy a constant stream of well thought out investment themes as well as specific investment vehicles such as individual funds and shares.

It is a great read, they have a brilliant editorial team and have been producing common sense and making me money for many years. If you do subscribe, you will find the magazine in your letter box every Friday. I tend to spend about twenty minutes every Saturday morning reading it over breakfast. I think you

2 As before please see www.plainenglishfinance.com/resources

will be surprised at what an easy read it is. It even has sections on wine, cars and property to lighten the tone. I can't recommend it highly enough. If you would like to take advantage of their standard offer of three free issues then please use the link in the resources section of www.plainenglishfinance.com.

2. SUBSCRIBE TO THE FOLLOWING FREE EMAIL SERVICES:

One of the best things about investment today is how much excellent information you can get entirely free of charge. All you need is an internet connection and an email address. I personally subscribe to dozens of free and paid email services and get as many as thirty such emails a day, many of which I read and all of which I skim. I do not for a minute suggest you do the same. I am obviously extremely interested in the subject. You also don't need to subscribe to all the services I do because I will highlight the most important things you need to be aware of every now and then in my Plain English Finance email.

These then are the email services I suggest you subscribe to. Remember that it only takes a second to hit delete and you can always unsubscribe from these services if you no longer feel they are providing you with valuable information. As ever, there are links to these services on the website.

- www.plainenglishfinance.com – I hope you will forgive the self promotion but obviously I truly believe you should subscribe to my free email service. Unlike many of the other free services I suggest below, I will only send an update from time to time to remind you of all the excellent steps you can take to get your finances humming and to highlight anything I think is particularly interesting or important for you to be aware of. This is categorically not a daily email as I will only send you information when I think it is very important. It is perhaps worth noting that Plain English Finance is fully regulated and authorised by the Financial Services Authority.

- MoneyMorning - This is MoneyWeek Magazine's free daily email and I think it is superb. You can subscribe on their website.

- Stansberry & Associates – This is a first class US based investment newsletter service. If you want to receive their research products you can pay hundreds or even thousands of pounds to do so but, fantastically, you can get very useful information from their free email services. Three of their best are: The S&A Digest, The Growth Stock Wire and Daily Wealth. You can subscribe to them all by emailing: customerservice@stansberryresearch.com, or by going via the link on the Plain English Finance website.

One thing to note is that these free email services will inevitably try to sell you their paid subscription products. Many people find this annoying. My view is that it is a small price to pay to receive such good free information. I would also point out that I have subscribed to a number of paid research services over the years and, without exception, they have paid for themselves many times over. The key is ensuring you subscribe to the good ones. This isn't that hard a task if you employ common sense and the knowledge you have gained from reading this book and others suggested here.

There are dozens of other excellent free email services, but I feel these three are a very good starting point and will provide you with plenty of extremely useful information entirely free of charge.

3. READ "THE ASCENT OF MONEY" BY NIALL FERGUSON (OR WATCH THE DVD OF THE TELEVISION SERIES).

Professor Ferguson was named one of the one hundred most influential people in the world by Time Magazine recently. This book is a superb summary of the history of money. It takes you all the way from ancient history to the financial crisis of the last few years. It is of practical importance for your development as an investor that you have a basic grasp of the history of money and the various financial products. This is the best book for this purpose that I have read to date. There is also an accompanying television series which you can buy on DVD which might be a more fun way of acquiring the relevant knowledge if you are not a big reader. Again, you can link directly through to the book and TV series from the Plain English Finance website.

Let's now move on to our next Key Concept: "Bottom Up" analysis and understanding fundamental and technical analysis:

KEY CONCEPT THREE: "BOTTOM UP" ANALYSIS. HOW TO USE BASIC FUNDAMENTAL AND TECHNICAL ANALYSIS TO CHOOSE THE RIGHT INVESTMENT VEHICLES AND MAXIMISE YOUR CHANCES OF BUYING LOW AND SELLING HIGH.

It is my hope that you will come up with some compelling investment themes relatively quickly once you start thinking like an investor and are plugged into the wealth of investment information we have looked at above. Now comes arguably the most important part: Working out the specific investment vehicles which will give you the best chance of benefitting from those themes. This is the hardest part but, I would argue, can actually be rather fun once you start to get into it.

Bottom up analysis will also help you to make your big asset allocation decisions since it is fundamental and technical analysis that will help you to work out which of the main asset classes are looking most interesting at any point in time.

AN EXAMPLE THEME: OIL

Once you have a theme, you are going to start to look for investment vehicles that give you exposure to that theme. Let's use oil as an example. You have decided that it is probably a good idea to have exposure to oil as the world population grows and becomes more industrialised, driving demand for energy and oil in particular.

You are now going to make a second list: A list of possible investments in the oil space. Off the top of your head, you have probably immediately thought of Shell and BP as *companies* that you might add to the list. You may also have realised that you are able to own oil itself, via an ETF for example.[3] A little bit more effort and you may come up with foreign oil firms such as Chevron in the US or Petrobras which is a Brazilian company but which trades on the US stock exchange, making it relatively easy to buy through your UK stockbroker (assuming, as ever, that you have the right sort of account).

If you are prepared to put in even more effort you might add oil service companies that are experts in drilling or prospecting for oil. There will also be ETFs of oil companies and ETFs of oil services companies – i.e. a fund where one investment will give you exposure to a basket of companies in the sector.

Although the above might sound quite daunting, if you are reading MoneyWeek and plugged into the kinds of free email services I have suggested above, you will learn more and more about companies from all sorts of industries as you go along. As ever, I would reiterate that there is no hurry here. Better to get it right than to rush into anything. Do not be afraid to take time building your shopping list of themes and companies.

Once you have a reasonable list of possible investments for each of your themes, it is time to think about which one, or possibly two investment vehicles you are going to use to put your money to work in that space. You will do this by subjecting each of the possible investments to some basic fundamental and technical analysis. It is to these ideas which we will now turn...

---

3 If you have forgotten what an ETF is then do please go and have a quick look at the section on funds in chapter eight.

FUNDAMENTAL ANALYSIS – STARTING WITH COMPANIES (SHARES)

Fundamental analysis is when you try to assess the inherent or fundamental value of an asset to work out whether it is cheap or expensive. We have already met certain types of fundamental analysis earlier in the book, when we looked at how to value property in chapter six, how to value shares in chapter eight and gold in chapter eleven.

As far as shares are concerned, we might think of fundamental analysis as quite simply listing all of the things that might affect the true value of a company by adding up all the positives (profits, cash, property, inventory etc.) and subtracting all the negatives (debt, salaries, all other costs etc.) to get to a number which is the value of the company. There are hundreds of thousands of people (accountants, stockbrokers, fund managers and financial analysts) all over the world doing this job every day with respect to hundreds of thousands of companies.

You might argue that working out the fundamental value of a company isn't actually that hard. It is what accountants do. At least once a year (although usually twice)[4] a company publishes a document called its Report and Accounts. This will contain almost exactly what I have described above, that is to say a calculation of the value of the company based on adding up all the positives (profits and assets) and subtracting all the negatives (liabilities).

So far, so simple. The complexity, which keeps so many thousands of people in gainful employment, broadly arises from three sources:

1. Debate about what the value of the company's assets is: How much is a certain factory, office building or brand worth, for example.
2. Expectations of what the value of profits and assets is going to do in the future. Financial analysts produce estimates for both of these.
3. Debate about what a sensible amount to pay for that value is. This is done by using a variety of valuation tools.

A very large proportion of the finance industry spends its day thinking about these three questions. We can perhaps illustrate this in further detail if we think about earnings per share again (remember we met this idea in chapter eight when we looked at shares. Do please go back and have a quick look if you have forgotten the term). What we are saying here is that accountants can give us this year's earnings number and asset value quite easily. The trick is to work out next year's earnings number and asset value as accurately as possible and then think about

---

4 Most companies issue an Annual Report once a year and an Interim Report half way through the year.

what you should "pay" for both numbers.

Different types of company have very different fundamental financial metrics. Some companies are capital intensive. This means that they need huge factories and tonnes of very expensive equipment to do what they do. Examples of these would include car (automotive), mining, oil, steel and pharmaceutical companies. Other companies, ones that deal with people and ideas for example, need hardly any equipment at all. These would include advertisers and other media firms, lawyers, bankers, software programmers and consultants.

Equally, some companies can grow their sales and profits very quickly, for example a company with a new technology that did not previously exist, such as Apple. A dozen years ago iPods, iPhones and iPads didn't even exist. Today a meaningful percentage of the world's population own these products. Apple shares have skyrocketed as a result as have shares in many of the companies that supply them with components for these products.

Other companies find themselves in a market that is dying, sometimes called an "ex growth" market. Good examples of these would be Eastman Kodak, the photography company, who recently filed for bankruptcy or HMV in the UK who have been suffering a fundamental decline in UK shoppers buying CDs and DVDs in the high street for some years and seen their share price hammered as a result. You might argue that foreseeing the problems faced by both of these companies wasn't really that difficult.

THE P/E RATIO AGAIN
Given these differences between companies, the fundamental value you might place on the profits and assets will therefore also be very different. If you remember the section on shares from chapter eight, you will hopefully remember the idea of a p/e ratio – the multiple of a company's profits that an investor is willing to pay to own that share. This is one of the most fundamental ways of assessing a company's value.

All other things being equal you might imagine that you would be willing to pay quite a high multiple of profits (a high p/e ratio) for a company growing very fast with no debt and no need to invest in huge factories and machines and a great deal less (a low p/e ratio) for a company with no growth and large debts. If you find a fast growing company with a great technology on a low p/e ratio, therefore, you will most likely have found a bargain!

The longer you look at investments, the more you will get an intuitive feel for what a company should trade at in terms of fundamental valuation metrics: A dairy company based in only one country and not growing at all should arguably trade on a p/e ratio of maybe only 5x and is likely to be expensive and liable to fall in value if it is trading at 10x, whereas a brilliant global software company with very high profit margins and massive growth potential might even be cheap on 25x earnings. That is to say that you might be willing to pay as much as five times the price, in terms of a multiple of profits, for a company that you think has five times (or more) the prospects of another company.

THE PEG RATIO

One of my favourite valuation tools in this respect is something called the PEG (Price / Earnings / Growth) ratio. It is worked out by dividing the p/e of a company by its estimated earnings growth. For example: If a company is trading on a p/e of 10x and growing its profits by 10% you would say it has a PEG ratio of 1x. If that company was trading on 20x earnings, the PEG would be 2x. Another company growing at 20% but trading on 10x p/e would have a PEG of 0.5x. Hopefully you can see that, all other things being equal, the lower the PEG the better as the number implies you are paying less to "own" more profit growth.

There are a large number of financial ratios and metrics to look at in fundamental analysis and they each have their benefits and drawbacks. PEG is just one example and no exception in terms of having benefits and drawbacks. The only reason I include it here is to show how these sorts of tools of fundamental analysis can be quite elegant and often really aren't that complicated. At the most basic level they enable you to "compare apples with apples" when you are trying to find the right company to invest in.

Let us now look at some of the most elementary valuation tools you will want to become aware of to give yourself a real head start in choosing a company to invest in.

USING BASIC VALUATION TOOLS

We have looked briefly at the p/e and PEG ratios and I have pointed out that there is a wealth of financial ratios used by financial analysts. That said, in my opinion, you can make a perfectly informed assessment of whether a company is cheap or expensive using relatively few of these valuation tools.

In chapter eight, as well as p/e, we looked briefly at earnings yield, dividend yield and book value. These are all reasonably simple things to understand and freely available on websites such as Yahoo or Google finance or from your stockbroker's website.

As such, once you have chosen a theme and made a list of companies you might consider to give you exposure to that theme, the next piece of the jigsaw puzzle would be to find out these numbers based on the company's current share price. Again, you can find these numbers on various free websites and you will see more specifically how to do this on the Plain English Finance website.

For each company, you might find the current year's p/e, PEG, dividend yield and price to book (book value per share) and, where possible, the same numbers for next year. Sometimes you will even be able to get numbers for the year after that but I wouldn't worry too much about those numbers; As you can imagine, forecasts of a company's numbers two years in the future can often be subject to significant revision unless the company has a particularly predictable business model.

PEER GROUP ANALYSIS / COMPARISON

Once you have these numbers you are able to perform a very useful and instructive simple analysis of which company might be the best in a given space (sector) by *comparing the numbers to each other*. This is called "peer group analysis". In chapter eight we looked at Sainsburys, Tesco and Morrisons. In our oil example we may simply want to decide whether to own Shell or BP (keeping things simple and putting dozens of other companies in our "too hard bucket").

All you need to do, then, is compare companies in the same space to see which one is the best value. To keep the example simple, if we know that Shell has more attractive financial ratios than BP, this might make us decide that the vehicle we want to own to make a solid long term investment in our "oil" theme is Shell.[5] Before you take the decision to pull the trigger and buy it, however, you will want to think about a couple of other things: You will want to see how Shell's metrics today compare to how they have been historically and you will want to think about where the stock market as a whole is at the moment.

HISTORICAL ANALYSIS

In our example so far you have established:

- That oil is probably a good theme over all.
- That Shell is probably a great company within that theme.
- That it currently has more attractive valuation metrics than its main rival, BP.

This is all useful stuff and moves us closer to our goal of actually pulling the trigger and buying some shares in Shell. An additional factor to consider, however, is how Shell's current valuation metrics compare to those same metrics in the past. Shell might look more attractive than BP at the moment but what if it is the most expensive it has ever been in the last twenty years? For example, what if the p/e

---

5 Again, you will learn more about how to evaluate these financial ratios on the website and from the resources I recommend in this chapter.

ratio of Shell going back twenty years has ranged from 5x next year's earnings to 25x next year's earnings and it is now trading at 24.5x?

What if Shell's dividend yield has been as low as 1.5% and as high as 6.5% and it is currently 2%? This type of approach is known as historical analysis as you might imagine. Hopefully it is not a complicated idea to suggest that your best chance of buying Shell at the right share price for a long term investment will be when the valuation metrics are historically attractive as well as being attractive compared to their peer group. If Shell shares are the most expensive they have been for twenty years then, all other things being equal, it may not be a good time to buy the shares.

That said, this might not be true if there is a compelling reason for Shell shares to trade very expensively. To give a slightly silly but potentially instructive example: Imagine if Shell's scientists were to announce that they have just developed a technology which can turn lead into gold. In this instance, you would be forgiven for arguing that the shares now deserve to trade on a higher p/e ratio than in the past. In fact, solving the age-old alchemists problem would mean that Shell shares should, in theory, suddenly skyrocket and trade on a p/e ratio far higher than ever before when they were just a boring old oil company.

It is obviously unlikely that Shell will ever solve the problem of turning lead into gold but you can of course see that they might announce a huge new oil or gas discovery either of which would justify their p/e ratio being higher than other peers who have not made such a discovery and higher than it was in the past before they made the discovery. You will want to be aware of these sorts of qualitative differences between companies as well as their financial ratios alone.

MARKET AND SECTOR VALUATION

Another consideration we might make before pulling the trigger and actually buying some shares is to think about the valuation of the oil sector at the moment and the stock market as a whole. As I have said earlier in the book, it is possible to find valuation metrics such as the p/e ratio or dividend yield for the market as a whole (in this instance we would use the FTSE 100 or S&P 500 p/e ratio) and for the sector (it is also possible to find financial ratios for the oil sector as a whole).

A final check we might make before deciding to build a position in Shell would be to see if the market and sector are cheap or expensive historically. This is because share prices are correlated to the value of their sector and the market as a whole. Even though our analysis so far might suggest that it is a good time to buy Shell: Oil is a great theme, it is good value compared to other oil companies and it is good value historically, we might want to be a little bit careful of what the oil sector and the market as a whole is doing.

If the FTSE 100 and S&P 500 are up 20% in the last two months or so, there is a chance that the market might fall back. When the market falls back, it takes share prices down with it. To be honest, this is probably the least important analysis we need to perform when thinking about making a long term investment in a good quality company. If a company is looking like it is fundamentally good value today for all the reasons we have already discussed, it is likely that it will be a good investment over the long term. Nevertheless, it is arguably worth just doing a quick sense check to make sure you are not buying in when shares as a whole are extremely expensive. If the market or the sector is up 20% in the last few weeks and your analysis tells you that this might correct, then you might hesitate to buy any stocks until it has.

FUNDAMENTAL ANALYSIS FOR THE OTHER ASSET CLASSES

We have just had a very quick look at the idea of using fundamental analysis to find a good quality company. It may be obvious to you that the metrics we used to look at a company share can't be applied to the other asset classes. Bonds, property and commodities have their own distinct characteristics and we must evaluate them in a different way as a result. As such, it is worth saying a little bit about how we might perform a fundamental analysis of each of the other asset classes.

BONDS

We looked at the basics of what a bond is in chapter eight. A bond does not have a p/e ratio or book value.

What a bond does have, however, are two fundamentally important metrics: Its yield and its credit quality. The yield is simply the annual return implied by the bond's price – something we looked at in chapter eight. The credit quality of a bond is a somewhat subjective assessment of the quality of the bond made by financial analysts who work at what is called a rating agency. The three most famous of these are Moody's, S&P and Fitch.

All these companies do is evaluate the financial strength of the company or government which has issued the bond. Once they have done this, they publish a rating which tells bond investors the quality of the bond. Each of the agencies has their own rating scale. You may have heard a bond described in the press as "triple A" (AAA), or read that a certain government's bonds are no longer rated "triple A". This is the top rating on the rating scale. Each of the rating agencies has its own distinct rating system and you don't really need to know any more than that.

The yield is simply the percentage return of the bond implied by its current price. Again, we looked at this concept in chapter eight. At the very basic level, bond investors will generally be looking to achieve the highest yield for any given credit rating. If you were to compare two triple A-rated bonds and find that one was yielding 2% and the other 2.2%, all other things being equal you would want to own the second one with the higher yield. In fairness this is a highly simplistic analysis as there is a wide degree of differentiation even between bonds of the same rating. It is these differences that professional bond investors are looking to exploit.

The most important point I would like to make about bonds is that, more than any other main asset class, I believe they are the hardest for the amateur investor to understand and analyse. What I have written above and in chapter eight is only designed to give you a very basic idea of what they are about, if only so you can understand their terminology a little when you read about them.

I feel strongly that any bond exposure you have in your portfolio should be via bond funds. Direct investment in individual bonds is generally only possible with large sums of money as most of these products have reasonably large minimum investments and many are also only available to professional investors. There are exceptions, particularly for US-based private investors but I still feel that bond analysis is too complex for the great majority of people. It is only worth learning about bond investment in great detail if you have a relatively large amount of money to put to work. For everyone else, I would suggest that whatever bond exposure you have from "owning the world" will be perfectly sufficient.

PROPERTY

We looked in some detail at various ways of valuing property in chapter six. As a reminder, we can think about a property's total return as a function of the assumed net rental yield (after costs, void periods et al.) plus any assumption you might make for capital growth. This percentage return number can then be compared to return numbers for other asset classes: The interest rate on a current account, the dividend yield (plus expected capital gain) of a share or the yield on a bond for example.

We also looked at the idea of house prices as a multiple of people's salaries. I like to think of this as the "p/e ratio" of the property market. In the same way that a p/e of 5x tells us a share is cheaper than a p/e of 10x (at a very basic level), if house prices are currently 6x people's salary on average, we know they are more expensive than when they are 3x salary. This is useful information for making big decisions about when property is cheap or expensive versus the other asset classes (again, at a reasonably basic level: We will still want to account for plenty of other metrics such as demand and supply and the conditions of any local market but it is useful nevertheless).

COMMODITIES

Just as with bonds and property, we cannot conduct fundamental analysis on commodities using the tools we might use on a share. Gold, oil, wheat, timber and uranium do not produce quarterly earnings numbers or see their price fall when a Chief Executive has to resign in disgrace.

Fundamental analysis of commodity markets is still possible however and there are plenty of individuals and institutions all over the world who spend their time on it. At the simplest level, fundamental analysis of commodities involves tracking data on their demand and supply. For metals, analysts all over the world try to assess what mine production is doing, what is happening to inventory levels at various points in the supply chain and make estimates about which direction end-demand is going. We have already seen examples of this kind of analysis earlier in the book when, for example, we talked about how a slow down in the Chinese economy will have a significant effect on the demand for a raft of commodities such as copper, iron ore or coal.

When it comes to the "soft" (agricultural) commodities, a similar analysis is made, this time the factors would include what is happening to the total amount of the crop being planted globally and what has happened to the harvest in various parts of the world as a result of the weather, for example.

As with bonds, I would argue that it is reasonably hard for the amateur investor to become proficient at the fundamental analysis of commodities. Again, as with bonds, this need not necessarily be a problem. First, we have already seen how you will gain sufficient commodity exposure from owning the world and owning inflation as described in chapter eleven. Secondly, if you do decide you want to get more heavily involved in commodities you will be able to get a wealth of free advice on them from the resources I have suggested in this chapter. Finally, I would argue that commodities lend themselves to technical analysis more than many of the other asset classes, particularly the bigger more liquid ones such as oil or precious metals.

If you are willing to invest a little time in learning about technical analysis, you can start to make a nice return trading the bigger commodities in reasonably short order. We will look at this in more detail in the next section.

A NOTE ON FOREIGN EXCHANGE (FOREX / FX)

There is a large degree of overlap between the FX market and the bond market in terms of fundamental analysis. This is because interest rates (bond yields) and the financial strength of a country are two of the most important factors in the performance of its currency.

As with bonds and commodities, I would stress that the fundamental analysis of foreign exchange is rather specialist and not something the private investor can learn overnight. As before, you will have natural exposure to a wide range of currencies by virtue of owning assets from all over the world and I would suggest that this is sufficient to give you the asset diversification into foreign exchange that you need.

That said, just as with commodities above, if you have got to the point where you have a reasonably large amount of money and are interested in using some of it to trade more aggressively, there are great returns to be made in foreign exchange, particularly for the UK based investor who is able to use a spread betting account. Just as with commodities, FOREX also lends itself to technical analysis which we will look at below...

ACTION POINTS AND RESOURCES FOR FUNDAMENTAL ANALYSIS

As ever, there are literally thousands of books you could read to learn about fundamental analysis. To really get to grips with the subject you should probably read a few of them but it is my belief that you will get a pretty good idea about things and most likely get quite inspired about investment generally if you read just this one, at least just to get you started:

"ONE UP ON WALL STREET" BY PETER LYNCH

Mr. Lynch is one of the most famous American investors of all time. He made just short of 30% a year for thirteen years running Fidelity's Magellan fund and he appears at number six in the table in chapter four where we looked at some top performing fund managers. This book shows you how, with a little bit of knowledge, you can have a very good chance of making a better return on your money than many professional investors and I can highly recommend it as a result.

MONEYWEEK MAGAZINE AGAIN

If you subscribe to MoneyWeek you will begin to get a feel for how fundamental analysis works as there are weekly columns teaching you about these things. There are also very good video tutorials on the MoneyWeek website.

There are plenty of other books which will help you to learn more about fundamental analysis in the bibliography and in the resources section of the website. Now let us turn our attention to technical analysis...

TECHNICAL ANALYSIS

Wikipedia defines technical analysis in the following way:

"Technical analysis is a financial term used to denote a security analysis discipline for forecasting the direction of prices through the study of past market data, primarily price and volume..."

To put this in Plain English: Over a long period of time academics looking at financial markets worked out a number of methods for predicting where prices in a market would go based on where they had come from.

This may seem quite crazy intuitively but it isn't when you think a little about human nature: If a share or market has been going up steadily then, all other things being equal, there is a good chance it will continue to do so, if only because of the herd mentality of the investment community. Technical analysis tries to generate rules along these lines which help the investor buy and sell with a high probability of success.

The discipline has been developing for several decades and there are now a bewildering array of techniques and theories available to the investment community with scary names like "Bollinger Bands", "Donchian channels", "Exponential Moving Averages" and so on. When you boil it down however, technical analysis is really about waiting until other people are investing in something and then jumping on the bandwagon. This works because the main thing that causes the price of an asset to move is lots of money flowing towards it (up) or away from it (down).

Just like fundamental analysis, technical analysis is a huge subject and you could spend a long time learning about it but it is my firm belief that you don't need to learn that much about it to start improving your ability to invest. Let us look at a couple of technical indicators to give you an example of how simple and powerful technical analysis can be.

AN EXAMPLE OF TECHNICAL ANALYSIS AT WORK: RSI – RELATIVE STRENGTH INDEX

This is a chart of the performance of a London-listed Silver ETF:

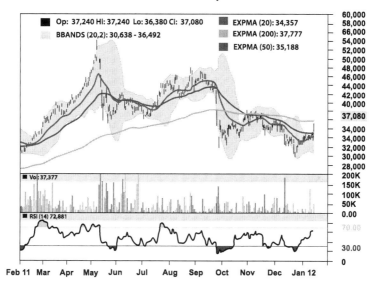

This graphic might look a bit complicated but please don't worry, let's look at each section in turn. The top half or so of the chart plots the daily moves in the price of silver. The middle graphic shows the volume traded. This is simply the number of shares of silver which changed hands that day. Days where the bar is light are up days (when the price ends higher than it started) and dark days are down days. The bigger the bar, the more shares in this fund traded. As a general rule, if there is big volume this gives you an indication that something is happening in the market, so a big dark bar is basically bad news and a big light bar good news, all other things being equal.

Most importantly, however, take a look at the bottom graphic with the heading "RSI (14)". This is a technical indicator called the Relative Strength Index (RSI). The RSI is simply a mathematical calculation that gives a range of 0 to 100.[6] You really don't need to understand the detail of how it is calculated. The point I want to make is simply for us to have a look at the relationship between what the RSI is

6 If you are interested in learning more about the detail behind RSI: http://en.wikipedia.org/wiki/Relative_Strength_Index

doing and what the price is doing. This is a form of technical analysis.

You can see that the RSI line turns shaded in this chart if it goes below the number 30 and if it goes above 70. Below 30 is what we call "oversold" and above 70 "overbought". All other things being equal the RSI tells us that an asset is cheap when it is oversold, so we should think about buying it and expensive when it is overbought, so we should think about selling it.

As such, in this example you would consider buying silver when it went below 30 and consider selling it when it went above 70. Hopefully you are with me so far and this doesn't seem at all complicated.

In reality someone using RSI would most likely finesse the above strategy based on looking at RSI going back a few years and look to buy silver when the RSI crosses back up through 30 and sell when it crosses back down through 70. You would also look for times when this happened with a larger than normal volume given that a big volume day would be a stronger indicator of a change in trend than a low volume day. Again, hopefully none of this so far is too complicated.

So let us look at how this strategy, using only one technical indicator, might have served us in the last few years. In chapter eleven we looked at a number of fundamental reasons that silver is in a bull market – that is to say we would like to have it on our investment shopping list. As always, however, we would ideally like to buy it when it is cheap and sell it when it is expensive. We must always be thinking about the price at which we buy something once we've decided that it is worth buying thanks to our big picture analysis.

Following the strategy outlined above you should be able to see that you would have bought silver in February 2011 when the RSI crossed back above 30. Can you see that the cost then would have been about $31 per share (perhaps use a ruler on the screen or page to help you see what the price is on the graph above)? You would then have held it until early May when it crossed down through 70 and there was heavy volume. You would have been able to sell your position for about $50 per share. That is a 61% return in about three months.

Using the same analysis, you then might have considered buying again at the end of May at about $40 and selling in August at about $48 (+20% in three months) and finally buying again in October at about $32 in which case you might have thought about selling again in February 2012 given silver was above 70 again at about $37 (+16% since October). In fact, you would not have been looking to sell your silver yet since it had not crossed back down through 70.

I should perhaps mention that this is not just theory, this is precisely what I have done with silver in the last couple of years. To do this I only needed to follow one share price, news about one investment (silver) and one broad strategy - the RSI with a weather eye on volumes. I should note that all of the information I am referencing here is available online entirely free of charge on various websites. These charts happen to come from www.barchart.com

If you think this is an isolated example and something of a freak it may be instructive to look at some other examples. Below is the same RSI analysis for a couple of other assets:

THE FTSE 100: HOW MIGHT BUYING AT 30 AND SELLING AT 70 HAVE WORKED OUT?

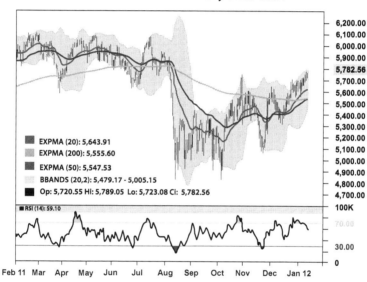

SFTSE - FTSE 100 Index - Daily OHLC Chart

GOLD: THE SAME AGAIN:

GBS.LS - Lyxor Gold Billion - Daily OHLC Chart

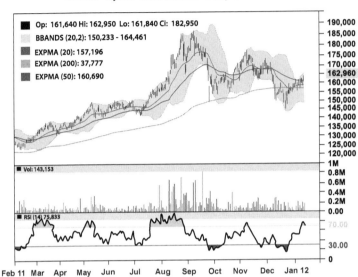

I could include plenty of other examples. Despite how compelling this looks, as with any technical indicator, the RSI is far from perfect. It does not have a 100% hit rate but in recent years it has been an amazing tool for timing entry and exit into gold and silver in particular and has helped me personally to make a much higher return with just this one strategy than what I would have made in pretty much any mainstream investment fund I could have put my money into. This is also a very cheap way of investing as the only fees you need to pay are the low dealing commissions on buying and selling a London listed share. There are obviously no commissions to be paid to financial advisers and a minimal fee structure within the product itself.

It is worth repeating that I did not use this strategy completely blindly. First, I had a strong fundamental view on precious metals as an investment as we have seen in chapter eleven. Secondly, once I had established that gold or silver was overbought or oversold I would do a little bit more work thinking about volumes and the time of year (both gold and silver have seasonal trends). Thirdly, I read emails nearly every day by market commentators, some of whom specialise in gold and silver. Importantly, I would take their latest opinions and numbers on board as a final check before buying or selling. All of this information is available free of charge.

Hopefully this brief example illustrates what can be achieved by using this combination of fundamental and technical analysis. As you can see such an approach can yield pretty fantastic results over and above obsessing about one or the other alone.

Some of you might be looking at the above and thinking that it all seems rather complicated and time consuming. Rest assured that you will not need to go to this level of detail or put in this amount of time and effort to still have a huge positive impact on your financial situation. I just wanted to use this as an example to illustrate what can be achieved with a little effort and an open mind.

ANOTHER EXAMPLE – MARK SHIPMAN'S LONG TERM MOVING AVERAGES

Another example of a very simple but consistently successful technical strategy is one outlined by Mark Shipman in his book "Big Money, Little Effort". I quoted Mr. Shipman at the beginning of the book. He was one of Britain's first hedge fund managers and has an incredible track record of investment success. In his books he does a superb job of showing how effective some very simple technical strategies can be, particularly if you are a patient, longer-term investor.

Mr. Shipman uses an indicator called a "moving average" (MA). As he says:

"...moving averages are one of the most basic yet effective trend-following technical analysis tools available to the investor...".

Basically all a moving average does is take a number of prices (for example the closing price) over a number of time periods and compute the average. Moving averages can take daily, weekly or even monthly prices. On the charts in the above section on RSI, you can see three moving averages that I have chosen to add to the chart: The various lines which are the 200, 50 and 20 day moving averages respectively.[7]

At the most basic level, if an asset's price today is above a moving average this suggests there is upward momentum in the price, all other things being equal. As with much of this chapter, I would stress that you do not need to understand this discussion in any depth, all we are trying to do is look at examples of how effective these strategies can be. If you find the examples compelling you can use the resources I recommend and the Plain English Finance website to increase your

---

7 These are actually "exponential" moving averages, which simply means that they weight more recent data more heavily than older data. You don't need to worry what this means at all but I mention it for the sake of accuracy for those who may have previously looked at technical analysis.

knowledge of all of these things to the point where you become confident enough to employ these strategies yourself.

Mr. Shipman's approach to using MAs is quite simply to use the 30 and 50 week MAs for large, liquid stock market indices (primarily the S&P 500) to find long term buy and sell signals. He suggests you take one of two stances with your money: Either you have your money in an S&P 500 tracker fund, or you have it on deposit as cash.

Specifically, he shows that:

...if the 30 week moving average is higher than the 50 week moving average, you should have your money in the market (i.e. own an S&P 500 tracker)...

...if, on the other hand, the 50 week average is greater than the 30 week average, you should sell your S&P 500 tracker fund and keep your money in cash until the 30 week is higher than the 50 again...

When Mr. Shipman started using this approach, he had to calculate the moving averages himself, initially with a pen and paper but latterly with a computer and his own software. Today you are able to find this sort of information on dozens, probably hundreds of websites for free. This is another example of the point I made in chapter four that today's financial products and information sources are better than ever before. The fact that you can learn how to find the RSI or MA for thousands of possible investments entirely free of charge is a huge development in investment and gives you tools that an investor from ten or more years ago could only dream of.

Mr. Shipman wrote his book in 2004. In it, he looked at the performance of this one simple method of technically driven investment going back to the beginning of 1951. From 1951 to 2004 the strategy generated 21 buy signals. 71.43% (15) of these positions were profitable, the best of which generated 178.78% (between 1995 and 2001). The average performance of all of them was 34.76% and the average loss on losing positions was 5.48%.

These sorts of returns are superior to what you are likely to see if you use almost any financial adviser, particularly once you have accounted for their fees. I highlight these sorts of strategies purely to show you what is possible today using free information and with a relatively small amount of effort on your part.

I would hope that you have found these two examples of technical analysis sufficiently compelling to want to learn more. This being the case, let us now look at some resources you might use to do so...

RESOURCES FOR TECHNICAL ANALYSIS

READ: "BIG MONEY, LITTLE EFFORT" BY MARK SHIPMAN

If you only read one book to inspire you about technical analysis, I recommend this one. You will learn more detail about the strategy outlined above. My other reason for choosing this book is that it is a very easy and quick read. It contains very important and compelling points in easy language early in the book. A few minutes of reading will reward you with some eureka moments and a tangible money making strategy.

FREE TECHNICAL ANALYSIS ON LINE

I have noted that the charts I have used in this section come from the website: www.barchart.com There are many sites that enable you to conduct technical analysis on a wide variety of assets. When you get more comfortable with using a little bit of technical analysis www.barchart.com will be a good place to start.

KEY CONCEPT FOUR: ARRANGING YOUR FINANCIAL AFFAIRS WITH THIRD PARTIES SO...

A. YOU ARE ABLE TO INVEST CHEAPLY IN ALL ASSET CLASSES

Happily we can dispatch this last section very quickly as we already looked at the best way to arrange your affairs earlier in the book when we learnt how to optimise your financial accounts.

We also looked very briefly at spread betting at the end of chapter seven. At this point I would like to stress that if you really want to "...take things further..." with investment and making money from your money you should consider learning about spread betting.

As I have already said, spread betting can be a very dangerous thing to do if you have not educated yourself about it enough but if you are really committed to making money from your money it is one of the very best ways to achieve our goal of being able "...to invest cheaply in all asset classes...".

Within a spread betting account you are able to take long and short positions on a huge range of shares, bonds, commodities and currencies and the gains you make will be tax free. You are also able to run positions worth a large multiple of the money you have to start with and build watch lists for your shopping themes. All of these facts make spread betting extremely powerful if you know what you are doing.

If you are interested in learning about spread betting then a good place to start is to read:

"The Naked Trader's Guide to Spread Betting: A guide to making money from shares in up or down markets" by Robbie Burns.

There are also tutorial videos on the MoneyWeek website www.moneyweek.com and you might consider having a look at the website www.igindex.co.uk . IG are the UK's biggest spread betting company (I have an account with them) and there is some great information about spread betting on their site as you might expect.

B. YOU RECEIVE A CONSTANT STREAM OF POSSIBLE INVESTMENT IDEAS

Again, we have already taken care of this requirement by virtue of the resources already recommended in this chapter. If you subscribe to MoneyWeek Magazine and the free email services I have outlined above, you will already be getting good quality investment ideas on a regular basis. There are more suggestions for this on the website, some of which are paid services, but if you have already followed the suggestions in this chapter you are well covered without having to spend a penny.

CONCLUSION

So that is it for our chapter on "...taking things further..." To be honest key concept four is somewhat surplus to requirements given that we have learnt most of the points it makes already. As I have already said, however, "repetition is the mother of invention" and one of the most important themes of Plain English Finance is that you have never been in a stronger position than you are today to take advantage of investing in financial assets. I wanted to repeat this right at the end of the book.

There are many more resources on the website which will help you take things even further than that but if you start by looking at the resources outlined in this chapter you will most likely be on the road to a deeper understanding of finance than anyone you know and a very large number of investment professionals...

I wish you the very best of luck learning about investment and making a huge difference to your life as a result...

TO CONCLUDE

"Tell 'em what you're going to tell 'em. Tell 'em. Tell 'em what you told 'em."

– Paul White, first Director of CBS news, paraphrasing Dale Carnegie.

The above quote is well known advice when making a presentation. I think it is also useful in a book like "Own The World". If you have come this far then I congratulate you heartily. Your financial knowledge is now better than an incredibly large proportion of the population including many finance professionals, economists and politicians. I hope you feel like you have learned enough to make a real and lasting difference to your financial affairs and, by extension, to your entire life.

Given my belief in the above quote, I thought it might be useful to have one final concluding chapter to summarise what we have learnt and draw things together. I would hope that by now you are to speed on the following crucial points:

1. You can and should invest your own money.
2. You must understand what is happening in the world today, particularly the pension predicament we face.
3. Even despite this pension predicament, you are capable of arranging your own affairs so it needn't worry you.
4. You can do a better job than professionals, particularly because if you do, you will avoid their fees and very likely end up with better financial arrangements too.
5. You need to learn about and benefit from the incredible power of compound interest.
6. Today's financial accounts, products and sources of information are the best they've ever been if you know where to go.
7. You can benefit from the fact that the world will continue to grow economically barring a major war or similar crisis (in which case, investment performance might be the least of your concerns!).
8. You can also actually benefit from the fact that there is high real inflation in the world.
9. You *can* find the money you need to invest, particularly if you are willing to change your living arrangements if you're spending too much on them.
10. You can set up your own personal financial accounts to benefit from top quality providers who are far better than the more mainstream financial services firms and save on costs as a result.
11. The various asset classes you might invest in aren't as complicated as you may previously have believed.
12. Making a financial plan is an important step on your road to financial success.
13. You can make superior returns with the relatively simple approach of "owning the world" and "owning inflation". Learning how to do this is no harder than learning how to drive.
14. Once you have a reasonable amount of money, you can aspire to learning much more about investment. Doing so can yield spectacular results longer term.

I hope you have enjoyed the book and that you have a sense of excitement and empowerment about what is possible with your money as a result of reading it.

The final point I would like to make is that I very much hope you join the Plain English Finance community by subscribing to the free email. This book is, by its very nature, a static source of information. Obviously finance is an incredibly dynamic subject. By subscribing to the email list and becoming part of the community you will ensure that you are kept in touch with the most important news and developments in finance in the months and years ahead.

So that is it. I thank you for taking the time to read the book and I wish you the very best for your future. If you are able to take control of your financial affairs I have every confidence that it will yield wonderful results for every area of your life.

Happy investing!

Andrew Craig, September 2012.

BIBLIOGRAPHY

"You cannot open a book without learning something…"

– Confucius.

"Eating words has never given me indigestion…"

– Winston Churchill.

Arnold, Glen. Financial Times Handbook of Corporate Finance: A Business Companion to Financial Markets, Decisions & Techniques. New York, NY: Pearson Financial Times, 2010. Print.

Arnold, Glen. The Financial Times Guide to Investing: The Definitive Companion to Investment and the Financial Markets. Harlow, England: Pearson Financial Times/Prentice Hall, 2010. Print.

Bakan, Joel. The Corporation: The Pathological Pursuit of Profit and Power. New York: Free, 2005. Print.

Bartholomew, James. The Welfare State We're in. London: Politico's, 2006. Print.

Bastiat, Frederic. The Law by Frederic Bastiat. N.p.: Lightning Source, 2007. Print.

Berman, Morris. The Twilight of American Culture. New York: Norton, 2006. Print.

Bernstein, Stefan. Understand Commodities in a Day. Hawkhurst: Global Professional, 2009. Print.

Blum, William. Rogue State: A Guide to the World's Only Superpower. Monroe, Me.: Common Courage, 2005. Print.

Boettke, Peter J. Living Economics: Yesterday, Today, and Tomorrow. Oakland, CA: Independent Institute, 2012. Print.

Bolton, Anthony, and Jonathan Davis. Investing with Anthony Bolton. Hampshire, Eng.: Harriman House, 2006. Print.

Bolton, Anthony. Investing against the Tide: Lessons from a Life Running Money. London: FT Prentice Hall, 2009. Print.

Bonner, William, and Addison Wiggin. Empire of Debt: The Rise and Fall of an Epic Financial Crisis. Hoboken, NJ: Wiley, 2006. Print.

Bonner, William, and Lila Rajiva. Mobs, Messiahs, and Markets: Surviving the Public Spectacle in Finance and Politics. Hoboken, NJ: John Wiley & Sons, 2007. Print.

Bonner, William. Dice Have No Memory: Big Bets and Bad Economics from Paris to the Pampas. Hoboken, NJ: Wiley, 2011. Print.

Borthwick, Mark. Pacific Century: The Emergence of Modern Pacific Asia. Boulder, CO: Westview, 2007. Print.

Botsman, Rachel, and Roo Rogers. What's Mine Is Yours: The Rise of Collaborative Consumption. New York: Harper Business, 2010. Print.

Bower, Tom. The Squeeze: Oil, Money and Greed in the Twenty-first Century. London: HarperPress, 2009. Print.

Bradfield-Moody, James, and Bianca Nogrady. Sixth Wave, the. London: ReadHowYouWant, 2010. Print.

Brussee, Warren. The Second Great Depression. [Bangor, ME]: Booklocker.com, 2005. Print.

Bryson, Bill. Notes from a Small Island. London: Black Swan, 1996. Print.

Bueno, De Mesquita, Bruce. Prediction: How to See and Shape the Future with Game Theory. London: Vintage, 2010. Print.

Burns, Robbie. The Naked Trader: How Anyone Can Make Money Trading Shares. Petersfield: Harriman House, 2007. Print.

Burns, Robbie. The Naked Trader's Guide to Spread Betting: How to Make Money from Shares in up or down Markets. Petersfield: Harriman House, 2010. Print.

Buzan, Tony. The Speed Reading Book. London: BBC, 1997. Print.

Carson, Rachel. Silent Spring. Boston: Houghton Mifflin, 2002. Print.

Casey, Douglas R. Crisis Investing: Opportunities and Profits in the Coming Great Depression. [S.l.]: Stratford, 1980. Print.

Cassidy, John. Dot.con: How America Lost Its Mind and Money in the Internet Era. New York, NY: Perennial, 2003. Print.

Chancellor, Edward. Devil Take the Hindmost: A History of Financial Speculation. New York: Farrar, Straus, Giroux, 1999. Print.

Chomsky, Noam, and David Barsamian. Imperial Ambitions: Conversations on the Post-9/11 World. New York: Metropolitan, 2005. Print.

Chomsky, Noam, John Schoeffel, and Peter R. Mitchell. Understanding Power: The Indispensable Chomsky. London: Vintage, 2003. Print.

Conway, Mark R. ., and Aaron N. . Behle. Professional Stock Trading: System Design and Automation. Waltham, MA: Acme Trader, 2003. Print.

Craig, David. Squandered: How Gordon Brown Is Wasting over One Trillion Pounds of Our Money. London: Constable, 2008. Print.

Csikszentmihalyi, Mihaly. Creativity: Flow and the Psychology of Discovery and Invention. New York: HarperCollinsPublishers, 1996. Print.

De, Botton Alain. Status Anxiety. London: Penguin, 2005. Print.

Deffeyes, Kenneth S. Beyond Oil: The View from Hubbert's Peak. New York: Hill and Wang, 2005. Print.

Dennis, Felix. How to Get Rich. London: Ebury, 2007. Print.

Dent, Harry S. The Great Depression Ahead: How to Prosper in the Crash following the Greatest Boom in History. New York: Free, 2009. Print.

Diamond, Jared M. Collapse: How Societies Choose to Fail or Survive. London: Penguin, 2006. Print.

Diamond, Jared M. Guns, Germs, and Steel: The Fates of Human Societies. New York: Norton, 2005. Print.

Diamond, Jared M. The Third Chimpanzee: The Evolution and Future of the Human Animal. New York, NY: HarperCollins, 1992. Print.

Dicken, Peter. Global Shift: Reshaping the Global Economic Map in the 21st Century. New York: Guilford, 2003. Print.

Doyen, Robert, and Meg Elaine. Schneider. Making Millions for Dummies. Hoboken, NJ: Wiley Pub., 2009. Print.

Elder, Alexander. The Complete Trading for a Living: The Legendary Approach to Trading with the Companion Study Guide. New York: J. Wiley, 2006. Print.

Estrada, Javier. Finance in a Nutshell: A No-nonsense Companion to the Tools and Techniques of Finance. London: Financial Times Prentice Hall, 2005. Print.

Faber, Mebane T. Ivy Portfolio: How to Invest like the Top Endowments and Avoid Bear Markets. Hoboken: John Wiley, 2011. Print.

Faith, Curtis M. Way of the Turtle. New York: McGraw-Hill, 2007. Print.

Feierstein, Mitch. Planet Ponzi: How Politicians and Bankers Stole Your Future. London: Bantam, 2012. Print.

Ferguson, Niall. Civilization the West and the Rest. London: Allen Lane, 2011. Print.

Ferguson, Niall. High Financier: The Lives and Time of Siegmund Warburg. New York: Penguin, 2010. Print.

Ferguson, Niall. The Ascent of Money: A Financial History of the World. New York: Penguin, 2008. Print.

Ferguson, Niall. The Cash Nexus: Money and Power in the Modern World, 1700-2000. New York: Basic, 2001. Print.

Fergusson, Adam. When Money Dies: The Nightmare of the Weimar Hyper-inflation. London: Old Street, 2010. Print.

Ferriss, Timothy. The 4-hour Work Week: Escape the 9-5, Live Anywhere, and Join the New Rich. London: Vermilion, 2007. Print.

Fischer, David Hackett. The Great Wave: Price Revolutions and the Rhythm of History. New York: Oxford UP, 1996. Print.

Fisher, Philip A. Common Stocks and Uncommon Profits and Other Writings. New York: Wiley, 2003. Print.

Fitz-Gerald, Keith. Fiscal Hangover: How to Profit from the New Global Economy. Hoboken, NJ: John Wiley & Sons, 2010. Print.

Franken, Al. Lies: And the Lying Liars Who Tell Them : A Fair and Balanced Look at the Right. New York: Dutton, 2003. Print.

Frieden, Jeffry A., and David A. Lake. International Political Economy: Perspectives on Global Power and Wealth. New York: St. Martin's, 1987. Print.

Friedman, Thomas L. The World Is Flat: A Brief History of the Twenty-first Century. New York: Farrar, Straus and Giroux, 2006. Print.

Fukuyama, Francis. The End of History and the Last Man. New York: Free, 1992. Print.

Fukuyama, Francis. Trust: The Social Virtues and the Creation of Prosperity. New York: Free Paperbacks, 1996. Print.

Funnell, Warwick, Jane Andrew, and Robert E. Jupe. In Government We Trust. London: Pluto, 2009. Print.

Galbraith, Kenneth. The Affluent Society. N.p.: Penguin, 1991. Print.

Galbraith, Kenneth. The Great Crash 1929. London: Penguin, 1992. Print.

Garrett, Garet. A Bubble That Broke the World,. Boston: Little, Brown, and, 1932. Print.

Getty, J. Paul. How to Be Rich. New York: Jove, 1983. Print.

Gladwell, Malcolm. Blink: The Power of Thinking without Thinking. New York: Little, Brown and, 2005. Print.

Gladwell, Malcolm. Outliers: The Story of Success. New York: Little, Brown and, 2008. Print.

Gladwell, Malcolm. The Tipping Point: How Little Things Can Make a Big Difference. Boston: Back Bay, 2002. Print.

Goleman, Daniel. Emotional Intelligence. New York: Bantam, 2006. Print.

Goodman, Leah McGrath. The Asylum: The Renegades Who Hijacked the World's Oil Market. New York, NY: William Morrow, 2011. Print.

Gough, Leo, and Leo Gough. How the Stock Market Really Works: The Guerrilla Investor's Secret Handbook. London: Financial Times Prentice Hall, 2001. Print.

Graham, Benjamin, and Jason Zweig. The Intelligent Investor. New York: HarperBusiness Essentials, 2003. Print.

Green, Alexander. The Gone Fishin' Portfolio: Get Wise, Get Wealthy-- and Get on with Your Life. Hoboken, NJ: Wiley, 2010. Print.

Greenblatt, Joel. You Can Be a Stock Market Genius: Uncover the Secret Hiding Places of Stock Market Profits. New York: Simon & Schuster, 1999. Print.

Greene, Robert, and Joost Elffers. The 48 Laws of Power. London: Profile, 2002. Print.

Griffis, Michael, and Lita Epstein. Trading for Dummies. Hoboken, NJ: Wiley, 2009. Print.

Haakonssen, Knud. Adam Smith: The Theory of Moral Sentiments. Cambridge: Cambridge UP, 2002. Print.

Hagstrom, Robert G. The Warren Buffet Way: Investment Strategies of the World's Greatest Investor. New York: Wiley, 1995. Print.

Hawken, Paul. The Ecology of Commerce: A Declaration of Sustainability. New York: Harper Business, 2010. Print.

Hayek, Friedrich A. Von, and Bruce Caldwell. The Road to Serfdom: Text and Documents. Chicago: University of Chicago, 2007. Print.

Hayek, Friedrich A. Von, Sudha R. Shenoy, and Friedrich A. Von Hayek. A Tiger by the Tail: A 40-years' Running Commentary on Keynesianism by Hayek;. London: Institute of Economic Affairs, 1972. Print.

Hazlitt, Henry. Economics in One Lesson: Fiftieth Anniversary Edition. Little Rock, AR: Laissez Faire, 1996. Print.

Heinberg, Richard. The Party's Over: Oil, War and the Fate of Industrial Societies. Gabriola, BC: New Society, 2003. Print.

Hill, Napoleon, Bill Hartley, and Ann Hartley. Think and Grow Rich. Los Angeles, CA: Highroads Media, 2008. Print.

Hobbes, Thomas, and Marshall Missner. Leviathan. New York: Pearson Longman, 2008. Print.

Hobsbawm, E. J., and Chris Wrigley. Industry and Empire: From 1750 to the Present Day. New York: New, 1999. Print.

Huntington, Samuel Phillips. The Clash of Civilizations and the Remaking of World Order. New York: Free, 2002. Print.

Hutton, Will. The State We're in. London: Vintage, 1996. Print.

Hutton, Will. The World We're in. London: Abacus, 2007. Print.

Ivins, Molly. Who Let the Dogs In?: Incredible Political Animals I Have Known. New York: Random House, 2004. Print.

Jackson, Tim. Prosperity without Growth Economics for a Finite Planet. London [u.a.: Earthscan, 2010. Print.

James, Oliver. Affluenza. London: Vermilion, 2008. Print.

James, Oliver. Britain on the Couch: How Keeping up with the Joneses Has Depressed Us since 1950. London: Vermilion, 2010. Print.

James, Oliver. The Selfish Capitalist: Origins of Affluenza. London: Vermilion, 2008. Print.

Kahn, Michael N. Technical Analysis Plain and Simple: Charting the Markets in Your Language. Upper Saddle River, NJ: FT, 2010. Print.

Kahneman, Daniel. Thinking, Fast and Slow. London: Penguin, 2011. Print.

Kay, J. A. The Truth about Markets: Their Genius, Their Limits, Their Follies. London: Penguin, 2004. Print.

Keen, Steve. Debunking Economics: The Naked Emperor of the Social Sciences. Annandale, NSW: Pluto Australia, 2001. Print.

Kennedy, Paul M. The Rise and Fall of the Great Powers: Economic Change and Military Conflict from 1500 to 2000. New York, NY: Random House, 1987. Print.

Keynes, John Maynard. The General Theory of Employment, Interest, and Money. [S.l.]: BN Pub., 2008. Print.

Kiyosaki, Robert T., and Sharon L. Lechter. Rich Dad, Poor Dad: What the Rich Teach Their Kids about Money-- That the Poor and Middle Class Do Not! New York: Warner Business, 2000. Print.

Klein, Naomi. No Logo: No Space, No Choice, No Jobs. New York: Picador, 2010. Print.

Kunstler, James Howard. The Long Emergency: Surviving the Converging Catastrophes of the Twenty-first Century. New York: Atlantic Monthly, 2005. Print.

Lanchester, John. Whoops!: Why Everyone Owes Everyone and No One Can Pay. London: Allen Lane, 2010. Print.

Lefevre, Edwin. Reminiscences of a Stock Operator. Hoboken, N.J .: J. Wiley,

2006. Print.

Levitt, Stephen D., and Stephen J. Dubner. Super Freakonomics. N.p.: HarperCollins Canada, Limited, 2009. Print.

Levitt, Steven D., and Stephen J. Dubner. Freakonomics: A Rogue Economist Explores the Hidden Side of Everything. New York, NY: William Morrow, 2006. Print.

Lewis, Michael. Liar's Poker: Rising through the Wreckage on Wall Street. New York: W. W. Norton, 2010. Print.

Lewis, Michael. The Big Short: Inside the Doomsday Machine. New York: W.W. Norton, 2010. Print.

Lewis, Michael. The New New Thing: A Silicon Valley Story. New York: Penguin, 2001. Print.

Lieven, Anatol, and John Hulsman. Ethical Realism: A Vision for America's Role in the World. New York: Pantheon, 2006. Print.

Lovelock, James. The Revenge of Gaia: Earth's Climate in Crisis and the Fate of Humanity. New York: Basic, 2007. Print.

Lynch, Peter, and John Rothchild. Beating the Street. New York: Simon & Schuster, 1993. Print.

Lynch, Peter, and John Rothchild. One up on Wall Street: How to Use What You Already Know to Make Money in the Market. New York: Simon & Schuster, 2000. Print.

Machiavelli, Niccolo, and George Bull. The Prince. London: Penguin, 2003. Print.

Mackay, Charles. Extraordinary Popular Delusions. New York: Dover Publications, 2003. Print.

Mallaby, Sebastian. More Money than God: Hedge Funds and the Making of a New Elite. New York: Penguin, 2010. Print.

Mallaby, Sebastian. The World's Banker: A Story of Failed States, Financial Crises, and the Wealth and Poverty of Nations. New York: Penguin, 2006. Print.

Marcus, Aurelius, Martin Hammond, and Diskin Clay. Meditations. London:

Penguin, 2006. Print.

Markusen, James R., James R. Melvin, and William H. Kaempfer. International Trade: Theory and Evidence. Boston (Mass.): McGraw-Hill, 1995. Print.

Marx, Karl, Friedrich Engels, and Gareth Stedman. Jones. The Communist Manifesto. London: Penguin, 2002. Print.

Marz, Eduard, Joseph Schumpeter: Scholar, Teacher, and Politician. New Haven: Yale UP, 1991. Print.

Mauldin, John, and Jonathan Tepper. Endgame: The End of the Debt Supercycle and How It Changes Everything. Hoboken, NJ: John Wiley, 2011. Print.

Mauldin, John. Bull's Eye Investing: Targeting Real Returns in a Smoke and Mirrors Market. Hoboken, NJ: Wiley, 2004. Print.

Mayer, Christopher W. World Right Side Up: Investing across Six Continents. Hoboken, NJ: Wiley, 2012. Print.

McLean, Bethany, and Peter Elkind. The Smartest Guys in the Room: The Amazing Rise and Scandalous Fall of Enron. New York: Portfolio, 2004. Print.

Mill, John Stuart, and John Gray. On Liberty and Other Essays. Oxford: Oxford UP, 1991. Print.

Mill, John Stuart, Jeremy Bentham, and Alan Ryan. Utilitarianism and Other Essays. Harmondsworth, Middlesex, England: Penguin, 1987. Print.

Mobius, Mark. The Little Book of Emerging Markets: How to Make Money in the World's Fastest Growing Markets. Singapore: John Wiley & Sons Singapore Pte., 2012. Print.

Monnery, Neil. Safe as Houses?: A Historical Analysis of Property Prices. London: London Partnership, 2011. Print.

Moore, Michael. Dude, Where's My Country? New York: Warner, 2003. Print.

Moore, Michael. Stupid White Men-- and Other Sorry Excuses for the State of the Nation! New York: Regan, 2001. Print.

More, Thomas, and Richard Marius. Utopia. London: J.M. Dent, 1994. Print.

Mount, Ferdinand. The New Few: A Very British Oligarchy. London: Simon &

Schuster, 2012. Print.

Moyo, Dambisa. Winner Take All: China's Race for Resources and What It Means for the World. New York: Basic, 2012. Print.

Naish, John. Enough: Breaking Free from the World of More. London: Hodder & Stoughton, 2008. Print.

Needleman, Lionel. The Economics of Housing. N.p.: Staples, 1965. Print.

Oldfield, Richard. Simple but Not Easy: An Autobiographical and Biased Book about Investing. London: Doddington Pub., 2007. Print.

O'Neil, William J. How to Make Money in Stocks: Complete Investing System. New York: McGraw-Hill, 2011. Print.

O'Shaughnessy, James P. What Works on Wall Street: The Classic Guide to the Best-performing Investment Strategies of All Time. Maidenhead: McGraw-Hill Professional, 2011. Print.

Pape, Scott. The Barefoot Investor: Five Steps to Financial Freedom in Your 20s and 30s. Chichester: Capstone, 2006. Print.

Penn, Mark J., and E. Kinney. Zalesne. Microtrends: The Small Forces behind Tomorrow's Big Changes. New York: Twelve, 2007. Print.

Perkins, John. Confessions of an Economic Hit Man. New York: Plume, 2006. Print.

Pilger, John. The New Rulers of the World. London: Verso, 2003. Print.

Porritt, Jonathon. Capitalism as If the World Matters. London: Earthscan, 2005. Print.

Rand, Ayn. Atlas Shrugged. London: Penguin, 2007. Print.

Reich, Robert B. . Supercapitalism. New York: Vintage , a Division of Random House, 2008. Print.

Rickards, James. Currency Wars: The Making of the next Global Crisis. New York: Portfolio/Penguin, 2011. Print.

Roberts, J. M., and Odd Arne. Westad. The New Penguin History of the World. London: Penguin, 2007. Print.

Robinson, Lee. Gathering Storm. Monaco: Derivatives Vision, 2010. Print.

Rockefeller, Barbara. Technical Analysis for Dummies. Hoboken, NJ: Wiley, 2011. Print.

Rogers, Jim. A Bull in China: Investing Profitably in the World's Greatest Market. Hoboken, NJ: Wiley, 2009. Print.

Rogers, Jim. A Gift to My Children: A Father's Lessons for Life and Investing. Chichester: Wiley, 2009. Print.

Rogers, Jim. Adventure Capitalist: The Ultimate Road Trip. Chichester, U.K.: Wiley, 2004. Print.

Rogers, Jim. Hot Commodities: How Anyone Can Invest Profitably in the World's Best Market. New York: Random House, 2007. Print.

Rogers, Jim. Investment Biker: Around the World with Jim Rogers. New York: Random House Trade Paperbacks, 2003. Print.

Rosefielde, Steven, and Daniel Quinn. Mills. Masters of Illusion: American Leadership in the Media Age. Cambridge: Cambridge UP, 2007. Print.

Roubini, Nouriel, and Stephen Mihm. Crisis Economics: A Crash Course in the Future of Finance. New York, NY: Penguin, 2010. Print.

Rousseau, Jean-Jacques. A Discourse on Equality. London: Penguin, 2003. Print.

Rousseau, Jean-Jacques. The Social Contract. Harmondsworth: n.p., 1975. Print.

Sachs, Jeffrey. Common Wealth: Economics for a Crowded Planet. New York: Penguin, 2008. Print.

Sachs, Jeffrey. The End of Poverty: Economic Possibilities for Our Time. New York: Penguin, 2005. Print.

Sachs, Jeffrey. The Price of Civilization: Reawakening American Virtue and Prosperity. New York: Random House, 2011. Print.

Sardar, Ziauddin, and Merryl Wyn. Davies. Why Do People Hate America? Cambridge [England: Icon, 2003. Print.

Schiff, Peter D., and Andrew Schiff. How an Economy Grows and Why It

Crashes: A Tale. Hoboken, NJ: Wiley, 2010. Print.

Schiff, Peter D., John Downes, and Peter D. Schiff. Crash Proof 2.0: How to Profit from the Economic Collapse. Hoboken, NJ: John Wiley, 2009. Print.

Schiff, Peter D. The Real Crash: America's Coming Bankruptcy--how to save Yourself and Your Country. New York: St. Martin's, 2012. Print.

Schlosser, Eric. Fast Food Nation: The Dark Side of the All-American Meal. New York, NY: Perennial, 2002. Print.

Schlosser, Eric. Reefer Madness: Sex, Drugs, and Cheap Labor in the American Black Market. Boston: Houghton Mifflin, 2003. Print.

Schwager, Jack D. Market Wizards: Interviews with Top Traders. Columbia, MD: Marketplace, 2006. Print.

Shiller, Robert J. Finance and the Good Society. Princeton, NJ: Princeton UP, 2012. Print.

Shipman, Mark. Big Money, Little Effort a Winning Strategy for Profitable Long-term Investment. London: Kogan Page, 2008. Print.

Shipman, Mark. The next Big Investment Boom: Learn the Secrets of Investing from a Master and How to Profit from Commodities. London: Kogan Page, 2008. Print.

Siegel, Jeremy J. Stocks for the Long Run: The Definitive Guide to Financial Market Returns and Long-term Investment Strategies. New York: McGraw-Hill, 2008. Print.

Simmons, Matthew R. Twilight in the Desert: The Coming Saudi Oil Shock and the World Economy. Hoboken, NJ: John Wiley & Sons, 2005. Print.

Smith, Adam, and Andrew S. Skinner. The Wealth of Nations,. London: Penguin, 1999. Print.

Smith, David. The Age of Instability: The Global Financial Crisis and What Comes next. London: Profile, 2010. Print.

Smith, Terry. Accounting for Growth: Stripping the Camouflage from Company Accounts. London: Century Business, 1992. Print.

Soros, George, and George Soros. The Crash of 2008 and What It Means: The

New Paradigm for Financial Markets. New York: PublicAffairs, 2009. Print.

Soros, George, and George Soros. Underwriting Democracy. New York: Free, 1991. Print.

Soros, George, Byron Wien, and Krisztina Koenen. Soros on Soros: Staying Ahead of the Curve. New York: J. Wiley, 1995. Print.

Soros, George. On Globalization. Oxford: PublicAffairs, 2002. Print.

Soros, George. Open Society: Reforming Global Capitalism. New York: Public Affairs, 2000. Print.

Soros, George. The Age of Fallibility: The Consequences of the War on Terror. New York: Public Affairs, 2006. Print.

Soros, George. The Alchemy of Finance. Hoboken, NJ: J. Wiley, 2003. Print.

Soros, George. The Bubble of American Supremacy: Correcting the Misuse of American Power. New York: Public Affairs, 2004. Print.

Soros, George. The Crisis of Global Capitalism: Open Society Endangered. New York: PublicAffairs, 1998. Print.

St, Clair Jeffrey. Grand Theft Pentagon : Tales of Corruption and Profiteering in the War on Terror. Monroe, Me.: Common Courage, 2005. Print.

Stiglitz, Joseph E. Globalization and Its Discontents. New York: W.W. Norton, 2003. Print.

Strauss, William, and Neil Howe. The Fourth Turning: An American Prophecy. New York: Broadway, 1998. Print.

Sunzi, Ralph D. Sawyer, Mei-chu?n Sawyer, and Bin Sun. The Complete Art of War. Boulder, CO: Westview, 1996. Print.

Suskind, Ron. The Way of the World: A Story of Truth and Hope in an Age of Extremism. New York: Harper, 2008. Print.

Sutherland, Stephen. Liquid Millionaire: How to Make Millions from the up and Coming Stock Market Boom. Milton Keynes: AuthorHouse, 2008. Print.

Taleb, Nassim Nicholas. Fooled by Randomness. London: Penguin, 2007. Print.

Taleb, Nassim. The Black Swan: The Impact of the Highly Improbable. New York: Random House Trade Paperbacks, 2010. Print.

Tannehill, Morris, and Linda Tannehill. The Market for Liberty: Is Government Really Necessary? ; Is Government Our Protector ... or Our Destroyer? New York: Laissez Faire, 1984. Print.

Templar, Richard. The Rules of Wealth: A Personal Code for Prosperity. Harlow, England: Pearson/Prentice Hall Business, 2007. Print.

Templar, Richard. The Rules of Work: A Definitive Code for Personal Success. Harlow, England [u.a.: Pearson - Prentice Hall Business, 2010. Print.

Tharp, Van K. Super Trader: Make Consistent Profits in Good and Bad Markets. New York: McGraw-Hill, 2011. Print.

Tharp, Van K. Trade Your Way to Financial Freedom. New York: McGraw-Hill, 2007. Print.

Toffler, Alvin. Future Shock. Toronto: Bantam, 1971. Print.

Toffler, Alvin. Powershift: Knowledge, Wealth, and Violence at the Edge of the 21st Century. New York: Bantam, 1990. Print.

Toffler, Alvin. The Third Wave. Toronto: Bantam, 1981. Print.

Turk, James, James Turk, and John A. Rubino. The Collapse of the Dollar and How to Profit from It: Make a Fortune by Investing in Gold and Other Hard Assets. New York: Doubleday, 2007. Print.

Vaitilingam, Romesh. The Financial Times Guide to Using the Financial Pages. Harlow, UK: Financial Times Prentice Hall, 2006. Print.

Vonnegut, Kurt, and Daniel Simon. A Man without a Country. New York: Random House Trade Paperbacks, 2007. Print.

Wapshott, Nicholas. Keynes Hayek: The Clash That Defined Modern Economics. New York: W.W. Norton &, 2011. Print.

Webb, Merryn Somerset. Love Is Not Enough: A Smart Woman's Guide to Making (and Keeping) Money. London: Harper Perennial, 2008. Print.

Weiner, Eric J. The Shadow Market: How a Group of Wealthy Nations and Powerful Investors Secretly Dominate the World. New York: Scribner, 2010.

Print.

Weissman, Richard L. Mechanical Trading Systems: Pairing Trader Psychology with Technical Analysis. Hoboken, NJ: John Wiley & Sons, 2005. Print.

Wiggin, Addison, and Justice Litle. Gold: The Once and Future Money. Chichester: John Wiley, 2006. Print.

Wiggin, Addison. The Demise of the Dollar... and Why It's Even Better for Your Investments. Hoboken, NJ: J. Wiley & Sons, 2008. Print.

Wiggin, Addison. The Little Book of the Shrinking Dollar: What You Can Do to Protect Your Money Now. Hoboken, NJ: John Wiley, 2012. Print.

38090561R00151

Made in the USA
Charleston, SC
01 February 2015